# Once Upon an Algorithm

# Once Upon an Algorithm

How Stories Explain Computing

Martin Erwig

The MIT Press
Cambridge, Massachusetts
London, England

This book was set in Garamond by the author using the LaTeX document preparation system. Printed and bound in the United States of America.

Library of Congress Cataloging-in-Publication Data

Names: Erwig, Martin, author.
Title: Once upon an algorithm : how stories explain computing / Martin Erwig.
Description: Cambridge, MA : MIT Press, [2017] | Includes bibliographical
    references and index.
Identifiers: LCCN 2016053945 | ISBN 9780262036634 (hardcover : alk. paper)
Subjects: LCSH: Computer algorithms–Popular works.
Classification: LCC QA76.9.A43 E78 2017 | DDC 005.1–dc23 LC record available at
    https://lccn.loc.gov/2016053945

10    9    8    7    6    5    4    3    2    1

# Contents

Preface   vii
Acknowledgments   xi
Introduction   1

## Part I  ALGORITHMS

**Computation and Algorithms** — *Hansel and Gretel*
1  A Path to Understanding Computation                          19
2  Walk the Walk: When Computation Really Happens              33

**Representation and Data Structures** — *Sherlock Holmes*
3  The Mystery of Signs                                        49
4  Detective's Notebook: Accessory after the Fact             63

**Problem Solving and Its Limitations** — *Indiana Jones*
5  The Search for the Perfect Data Structure                   83
6  Sorting out Sorting                                        103
7  Mission Intractable                                        121

## Part II  LANGUAGES

**Language and Meaning** — *Over the Rainbow*
8  The Prism of Language                                      141
9  Finding the Right Tone: Sound Meaning                      159

**Control Structures and Loops** — *Groundhog Day*
10  Weather, Rinse, Repeat                                    175
11  Happy Ending Not Guaranteed                               189

**Recursion** — *Back to the Future*
12  A Stitch in Time Computes Fine                            205
13  A Matter of Interpretation                                225

**Types and Abstraction** — *Harry Potter*
14  The Magical Type                                          245
15  A Bird's Eye View: Abstracting from Details               263

Glossary   287
Notes   303
Index   313

# Preface

When people ask about my work, the conversation quickly turns to the question of what computer science is. To say computer science is the science of computers is misleading (though strictly speaking not incorrect) because most people will take *computer* to mean PC or laptop and conclude that computer scientists spend their time constructing hardware. On the other hand, defining computer science as the study of computation is simply kicking the can down the road, since it immediately raises the question of what computation is.

Over the years, I have come to realize that teaching by just introducing concept after concept doesn't work very well; it is simply too abstract. Nowadays, I typically start by describing computer science as the study of systematic problem solving. Everybody knows what a problem is, and everybody has seen solutions as well. After explaining this view through an example, I often get the chance to introduce the concept of an algorithm, which allows me to point out important differences between computer science and mathematics. Most of the time, I don't need to talk about programming languages, computers, and related technical matters, but even if it comes to that, the concrete problem makes it easy to illustrate these concepts. *Once Upon an Algorithm* is an elaboration of this approach.

Computer science is a relatively new member of the science club, and sometimes it seems it has not yet earned the respect granted to serious scientific disciplines like physics, chemistry, and biology. Think of a movie scene involving a physicist. You will probably see someone discussing complicated formulas written on a blackboard or supervising an experiment wearing a lab coat. The physicist is shown as a reputable scientist whose knowledge is treasured. Now imagine a similar scene involving a computer scientist. Here you will likely see some nerdy guy sitting in a dark, messy room and staring at a computer screen. He is frantically typing on a keyboard, probably trying to break some code or password. In both scenes, an important problem is being solved, but while the physicist might provide some plausible explanation of how it can be solved, the solution of the computer problem remains mysterious, often magical, and much too complex to be explained to a nonspecialist. If computer science is unexplainable to laypeople, why would anyone ever try to know more about it or understand it?

The subject of computer science is *computation*, a phenomenon that affects everybody. I am not talking only about cell phones, laptops, or the internet. Consider folding a paper airplane, driving to work, cooking a meal, or even DNA transcription, a process that occurs in your cells millions of times while you are reading this sentence. These are all examples of computation—a systematic way of problem solving—even though most people would not perceive them as such.

Science provides us with a basic understanding of how the natural world works, and it gives us the scientific method for reliably establishing that knowledge. What applies to science in general holds for computer science, too, especially since we encounter computation in so many different forms and so many different situations. A basic understanding of computation thus provides benefits similar to a basic knowledge of physics, chemistry, and biology in making sense of the world and tackling many real-world problems more effectively. This aspect of computation is often referred to as *computational thinking*.

A major goal of this book is to emphasize the general nature of computation and thus the wide applicability of computer science. My hope is that this will spark a broader interest in computer science and a desire to learn more about it.

I first identify computation in everyday activities and then explain corresponding computer science concepts through popular stories. The everyday situations are taken from a typical workday: getting up in the morning, having breakfast, commuting to work, episodes at the workplace, a doctor's appointment, a hobby activity in the afternoon, having dinner, and reflecting on the day's events in the evening. Each of these fifteen vignettes introduces a book chapter. The chapters then explain the computation concepts using seven popular stories. Each story spans two or three chapters and deals with a specific topic of computer science.

The book has two parts: *algorithms* and *languages*. These are the two main pillars on which the concept of computation rests. Table 1 summarizes the stories and the computer science concepts they illustrate.

We all appreciate a good story. Stories console us, give us hope, and inspire us. They tell us about the world, make us aware of the problems we face, and sometimes suggest solutions. Stories can also provide guidance for our lives. When you think about what stories have to teach us, you probably think about love, conflict, the human condition. But I also think about computation. When Shakespeare's Juliet asks, "What's in a name?" she is on to an important question about representation. Albert Camus's

**Table 1**

| Story | Chapters | Topics |
|---|---|---|
| *Part I* | | |
| Hansel and Gretel | 1, 2 | Computation and Algorithms |
| Sherlock Holmes | 3, 4 | Representation and Data Structures |
| Indiana Jones | 5, 6, 7 | Problem Solving and Its Limitations |
| | | |
| *Part II* | | |
| Over the Rainbow | 8, 9 | Language and Meaning |
| Groundhog Day | 10, 11 | Control Structures and Loops |
| Back to the Future | 12, 13 | Recursion |
| Harry Potter | 14, 15 | Types and Abstraction |

*The Myth of Sisyphus* raises the question of how to face the absurdity of life and also how to detect a never-ending computation.

Stories have multiple layers of meaning. They often include a computational layer. *Once Upon an Algorithm* is an effort to unveil this layer and offer readers a new perspective on stories and computation. I hope that stories will be appreciated for their computational content and that this novel point of view will spark interest in computer science.

# Acknowledgments

The idea for *Once Upon an Algorithm* arose from many conversations with friends, students, colleagues, and people I talk to on the bus on my way to work. I thank all of them for their patience in listening to my explanations about computer science and for their friendly impatience when the explanations became too long and complicated. The goal of writing a widely accessible book about computer science was fueled to a large degree by these experiences.

Over the last decade I've had the opportunity to work with many high school students as summer interns, which provided additional encouragement. These internships were supported by several grants from the National Science Foundation, to which I am grateful for its support of scientific research and science education in the United States.

In researching the material for *Once Upon an Algorithm* I have relied on the internet, in particular, Wikipedia (wikipedia.org) and the TV Tropes website (tvtropes.org). Thanks to all those contributors for their commitment and enthusiasm in sharing their knowledge with the world.

While I was writing this book, Eric Walkingshaw, Paul Cull, and Karl Smeltzer read some of the chapters and provided expert feedback on content and writing style. I want to thank them for their helpful advice. Thanks also to Jennifer Parham-Mocello for reading some of the chapters and testing several of the examples with her students in a college freshman class. I also thank my son, Alexander, for proofreading the manuscript and providing expert advice on questions related to Harry Potter. Most of this book was written during a sabbatical from my position at Oregon State University. I thank my department and the university for their support for this project.

Turning the idea for this book into reality was a much greater challenge than I had anticipated. My sincere thanks to Marie Lufkin-Lee, Katherine Almeida, Kathleen Hensley, and Christine Savage at MIT Press for supporting this project and helping me with it along the way.

Finally, I am fortunate to be married to my most patient and candid reader. My wife, Anja, encouraged me throughout the adventure of this book project. She always had an open ear for my questions, which more often than not were quite nerdy and abstract. She read many drafts and patiently tried to rein me in whenever my writing was too academic and relied too much on technical jargon. The completion of *Once Upon an Algorithm* owes more to her than to anyone else, and I dedicate this book to her.

# Introduction

Computation plays a prominent role in society now. But unless you want to become a computer scientist, why should this prompt you to learn more about it? You could simply enjoy the technology powered by computation and take advantage of its benefits. You likely also don't study avionics to make use of air travel or seek a medical degree to benefit from the achievements of modern health care.

However, the world we live in consists of more than man-made technology. We still have to interact with nonautonomous objects ruled by physical laws. Therefore, it is beneficial to understand the basics of mechanics simply to predict the behavior of objects and to safely navigate one's environment. A similar case can be made for the benefits of studying computation and its related concepts. Computation is not only revealed in computers and electronic gadgets but also occurs outside of machines. In the following I briefly discuss some of the major computer science principles and explain why they matter.

## Computation and Algorithms

I invite you to perform the following simple exercise. For this you need a ruler, a pencil, and a piece of (quadrille-ruled) paper. First, draw a horizontal line that is 1 inch long. Then draw a vertical line of the same length, perpendicular to the first, starting at one of its ends. Finally, connect the two open ends of the lines you drew with a diagonal to form a triangle. Now measure the length of the diagonal just drawn. Congratulations; you have just computed the square root of 2. (See figure 1.)

What does this exercise in geometry have to do with computation? As I explain in chapters 1 and 2, it is the execution of an algorithm by a computer that brings about a computation. In this example, you acted as a computer that executed an algorithm to draw and measure lines, which led to the computation of $\sqrt{2}$. Having an algorithm is crucial because only then can different computers perform a computation repeatedly and at different times. An important aspect of computation is that it requires resources

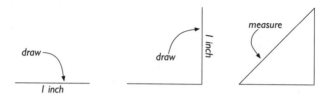

**Figure 1**    Computing the square root of 2 using a pencil and a ruler.

(such as pencil, paper, and a ruler) and takes time to carry out. Here again, having an algorithmic description is important because it helps in analyzing the resource requirements for computations.

Chapters 1 and 2 explain

- what algorithms are,
- that algorithms are used for systematic problem solving,
- that an algorithm needs to be executed by a computer (human, machine, etc.) to produce a computation,
- that the execution of algorithms consumes resources.

### Why does it matter?

Recipes are examples of algorithms. Whenever you make a sandwich, bake a chocolate cake, or cook your favorite dish by following the instructions of a recipe, you are effectively executing an algorithm to transform the raw ingredients into the final product. The required resources include the ingredients, tools, energy, and preparation time.

Knowledge about algorithms makes us sensitive to questions about the correctness of a method and what its resource requirements are. It helps us identify opportunities for improving processes in all areas of life through the (re)organization of steps and materials. For instance, in the geometric square root computation, we could have omitted drawing the diagonal line and just measured the distance between the two unconnected end points.

In cooking the improvement can be as simple and obvious as saving trips to the fridge by planning ahead or gathering ingredients ahead of time. You could plan how to use your oven or stove more efficiently and save time by parallelizing steps, such as preheating the oven or washing the salad while the potatoes are cooking. These techniques also apply to many other areas, from simple assembly instructions for furniture to organizational processes for running an office or managing a factory floor.

In the realm of technology, algorithms control basically all the computations in computers. One prominent example is data compression, without which the transmission of music and movies over the internet would be nearly impossible. A data compression algorithm identifies frequent patterns and replaces them with small codes. Data compression directly addresses the resource problem of computation by reducing the space required to represent songs and movies and thus also the time it takes to load them over the internet. Another example is Google's page-rank algorithm, which determines the order in which search results are presented to a user. It works by assessing the importance of a web page through counting how many links point to it and weighing how important those links are.

## Representation and Data Structures

One might expect that numerical computations are carried out with the help of numbers because we use the Hindu-Arabic numeral system, and machines work with 0s and 1s. So the geometric method for computing $\sqrt{2}$ with the help of lines might be surprising. The example demonstrates, however, that one and the same thing (for example, a quantity) can be represented in different ways (number symbols or lines).

The essence of a computation is the transformation of representation. I explain in chapter 3 what representations are and how they are employed in computations. Since many computations deal with large amounts of information, I explain in chapter 4 how collections of data can be efficiently organized. What complicates this question is the fact that any particular data organization may support some forms of accessing the data efficiently but not others.

Chapters 3 and 4 discuss

- different forms of representation,
- different ways of organizing and accessing data collections,
- the advantages and disadvantages of different data organizations.

### *Why does it matter?*

Measurements of ingredients in recipes can be given by weight or by volume. These are different forms of representation, which require different cooking utensils (scales or measuring cups) for properly executing the recipe/algorithm. As for data organization, the way your fridge or pantry is organized has an impact on how fast you can retrieve all the ingredients required for the recipe. Or consider how the question of representation applies to the recipe itself. It may be given as a textual description, through a series of pictures, or even in the form of a YouTube video. The choice of representation often makes a big difference in the effectiveness of algorithms.

In particular, the question of how to arrange a collection of items or people has many applications, for instance, how to organize your desk or garage to help you find items more quickly or how to organize the book shelves in a library. Or consider the different ways you wait in line: in a grocery store (standing in a queue) or at a doctor's office (sitting in a waiting room having picked a number) or when boarding an airplane (multiple queues).

In the realm of technology, spreadsheets are among the most successful programming tools. The organization of data in tabular form has contributed to much of their success because it supports the quick and easy formulation of sums over rows and columns and represents the data and computation results for them in one place. On the other hand, the internet, one of the most transformative inventions of the late twentieth century, organizes web pages, computers, and the connections between them as a network. This representation supports flexible access to information and efficient transmission of data.

## Problem Solving and Its Limitations

An algorithm is a method for solving problems, be it finding the square root of a number or baking a cake. And computer science is a discipline that is concerned with systematic problem solving.

Of the many problems that can be solved through algorithms, two deserve to be discussed in detail. In chapter 5, I explain the problem of searching, one of the most frequently used computations on data. Chapter 6 then explains the problem of sorting, which illustrates a powerful problem-solving method and also the notion of intrinsic problem complexity. In chapter 7, I describe the class of so-called intractable problems. Algorithms exist for these problems, but take too long to execute, so the problems are not solvable in practice.

Chapters 5, 6, and 7 clarify

- why searching can be difficult and time consuming,
- methods to improve searching,
- different algorithms for sorting,

- that some computations can support others, such as sorting can support searching,
- that algorithms with exponential runtimes cannot really be considered solutions to problems.

### Why does it matter?

We spend countless hours of our lives searching, be it for our car keys or for information on the internet. It is therefore helpful to understand searching and to know about techniques that can help make it more efficient. In addition, the problem of searching illustrates how the choice of representation affects the efficiency of algorithms, reflecting John Dewey's observation, "A problem well put is half solved."[1]

Knowing when a problem *cannot* be solved efficiently is just as important as knowing algorithms for solvable problems because it helps us avoid searching for efficient solutions where none can exist. It suggests that in some cases we should be content with approximate answers.

In the realm of technology, the most obvious instance of searching is given by internet search engines such as Google. Search results for a query are not presented in arbitrary order but are typically sorted according to their anticipated importance or relevance. The knowledge about the hardness of problems is used to develop algorithms that compute approximate solutions where exact solutions would take too long to compute. One famous example is the traveling salesman problem, which is to find the round-trip that visits a certain number of cities in an order that minimizes the total distance traveled.

Knowledge about the lack of an efficient algorithm to solve a problem can also be exploited in a positive way. One example is public key encryption, which enables private transactions on the internet, including managing bank accounts and shopping online. This encryption only works because currently no efficient algorithm is known for prime factorization (that is, writing a number as the product of prime numbers). If that were to change, public key encryption would not be safe anymore.

## Language and Meaning

Any algorithm has to be expressed in some language. Current computers cannot be programmed in English because natural languages contain too many ambiguities, which humans, but not machines, can deal with easily. Therefore, algorithms that are to be executed by machines have to be written in languages that have a well-defined structure and meaning.

In chapter 8, I explain what a language is and how we can define its syntax. A syntax definition for a language ensures that each of its sentences has a well-defined structure, which is the basis for understanding and defining the meaning of sentences and languages. In chapter 9, I discuss the meaning of languages and the problem of ambiguity.

Chapters 8 and 9 describe

- how a grammar defines a language,
- how a grammar can be used to construct all sentences belonging to the language,
- what syntax trees are,
- how syntax trees represent the structure of sentences and resolve ambiguities in the meaning of sentences.

### *Why does it matter?*

We employ languages to communicate meaning. For communication to work, the communicating partners have to agree on what counts as a proper sentence and what each sentence means. For example, instructions in recipes must be precise about measurements, oven temperature, cooking time, and so on, to produce the desired outcomes.

In most areas of our lives we have produced special terminology and languages that facilitate more effective communication. This is particularly true in computer science, in which a crucial part of communication happens via machines. Since machines are inferior to humans in their abilities to process language, the precise definition of languages is important to ensure that programmed machines behave as expected.

In the realm of technology, a widely used programming language is the formula language of spreadsheets. Anybody who has ever put a formula into a spreadsheet has written a spreadsheet program. Spreadsheets are notorious for being erroneous at times and causing losses of billions of dollars because of incorrect formulas. Another ubiquitous language is HTML (hypertext markup language). Whenever you load a web page onto your laptop, PC, or cell phone, it is very likely that the content is presented in your browser in HTML, which is a language that makes the structure of the web page explicit and presents it in an unambiguous way. While HTML is just for representing information and does not itself describe computation, another language any web browser understands these days is JavaScript, a language that especially defines the dynamic behavior of web pages.

# Control Structures and Loops

Instructions in an algorithm have two distinct functions: they either directly manipulate data, or they decide which instructions are to be performed next and how often. The latter kind of instructions are called control structures. Just like the plot of a movie or a story ties together individual actions and scenes into a coherent narrative, control structures build algorithms out of individual instructions.

In chapter 10, I explain different control structures and focus specifically on loops, which are used for expressing the repetition of actions. An important question, discussed in chapter 11, is whether a loop terminates or runs forever and whether this can be decided by an algorithm.

Chapters 10 and 11 discuss

- what control structures are,
- why control structures are a crucial part of any language for expressing algorithms,
- how repetitive tasks can be expressed by loops,
- what the halting problem is, and how it exemplifies a fundamental property of computation.

### Why does it matter?

You have to grease the pan before baking the pancakes. The order of steps in recipes matters. Moreover, recipes sometimes contain decisions that are based on properties of the ingredients or cooking utensils. For example, if you are using a convection oven, you have to use a shorter baking time or a lower temperature (or both). A recipe contains a loop when it instructs you to repeatedly perform some actions, such as repeatedly adding an egg and whisking the batter for a bundt cake.

The distinction between control structures and other operations amounts to the difference between doing something and organizing when and how often to do it. For any process or algorithm we may want to know whether it does what it is supposed to do, or even simply whether it can be completed at all. This rather simple question, posed by the halting problem, is only one example of many properties of algorithms that one would like to know about. Knowing which properties of algorithms can be determined automatically by other algorithms tells us about the reach of algorithms and the limits of computation.

In the realm of technology, control structures are used wherever algorithms are used, and thus they are everywhere. Any information sent over the internet is transmitted in a loop repeatedly until it has been properly received. Traffic lights are controlled by endlessly repeating loops, and many manufacturing processes contain tasks that are repeated until a quality measure is met. Predicting the behavior of algorithms for unknown future inputs has many applications in security. For example, one would like to know if a system is vulnerable to attacks by hackers. It also applies to rescue robots that have to be used in situations different from the ones they are trained in. Accurately predicting robot behavior in unknown situations can mean the difference between life and death.

## Recursion

The principle of reduction—the process of explaining or implementing a complex system by simpler parts—plays an important role in much of science and technology. Recursion is a special form of reduction that refers to itself. Many algorithms are recursive. Consider, for example, the instructions for looking up a word in a dictionary that contains one entry per page: "Open the dictionary. If you can see the word, stop. Otherwise, look up the word in the dictionary part before or after the current page." Notice how the look-up instruction in the last sentence is a recursive reference to the whole process that brings you back to the beginning of the instructions. There is no need for adding something like "repeat this until the word is found" to the description.

In chapter 12, I explain recursion, which is a control structure but is also used in the definition of data organization. In chapter 13, I illustrate different approaches for understanding recursion.

Chapters 12 and 13 examine

- the idea of recursion,
- how to distinguish between different forms of recursion,
- two different methods to unravel and make sense of recursive definitions,
- how these methods help in understanding recursion and the relationship between its different forms.

### Why does it matter?

The recursive definition of "season to taste" is as follows: "Taste the dish. If it tastes fine, stop. Otherwise, add a pinch of seasoning, and then season to taste." Any repeated action can be described recursively by using the action to be repeated (here "season to taste") in its description and a condition when to stop.

Recursion is an essential principle for obtaining finite descriptions of potentially infinite data and computations. Recursion in the grammar of a language facilitates an infinite number of sentences, and a recursive algorithm allows it to process inputs of arbitrary size.

Since recursion is a general control structure and a mechanism for organizing data, it is part of many software systems. In addition, there are several direct applications of recursion. For example, the Droste effect, in which a picture contains a smaller version of itself, can be obtained as a result of a feedback loop between a signal (a picture) and a receiver (a camera). The feedback loop is a recursive description of the repetitious effect. Fractals are self-similar geometric patterns that can be described through recursive equations. Fractals can be found in nature, for example, in snowflakes and crystals, and are also used in analyzing protein and DNA structures. Moreover, fractals are employed in nanotechnology for designing self-assembling nanocircuits. Self-replicating machines are a recursive concept because once they are operating, they reproduce copies of themselves that reproduce further copies, and so on. Self-replicating machines are investigated for space exploration.

## Types and Abstraction

Computation works by transforming representations. But not every transformation is applicable to every representation. While we can multiply numbers, we cannot multiply lines, and similarly, while we can compute the length of a line or the area of a rectangle, it does not make sense to do that for a number.

Representations and transformations can be classified into different groups to facilitate the distinction between transformations that are viable and those that don't make sense. These groups are called types, and the rules that determine which combinations of transformations and representations are allowed are called typing rules. Types and typing rules support the design of algorithms. For example, if you need to compute a number, you should employ an operation that produces numbers, and if you need to process a list of numbers, you have to use an operation that accepts lists of numbers as input.

In chapter 14, I explain what types are and how they can be used to formulate rules for describing regularities of computations. Such rules can be used to find errors in algorithms. The power of types lies in their ability to ignore details about individual objects and therefore to formulate rules on a more general level. The process of ignoring details is called abstraction, which is the subject of chapter 15, where I explain why abstraction is central to computer science and how it applies not only to types but also to algorithms, and even computers and languages.

Chapters 14 and 15 discuss

- what types and typing rules are,
- how they can be used to describe laws about computation that help to detect errors in algorithms and to construct reliable algorithms,
- that types and typing rules are just a special case of the more general idea of abstraction,
- that algorithms are abstractions of computation,
- that types are abstractions of representations,
- that runtime complexity is an abstraction of execution time.

### Why does it matter?

If a recipe requires the opening of a can of beans, you'd be surprised if someone approached this task using a spoon because that would violate a typing rule that deems spoons inadequate for that task.

The use of types and other abstractions to describe rules and processes is ubiquitous. Any procedure that has to be repeated suggests an algorithmic abstraction, that is, a description that ignores unnecessary details and replaces variable parts by parameters. Recipes also contain algorithmic abstractions. For example, many cookbooks contain a section describing basic techniques, such as peeling and seeding tomatoes, which can then be referred to in recipes by simply requesting a particular amount of peeled and seeded tomatoes. Moreover, the roles of the different objects that take part in such an abstraction are summarized by types that characterize their requirements.

In the realm of technology, there are many examples of types and abstractions. Examples of physical types are all kinds of differently shaped plugs and outlets, screws and screwdrivers and drill bits, and locks and keys. The shapes' purpose is to prevent improper combinations. Software examples of types can be found in web forms that require entering phone numbers or email addresses in a specific format. There are many examples of costly mistakes that were caused by ignoring types. For instance, in 1998, NASA lost its $655 million Mars Climate Orbiter because of incompatible number representations. This was a type error that could have been prevented by a type system. Finally, the notion of a computer is itself an abstraction of humans, machines, or other actors that are capable of executing algorithms.

# How to Read This Book

Figure 2 presents an overview of the concepts discussed in this book and how they are related. Chapters 7, 11, and 13 (dark-shaded boxes in figure 2) contain more technical material. These chapters may be skipped and are not required in order to understand the rest of the book.

While the material in this book is arranged in a specific order, it doesn't have to be read in that order. Many of the chapters can be read independently of one another, even though later chapters of the book sometimes refer to concepts an examples that have been introduced earlier.

The following provides guidance for selecting chapters to read and the order in which to read them. It also provides exits and shortcuts that allow readers to skip ahead while reading chapters. While I discuss the computing concepts via events, people, and objects that occur in stories, I also sometimes introduce new notation and work through examples to demonstrate important aspects in more detail. Hence, some parts of the book are easier to follow than others. As a reader of many popular science books, I am well aware of the fact that one's appetite for such details may vary. That is why I hope this guidance will help the reader to better navigate the book's content.

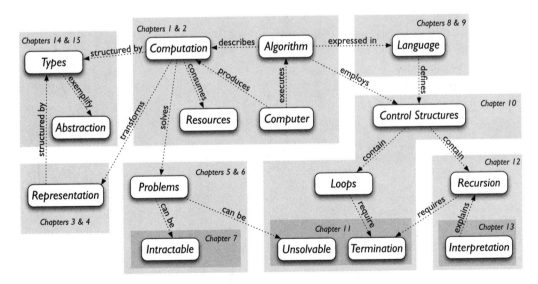

**Figure 2**   Concepts of computation and how they are related.

I suggest reading chapters 1 and 2 first, since they introduce fundamental concepts of computing that appear throughout the book, such as algorithm, parameter, computer, and runtime complexity. These two chapters should be easy to follow.

The other six topic areas (light-shaded boxes in figure 2) are largely independent of one another, but within each topic area the chapters should be read in order. Chapter 4 introduces several data structures, so it should be read before chapters 5, 6, 8, 12, and 13 (see diagram).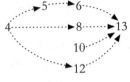

Finally, the Glossary at the end of the book provides additional information about how the chapters relate by grouping definitions into topic areas and cross-linking their entries.

# Part I

# ALGORITHMS

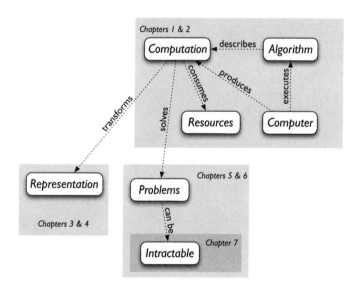

Chapters 1 & 2

Computation —describes→ Algorithm

consumes · produces · executes

transforms · solves

Resources · Computer

Representation

Chapters 3 & 4

Problems · Chapters 5 & 6

can be

Intractable · Chapter 7

# Computation and Algorithms

---

*Hansel and Gretel*

# Getting up

It is early in the morning. The alarm clock rings. You move your body out of bed—eventually. You get dressed. This simple daily getting-up routine solves a recurring problem through a series of well-defined steps. In computer science such a routine is called an *algorithm*. Taking a shower, brushing your teeth, having breakfast, and so on, are more examples of algorithms that solve specific problems.

But wait a minute. Except perhaps for not getting enough sleep, what is the problem here? We usually do not perceive mundane everyday activities as producing solutions to problems. Maybe this is because these problems have obvious solutions or the solutions are easily obtained. However, the word *problem* is commonly used for situations or questions that have well-known solutions. Think of exams, which contain problems with well-defined answers. A *problem* is thus any question or situation that demands a solution, even if it is clear how to get it. In this sense, having to get up in the morning is a problem that has a well-known method for producing a solution.

Once we know how to solve a problem, we seldom wonder how the corresponding method was conceived. In particular, when the method is obvious and simple to use, there seems to be no point in reflecting on it. But thinking about *how* we can solve problems can help us solve unknown problems in the future. Solutions to problems are not always obvious. In hindsight, most solutions seem evident, but what if you didn't know how to solve the getting-up problem. How would you approach it?

One crucial observation is that nontrivial problems can be decomposed into subproblems and that the solutions to the subproblems can be combined into a solution for the original problem. The getting-up problem consists of the two subproblems: getting out of bed and getting dressed. We have algorithms for solving both of these problems, that is, moving our body out of the bed and putting on clothes, respectively, and we can combine these algorithms into an algorithm for getting up, but we have to be careful to do it in the right order. Since it is rather difficult to get dressed in bed, we should take the step of getting out of bed first. If you don't find this example convincing, think about the order in which to take a shower and to get dressed. In this simple example there is only one ordering of the steps that leads to a viable solution, but this is not always the case.

Problem decomposition is not limited to one level. For example, the problem of getting dressed can be further decomposed into several subproblems, such as putting on pants, a shirt, shoes, and so on. The nice thing about problem decomposition is that it helps us to modularize the process of finding solutions, which means that solutions to different subproblems can be developed independently of one another. Modularity is important because it enables the parallel development of solutions to problems by teams.

Finding an algorithm for solving a problem is not the end of the story. The algorithm has to be put to work to actually solve the problem. Knowing how to do something and actually doing it are two different things. Some of us are made painfully aware of this difference each morning when the alarm clock rings. Thus there is a difference between an algorithm and its use.

In computer science each use of an algorithm is called a *computation*. So does that mean, when we actually do get up, that we are computing ourselves out of bed and into our clothes? That sounds crazy, but what would we say about a robot that did the same thing? The robot needs to be programmed to accomplish the task. In other words, the robot is told the algorithm in a language it understands. When the robot executes its program to get up, wouldn't we say it carries out a computation? This is not to say that humans are robots, but it does show that people compute when they execute algorithms.

The power of algorithms derives from the fact that they can be executed many times. Like the proverbial wheel that should not be reinvented, a good algorithm, once developed, is there to stay and serve us forever. It will be reused by many people in many situations to reliably compute solutions to recurring problems. This is why algorithms play a central role in computer science and why the design of algorithms is one of the most important and exciting tasks for computer scientists.

Computer science could be called the science of problem solving. Even though you won't find this definition in many textbooks, this perspective is a useful reminder of why computer science affects more and more areas of our lives. Moreover, many useful computations happen outside of machines and are performed by people (without a computer science education) to solve problems. Chapter 1 introduces the concept of computation and, through the story of Hansel and Gretel, highlights its problem-solving and human aspects.

# 1

# A Path to Understanding Computation

*What is computation?* This question lies at the core of computer science. This chapter provides an answer—at least a tentative one—and connects the notion of computation to some closely related concepts. In particular, I explain the relationship between computation and the concepts of problem solving and algorithms. To this end, I describe two complementary aspects of computation: what it does, and what it is.

The first view, *computation solves problems*, emphasizes that a problem can be solved through computation once it is suitably represented and broken down into subproblems. It not only reflects the tremendous impact computer science has had in so many different areas of society but also explains why computation is an essential part of all kinds of human activities, independent of the use of computing machines.

However, the problem-solving perspective leaves out some important aspects of computation. A closer look at the differences between computation and problem solving leads to a second view, *computation is algorithm execution*. An algorithm is a precise description of computation and makes it possible to automate and analyze computation. This view portrays computation as a process consisting of several steps, which helps explain how and why it is so effective in solving problems.

The key to harnessing computation lies in grouping similar problems into one class and designing an algorithm that solves each problem in that class. This makes an algorithm similar to a skill. A skill such as baking a cake or repairing a car can be invoked at different times and thus can be employed repeatedly to solve different instances of a particular problem class. Skills can also be taught to and shared with others, which gives them an even wider impact. Similarly, we can execute an algorithm repeatedly for different problem instances and generate with each execution a computation that solves the problem at hand.

## Dividing Problems into Triviality

Let us start with the first perspective and consider computation as a process that solves a specific problem. As an example, I use the well-known story of Hansel and Gretel, who were left to die in the woods by their parents. Let's examine Hansel's clever idea that allowed him and Gretel to find their way back home after being left behind in the forest. The story unfolds in the context of a famine, when Hansel and Gretel's stepmother urges their father to lead the children into the forest and abandon them, so that the parents can survive. Having overheard his parents' conversation, Hansel goes outside later that night and collects several handfuls of small pebbles that he stuffs into his pockets. The next day, during their walk into the forest, he drops the pebbles along the way as markers for the way back home. After the parents have left them, the children wait until it is dark and the pebbles begin to shine in the moonlight. They then follow the pebbles until they return home.

The story doesn't end here, but this part provides us with a peculiar example of how a problem is solved using computation. The problem to be solved is one of survival—certainly much more serious than the problem of getting up. The survival problem presents itself as a task of moving from a location in the forest to the location of Hansel and Gretel's home. This is a nontrivial problem particularly because it cannot be solved in one step. A problem that is too complex to be solved in one step has to be broken down into subproblems that are easy to solve and whose solutions can be combined into a solution for the overall problem.

The problem of finding the way out of the forest can be decomposed by identifying a sequence of intermediate locations that are close enough to each other that one can easily move between them. These locations form a path out of the forest back to Hansel and Gretel's home, and the individual movements from one location to the next are easy to achieve. When combined, they yield a move- 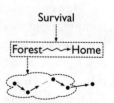 ment from the starting location in the forest to the home. This movement solves Hansel and Gretel's problem of survival in a systematic way. Systematic problem solving is one key characteristic of computation.

As this example illustrates, a computation usually consists of not just one but many steps. Each of these steps solves a subproblem and changes the problem situation a little bit. For example, each move by Hansel and Gretel to the next pebble is a step in the computation that changes their position in the forest, which corresponds to solving the subproblem of reaching the next target on the path home. While in most cases each individual step will bring the computation closer to the solution, this does not necessarily have to be the case for every step. Only all steps taken together have to yield the solution. In the story, while each position that Hansel and Gretel go through will generally be closer to home, it is also likely that the path is not a straight line. Some pebbles may even cause detours, for example, to move around obstacles or to cross a river using a bridge, but this does not change the effect of the combined movement.

The important lesson is that a solution is obtained through a systematic problem decomposition. While decomposition is a key strategy to obtaining a solution to a problem, it is not always sufficient by itself, and solutions may depend on supplementary items—in the case of Hansel and Gretel, the pebbles.

## No Computation without Representation

If a computation consists of a number of steps, what does each of these steps actually do, and how can all the steps together produce a solution to the given problem? To produce an aggregate effect, each step has to have an effect that the next steps can build on so that the cumulative effect produced by all the steps results in a solution for the problem. In the story the effect of each step is to change Hansel and Gretel's location, and the problem is solved when the location is finally changed to their home. In general, a step in a computation can have an effect on almost anything, be it concrete physical objects or abstract mathematical entities.

To solve a problem it is necessary that a computation manipulate a *representation* of something meaningful in the real world. Hansel and Gretel's locations represent one of two possible states: all locations in the forest represent the problem state of danger and possibly death, while their home represents the solution state of safety and survival. This is why the computation that brings Hansel and Gretel home solves a problem—it moves them from danger to safety. In contrast, a computation that leads from one place in the forest to another would not achieve that.

This example has another level of representation. Since the computation that is defined by moves between locations is carried out by Hansel and Gretel, the locations must be recognizable to them, which is why Hansel drops the pebbles along the way. The pebbles represent the locations in a form that enables the

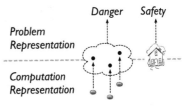

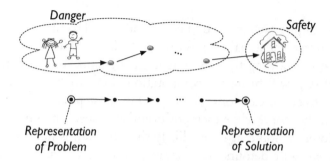

**Figure 1.1**  Computation is a process for solving a particular problem. Usually, a computation consists of several steps. Starting with a representation of the problem, each step transforms the representation until the solution is obtained. Hansel and Gretel solve the problem of surviving through a process of changing their position step-by-step and pebble-by-pebble from within the forest to their home.

computer, that is, Hansel and Gretel, to actually carry out the steps of the computation. It is common to have several layers of representation. In this case we have one that defines the problem (locations) and one that makes it possible to compute a solution (pebbles). In addition, all the pebbles taken together constitute another level of representation, since they represent the path out of the forest back home. These representations are summarized in table 1.1.

Figure 1.1 summarizes the problem-solving picture of computation; it shows Hansel and Gretel's way-finding as an instance of the view that computation manipulates representation in a sequence of steps. In the getting-up problem we also find representations, for example, as location (in bed, out of bed) and as an alarm clock representing time. Representations can take many different forms. They are discussed in more detail in chapter 3.

**Table 1.1**

| *Computation Representation* | | *Problem Representation* | |
|---|---|---|---|
| **Object** | **Represents** | **Concept** | **Represents** |
| One pebble | Location in forest | Location in forest | Danger |
|  | Home | Home | Safety |
| All pebbles | Path out of forest | Path out of forest | Problem Solution |

# Beyond Problem Solving

Regarding computation as a problem-solving process captures the purpose of computation but doesn't explain what computation really *is*. Moreover, the problem-solving view has some limitations, since not every act of problem solving is a computation.

As illustrated in figure 1.2, there are computations, and there is problem solving. Although these often overlap, some computations do not solve problems, and some problems are not solved through computation. The emphasis in this book is on the intersection of computations and problem solving, but to make this focus clear, I consider some examples for the other two cases.

For the first case, imagine a computation consisting of following pebbles from one place to another within the forest. The steps of this process are in principle the same as in the original story, but the corresponding change of location would not solve Hansel and Gretel's problem of survival. As an even more drastic example, imagine the situation when the pebbles are arranged in a loop, which means the corresponding computation doesn't seem to achieve anything, since the initial and final positions are identical. In other words, the computation has no cumulative effect. The difference between these two cases and the one in the story is the meaning that is attached to the process.

Processes without such an apparent meaning still qualify as computation, but they may not be perceived as problem solving. This case is not hugely important, since we can always assign some arbitrary meaning to the representation operated on by a particular computation. Therefore, any computation could arguably be considered problem solving; it always depends on what meaning is associated with the representation. For example, following a loop inside a forest may not be helpful for Hansel and Gretel, but it could solve the problem of getting exercise for a runner. Thus, whether a computation solves a problem is in the eye of the beholder, that is, in the utility of a computation. In any case, whether or not one grants a particular computation the status of problem solving does not affect the essence of computation.

The situation is markedly different for noncomputational problem solving, since it provides us with further criteria for computation. In figure 1.2 two such criteria are mentioned, both of which are, in fact, very closely related. First, if a problem is solved in an ad hoc way that doesn't follow a particular method, it is not a computation. In other words, a computation has to be systematic. We can find several instances of this kind of noncomputational problem solving in the story. One example occurs when Hansel and Gretel are held captive by the witch who tries to fatten up Hansel with the goal of eating him. Since she can't see well, she estimates Hansel's weight by feeling his finger. Hansel misleads the witch about his weight by using a little bone in place of his

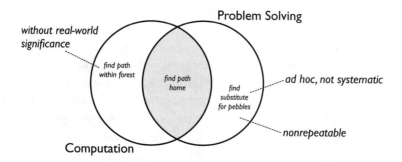

**Figure 1.2** Distinguishing problem solving from computation. A computation whose effect carries no meaning in the real world does not solve any problems. An ad hoc solution to a problem that is not repeatable is not a computation.

finger. This idea is not the result of a systematic computation, but it solves the problem: it postpones the witch's eating Hansel.

Another example of noncomputational problem solving occurs right after Hansel and Gretel have returned home. The parents plan to lead them into the forest again the next day, but this time the stepmother locks the doors the night before to prevent Hansel from collecting any pebbles. The problem is that Hansel cannot get access to the pebbles that served him so well the first time and that he relied on for finding the way back home. His solution is to find a substitute in the form of breadcrumbs. The important point here is how Hansel arrives at this solution—he has an idea, a creative thought. A solution that involves a eureka moment is generally very difficult, if not impossible, to derive systematically through a computation because it requires reasoning on a subtle level about objects and their properties.

Unfortunately for Hansel and Gretel, the breadcrumbs solution doesn't work as expected:

> When the moon came, they set out, but they found no crumbs, for the many thousands of birds which fly about in the woods and fields had picked them all up.[1]

Since the breadcrumbs are gone, Hansel and Gretel can't find their way home, and the rest of the story unfolds.

However, let us assume for a moment that Hansel and Gretel could somehow have found their way back home again and that the parents would have tried a third time to leave them behind in the forest. Hansel and Gretel would have had to think of yet another means to mark their way home. They would have had to find something else to drop along the way, or maybe they would have tried to mark trees or bushes. Whatever the solution, it would have been produced by thinking about the problem and having another creative idea, but not by systematically applying a method. This highlights the other criterion for computation, which is its ability to be repeated and solve many similar problems. The method for solving the way-finding problem by following pebbles is different in this regard because it can be executed repeatedly for many different pebble placements.

To summarize, while the problem-solving perspective shows that computation is a systematic and decomposable process, it is not sufficient to give a comprehensive and precise picture of computation. Viewing computation as problem solving demonstrates how computation can be employed in all kinds of situations and thus illustrates its importance but ignores some important attributes that explain how computation works and why it can be successfully applied in so many different ways.

## When Problems Reappear

Hansel and Gretel are faced with the problem of finding their way back home *twice*. Except for the practical problems caused by the lack of pebbles, the second instance could be solved in the same way as the first, namely, by following a series of markers. There is nothing really surprising about this fact, since Hansel and Gretel are simply applying a general method of way-finding. Such a method is called an *algorithm*.

Let us take a look at the algorithm that was used by Hansel and Gretel to find their way home. The exact method is not explained in detail in the original fairy tale. All we are told is the following:

> And when the full moon had risen, Hansel took his little sister by the hand, and followed the pebbles which shone like newly-coined silver pieces, and showed them the way.

A simple algorithm that fits this characterization is given, for example, by the following description:

> Find a shining pebble that was not visited before, and go toward it.
> Continue this process until you reach your parents' house.

An important property of an algorithm is that it can be used repeatedly by the same or a different person to solve the same or a closely related problem. An algorithm that generates a computation with a physical effect is useful even if it solves only one specific problem. For example, a recipe for a cake will produce the same cake over and over again. Since the output of the algorithm is transient—the cake gets eaten—reproducing the same result is very useful. The same holds for the problem of getting out of bed and dressed; the effect of the algorithm has to be reproduced every day, although likely with different clothes and at a different time on weekends. This also applies to Hansel and Gretel. Even if they are brought to the same place in the forest as on the first day, getting home has to be recomputed by repeating the algorithm to solve the exact same problem.

The situation is different for algorithms that produce nonphysical, abstract results, such as numbers. In such a case one can simply write down the result and look it up the next time it is needed instead of executing the algorithm again. For an algorithm to be useful in such situations it must be able to solve a whole class of problems, which means that it must be possible to apply the method to several different, but related, problems.[2]

In the story the method is general enough to solve many different way-finding problems, since the exact positions of the pebbles do not matter. No matter where exactly in the forest the parents lead the children to, the algorithm will work in every case[3] and consequently will cause a computation that solves Hansel and Gretel's survival problem. Much of the power and impact of algorithms comes from the fact that *one* algorithm gives rise to *many* computations.

The notion of an algorithm is one of the most important concepts in computer science because it provides the foundation for the systematic study of computation. Accordingly, many different aspects of algorithms are discussed throughout this book.

## Do You Speak "Algorithmish"?

An algorithm is a description of how to perform a computation and must therefore be formulated in some language. In the story the algorithm is only marginally mentioned. Hansel certainly has the algorithm in his head and might have told Gretel about it, but the algorithm is not written down as part of the story. However, the fact that an algorithm can be written down is an important  property because it enables the reliable sharing of the algorithm and thus allows many people to use it to solve problems. The ability to express an algorithm in some language supports the proliferation of computation because instead of one person producing many computations, it facilitates many people's producing even more computations. If the language in which the algorithm is expressed can be understood by a computing machine, then the proliferation of computation seems almost limitless, bounded only by the resources needed to build and operate computers.

Does the getting-up algorithm need a description in a language? Probably not. Through repeated execution we all have internalized the steps to the point that we execute them unconsciously and don't need a description. However, for some parts of this algorithm there do exist descriptions, often given as a sequence of pictures. Think about tying a tie or arranging a sophisticated braided hairstyle. If you do this for the first time and no one is available to demonstrate the technique, you can learn the skill from such a description.

The ability to express an algorithm in a language has another important effect. It allows the systematic analysis and formal manipulation of algorithms, which is the subject of computer science theory and programming languages research.

An algorithm must be expressible in a language that can be understood by the computer to execute it. Moreover, the description must be *finite*, that is, it is bounded and doesn't go on forever. Finally, each of its individual steps must be *effective*, that is, whoever executes the algorithm must be able to understand and perform all the steps. Hansel and Gretel's algorithm is clearly finite, since it contains only a few instructions, and the individual steps are also effective, at least when we assume that the pebbles are placed within viewing distance of one another. One might have some doubts about the requirement to always find a pebble that was not visited before; this can be difficult because of the need to remember all the previously encountered pebbles. This requirement could be easily realized, though, by simply picking up each pebble immediately after it has been visited. However, this would then be a different algorithm. Incidentally, that algorithm would have made it easy for Hansel and Gretel to find their way back on the second day, since Hansel would have held onto all the pebbles. The slightly changed algorithm would have made the story as told by the Brothers Grimm impossible (depriving us, alas, of a classic fairy tale).

## A Wish List

In addition to the defining characteristics, there are several desirable features for algorithms. For example, an algorithm should always produce a computation that *terminates* and that delivers *correct results*. Since Hansel has placed a finite number of pebbles that mark the way to the parents' house, an execution of the described algorithm will terminate because it visits each pebble no more than once. Surprisingly, however, it might not produce a correct result in all cases because the process could get stuck.

**Figure 1.3** A path that illustrates a possible dead end in an algorithm. *Left:* Visiting the pebbles in the reverse order leads to Hansel and Gretel's home. *Right:* Since pebbles $B$, $C$, and $D$ are all within viewing distance from one another, Hansel and Gretel could choose to go from $D$ to $B$ and then to $C$. At that point, however, they are stuck because no pebble that they haven't visited before is visible from $C$. Specifically, they cannot reach $A$, which is the next pebble on the path home.

As stated, the algorithm does not say which pebble exactly to go to. If the parents are leading Hansel and Gretel not in a straight line but, say, along a zig-zag path into the forest, it could happen that from one pebble several other pebbles are visible. Which pebble should Hansel and Gretel go to in such a case? The algorithm doesn't say. Under the assumption that all pebbles are placed in viewing distance from one another, we can encounter the following situation, illustrated in figure 1.3.

Imagine a series of pebbles $A$, $B$, $C$, and $D$, placed by Hansel on their way into the forest. Suppose that $A$ can be seen from $B$, and $B$ can be seen from $C$, but $A$ is too far away to be visible from $C$. (This is indicated in the figure by the circles of visibility around pebbles $B$ and $C$.) Moreover, suppose that $D$ is within viewing distance from both $B$ and $C$. This means that when Hansel and Gretel arrive at $D$, they can see the two pebbles $B$ and $C$ and have a choice to make. If they choose to go to $C$, then they will find $B$ next and finally $A$, and everything will be fine (see left part of figure 1.3). However, if they choose $B$ instead of $C$—which is possible according to the algorithm, since $B$ is a visible pebble not visited before—they can get into trouble because if they next choose $C$—which again is visible and has not been visited yet—they will be stuck at $C$. This is because the only pebbles that they can see from $C$ are $B$ and $D$, both of which have already been visited and therefore cannot be chosen, according to the algorithm (see right part of figure 1.3).

Of course, we could try to fix the algorithm by adding instructions to backtrack in cases like this and choose a different alternative, but the point of this example is to illustrate a case in which a given algorithm does not produce a correct result. It also shows that the behavior of an algorithm is not always easy to predict, which makes the design of algorithms a challenging and interesting endeavor.

The termination of algorithms is not an easy-to-recognize property either. If we remove the condition in the algorithm to find only nonvisited pebbles, a computation can easily slip into a nonterminating back-and-forth movement between two pebbles. One might object that Hansel and Gretel would never do such a silly thing and would recognize such a repeating pattern. This might be true, but then they would not be following the exact algorithm and would, in fact, be deliberately avoiding a previously visited pebble.

Whereas the case of a nonterminating back-and-forth between two pebbles would be easy to spot, the problem can be much more difficult generally. Imagine a path taken by the parents into the forest that crosses itself a few times. The resulting pebble placement  would include several loops, each of which Hansel and Gretel could be caught in; only by remembering visited pebbles could they be certain to avoid such loops. Chapter 11 considers the problem of termination in more detail.

Questions of correctness and termination do not seem that important for the getting-up algorithm, but people have been known to put on nonmatching socks or to violate the rules for correctly buttoning a shirt. And if you persist in repeatedly hitting the snooze button, the getting-up algorithm will not even terminate.

# Starting the Day

Most people's day doesn't really start before they've had breakfast. Cereal, fruit, eggs with bacon, juice, coffee—whatever is on the menu, chances are that breakfast needs some form of preparation. Some of these preparations can be described by algorithms.

If you like to vary your breakfast, for example, by adding different toppings to your cereal or brewing different amounts of coffee, the algorithm that describes the preparation must be able to reflect this flexibility. The key to providing controlled variability is to employ one or more placeholders, called *parameters*, that are replaced by concrete values whenever the algorithm is executed. Using different values for a placeholder causes the algorithm to produce different computations. For example, a parameter "fruit" can be substituted by different fruits on different days, allowing the execution of the algorithm to produce blueberry cereal as well as banana cereal. The getting-up algorithm also contains parameters so that we are not forced to wake up at the same time and wear the same shirt every day.

If you are grabbing coffee from a coffee shop on your way to work, or if you are ordering breakfast in a restaurant, algorithms are still employed in producing your breakfast. It is just that other people have to do the work for you. The person or machine that is executing an algorithm is called a *computer* and has a profound effect on the outcome of a computation. It may happen that a computer is unable to execute the algorithm if it doesn't understand the language in which the algorithm is given or if it is unable to perform one of its steps. Imagine you are a guest on a farm, and the algorithm for getting your morning milk involves your milking a cow. This step might prove prohibitive.

But even if a computer can execute all the steps of an algorithm, the time it takes to do so matters. In particular, the execution time can vary substantially between different computers. For example, an experienced cow milker can extract a glass of milk faster than a novice. However, computer science mostly ignores these differences because they are transient and not very meaningful, since the speed of electronic computers increases over time—and novice cow milkers can get more experienced and thus faster. What is of great importance, however, is the difference in execution time between different algorithms for the same problem. For example, if you want to get a glass of milk for everyone in your family, you could fetch each glass separately, or you could fetch a milk can once and then fill all glasses at the breakfast table. In the latter case you have to walk the distance to the stable only twice, whereas in the former case you have to walk it ten times for a family of five. This difference between the two algorithms exists independently of how fast you can milk or walk. It is thus an indicator for the complexity of the two algorithms and can be the basis for choosing between them.

In addition to execution time, algorithms may also differ with regard to other resources that are required for their execution. Say your morning drink is coffee and not milk, and you have the option to brew coffee with a coffee maker or use a French press. Both methods require water and ground coffee, but the first method additionally requires coffee filters. The resource requirements for different milking algorithms are even more pronounced. Getting fresh milk requires a cow, whereas milk bought at a grocery store requires a fridge for storing it. This example also shows that computation results can be saved for later use and that computation can be sometimes traded for storage space. We can save the effort of milking a cow by storing previously drawn milk in a fridge.

The execution of an algorithm has to pay for its effect with the use of resources. Therefore, in order to compare different algorithms for the same problem, it is important to be able to measure the resources they consume. Sometimes we may even want to sacrifice correctness for efficiency. Suppose you are on your way to your office and you have to grab a few items from the grocery store. Since you are in a hurry, you leave the change behind instead of storing the coins returned to you. The correct algorithm would exchange the exact amount of money for the bought items, but the approximation algorithm that rounds up finishes your transaction faster.

Studying the properties of algorithms and their computations, including the resource requirements, is an important task of computer science. It facilitates judging whether a particular algorithm is a viable solution to a specific problem. Continuing with the story about Hansel and Gretel, I explain in chapter 2 how different computations can be produced with one algorithm and how to measure the resources required.

# 2

# Walk the Walk: When Computation Really Happens

In the previous chapter we saw how Hansel and Gretel solved a problem of survival by computing their way back home. This computation transformed their position systematically in individual steps, and it solved the problem by moving from a position in the forest, representing danger, to the final position at home, representing safety. The back-to-home computation was the result of executing an algorithm to follow a path of pebbles. Computation happens when algorithms get to work.

While we now have a good picture of what computation *is*, we have only seen one aspect of what computation actually *does*, namely, the transformation of representation. But there are additional details that deserve attention. Therefore, to expand understanding beyond the *static* representation through algorithms, I discuss the *dynamic* behavior of computation.

The great thing about an algorithm is that it can be used repeatedly to solve different problems. How does this work? And how is it actually possible that one fixed algorithm description can produce different computations? Moreover, we have said that computation results from executing an algorithm, but who or what is executing the algorithm? What are the skills needed to execute an algorithm? Can anybody do it? And finally, while it is great to have an algorithm for solving a problem, we have to ask at what cost. Only when an algorithm can deliver a solution to a problem fast enough and with the resources allocated is it a viable option.

# Creating Variety

Getting back to Hansel and Gretel, we've seen that their pebble-tracing algorithm can be used repeatedly and in different situations. Let us now take a closer look at how this actually works. Since the description in the algorithm is fixed, some part of this description must account for the variability in computations. This part is called a *parameter*. A parameter in an algorithm stands for some concrete value, and when an algorithm is executed, a concrete value must be substituted for the parameter in the algorithm. Such a value is called an *input value*, or just *input*, for the algorithm.

For example, an algorithm for making coffee may use a parameter *number* to represent the number of cups to be brewed so that the algorithm's instructions can refer to this parameter. Here is an excerpt from such an algorithm:[1]

> Fill in *number* cups of water.
> Fill in 1.5 times *number* tablespoons of ground coffee.

To execute this algorithm for three cups of coffee, you have to substitute the input value 3 for the parameter *number* in the algorithm's instructions, which yields the following specialized version of the algorithm:

> Fill in 3 cups of water.
> Fill in 1.5 times 3 tablespoons of ground coffee.

The use of the parameter makes the algorithm applicable in a variety of different situations. Each situation is represented by a different input value (in the example, the number of cups of coffee to be brewed) to be substituted for the parameter, and the substitution adapts the algorithm to the situation represented by the input value.

Hansel and Gretel's algorithm uses a parameter for the pebbles placed in the forest. I did not specify the parameter exactly before because the instruction "Find a pebble not visited before" clearly referred to the pebbles placed by Hansel. The parameter can be made explicit by using the following instruction instead: "Find a pebble from the *pebbles-placed-by-Hansel* not visited before." For each execution of the algorithm, the parameter *pebbles-placed-by-Hansel* is then replaced by the pebbles that Hansel has dropped—at  least we can think of it this way. Since we obviously cannot physically place pebbles into the algorithm description, we treat the parameter as a reference or pointer to the input value. A *pointer* is a mechanism to access the input value; it tells us where to look for the input value when the algorithm needs it. In the way-finding algorithm, the input value is to be found on the forest floor. In the coffee-making algorithm, we have the input value in our mind, and whenever the parameter refers to it, we retrieve it. Nonetheless, the idea of substitution provides a useful analogy that helps to make the relationship between an algorithm and a computation concrete.

By introducing a parameter and using it to replace concrete values we can generalize an algorithm to work in many situations. For example, if a particular getting-up algorithm contains the instruction "Wake up at 6:30 a.m.," we can replace the concrete time value by a parameter *wake-up-time*, which leads to the generalized instruction "Wake up at *wake-up-time*." Similarly, the cereal experience can be expanded by making the parameter *fruit* part of the preparation algorithm.

The flip side is that in order to execute the getting-up algorithm we now need to supply it with an input value so that the instructions can be made concrete by replacing the parameter with a time value. This is generally not a problem, but it requires a decision and is a potential source of mistakes. It all depends how valuable the variability is. An alarm clock that can wake you up at only one preset time that can never be changed is probably unacceptable, but many people can do without a parameter for selecting different alarm sounds.

Finally, an algorithm that has no parameters and thus cannot take different input values will always produce the same computation. As mentioned before, this is not a problem for algorithms that have a transient physical effect, as in the case of cake recipes, where the produced cakes get eaten, or for fetching milk, when the milk is drunk. The recomputation of the same effect makes sense in these cases. However, algorithms for computing values that can be stored and reused at later times need one or more parameters to be reusable.

Parameters are a crucial component of algorithms, but the question of how general or specific an algorithm should be does not have a simple answer. It is discussed in chapter 15.

## Who Is Performing?

As we have seen, a computation is the result of executing an algorithm. This raises the question of who or what can execute an algorithm, and how. The examples have shown that people can certainly execute algorithms, but so can (electronic) computers. Are there other possibilities? And what are the requirements for executing an algorithm?

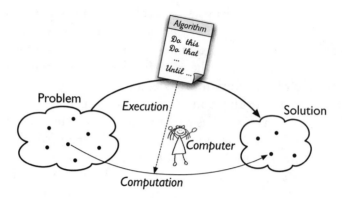

**Figure 2.1**    The execution of an algorithm generates a computation. The algorithm describes a method that works for a whole class of problems, and an execution operates on the representation of a particular example problem. The execution must be performed by a computer, for example, a person or a machine, that can understand the language in which the algorithm is given.

The word for somebody or something that can perform a computation is, of course, *computer*. In fact, the original meaning of the word referred to people who carried out computations.[2] In the following, I use the term in a general sense that refers to any natural or artificial agent that can perform computations.

We can distinguish two principal cases of algorithm execution based on the abilities of the performing computer. On the one hand, there are universal computers, such as people or laptops or smart phones. A universal computer can in principle execute any algorithm as long as it is expressed in a language understandable by the computer. Universal computers establish an execution relationship between algorithms and computation. Whenever the computer executes an algorithm for a particular problem, it performs steps that change some representation (see figure 2.1).

On the other hand, there are computers that execute just one algorithm (or perhaps a set of predefined algorithms). For example, a pocket calculator contains hard-wired electronic circuits for executing algorithms to perform arithmetic computations, as does an alarm clock for making sounds at particular times. Another intriguing example can be found in cell biology.

Think about what happens in your cells millions of times while you are reading this sentence. Ribosomes are producing proteins to support your cells' functions. Ribosomes are little machines that assemble proteins as described by RNA molecules. These are sequences of amino acids that tell the ribosome to produce specific proteins. You are alive thanks to the computation that results from the ribosomal computers in your cells reliably executing an algorithm to translate RNA molecules into proteins. But even though the algorithm used by a ribosome can produce a huge variety of proteins, this is the only algorithm that ribosomes can ever execute. While very useful, ribosomes are limited; they cannot get you dressed or find a way out of the forest.

In contrast to computers that consist of hard-wired algorithms, an important requirement for universal computers is that they understand the language in which their algorithms are given. If the computer is a machine, the algorithm is also called a *program*, and the language in which it is given is called a *programming language*.

If Hansel and Gretel wrote their memoirs and included a description of the algorithm that saved their lives, other children with access to that book could execute the algorithm only if they understood the language in which the book was written. This requirement does not apply to nonuniversal computers that carry out only fixed, hard-wired algorithms.

A requirement that applies to every kind of computer is the ability to access the representation that is used by the algorithm. In particular, a computer must be able to affect the required changes to the representation. If Hansel and Gretel were chained to a tree, the algorithm would be of no help to them, since they wouldn't be able to change their position, which is what an execution of the way-finding algorithm requires.

To summarize, any computer has to be able to read and manipulate the representations that the algorithms operate on. In addition, a universal computer has to understand the language in which algorithms are expressed. From now on, I use the term computer to mean a universal computer.

## The Cost of Living

A computer has some real work to do, a fact one is reminded of whenever the laptop gets hot while rendering high-end graphics in a video game or when the smart phone battery drains too quickly with too many apps running in the background. And the reason you have to set your alarm clock considerably earlier than the time of your first appointment is that the execution of the getting-up algorithm takes some time.

Having figured out an algorithm to solve a problem is one thing, but ensuring that an actual computation generated by the algorithm will produce a solution quickly enough is an entirely different matter. Related is the question of whether the computer in charge has enough resources available to perform the computation in the first place.

For example, when Hansel and Gretel follow the pebble trace back home, the entire computation takes as many steps as the number of pebbles that Hansel dropped.[3] Note that step here means "step of the algorithm" and not "step as a part of walking." In particular, one step of the algorithm generally corresponds to several steps taken by Hansel and Gretel through the forest. Thus the number of pebbles is a measure for the execution time 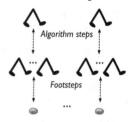 of the algorithm, since one step of the algorithm is required for each pebble. Thinking about the number of steps an algorithm needs to perform its task is judging its *runtime complexity*.

Moreover, the algorithm works only if Hansel and Gretel have enough pebbles to cover the path from their home to the place in the forest where they are left by their parents. This is an example of a re-  source constraint. A shortfall of pebbles could be due either to a limited availability of pebbles, which would be a limit of external resources, or to the limited space offered by Hansel's pockets, which would be a limit of the computer. To judge an algorithm's *space complexity* means to ask how much space a computer needs to execute the algorithm. In the example, this amounts to asking how many pebbles are needed to find a path of a particular length and whether Hansel's pockets are big enough to carry them all.

Therefore, while the algorithm may work in theory for any place in the forest, it is not clear ahead of time that a computation will succeed in practice because it may take too much time or require an amount of resources exceeding what is available. Before examining computation resources more closely, I explain two important assumptions about measuring computing costs that make this kind of analysis practical at all. In the following, I focus on the runtime aspect, but the discussion also applies to the question of space resources.

## The Big Picture of Costs

An algorithm can be viewed as a generalization of many computations. As explained earlier, the differences in the computations are captured in the algorithm description by parameters, and any particular computation can be obtained through an execution of the algorithm with particular input values substituted for the parameters. In the same way, we would like to obtain a generalized description of the resource requirements of an algorithm—a description that does not just apply to a particular computation but captures all computations. In other words, we are looking for a generalization of cost descriptions. This generalization can be achieved by using parameters that can make the number of steps required for executing an algorithm dependent on the size of its input. Thus runtime complexity is a function that yields the number of steps in a computation for an input of a given size.

For example, the number of computation steps, and thus the time, required to execute the pebble-tracing algorithm is roughly equal to the number of dropped pebbles. Since paths to different places in the forest generally contain different numbers of pebbles, computations for these paths also require different numbers of steps. This fact is reflected in expressing runtime complexity as a function of the size of input. For the pebble-tracing algorithm it is easy to derive a precise measure for each computation, since the number of computation steps seems to be in one-to-one correspondence with the number of pebbles. For example, for a path with 87 pebbles, the computation requires 87 steps.

However, this is *not* always the case. Take another look at the path depicted in figure 1.3. That example was used to illustrate how the algorithm can get stuck, but we can also use it to demonstrate how the algorithm can produce computations that take fewer steps than there are pebbles. Since $B$ and $C$ are visible from $D$, we can pick $B$, and since both $A$ and $C$ are visible from $B$, we can next pick $A$, that is, the path $D$, $B$, $A$ is a valid path, and since it bypasses $C$, the computation contains at least one less step than the number of pebbles in the path.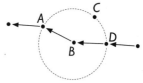

Note that in this case the number of steps in the computation is actually *lower* than predicted by the measure for the algorithm, which means that the cost of the computation is overestimated. Thus, runtime complexity reports the complexity a computation can have in the *worst case*. This helps us decide whether or not to execute the algorithm for a particular input. If the estimated runtime is acceptable, then the algorithm can be executed. If the computation actually performs faster and takes fewer steps, then all the better, but the worst-case complexity provides a guarantee that the algorithm will not take more time. In the case of getting up, your worst-case estimate for the time it takes to take a shower in the morning might be 5 minutes. Since this includes the time it takes for the water to get warm, your actual shower time might be shorter if someone has taken a shower before you.

Since runtime analysis is applied on the level of algorithms, only algorithms (not individual computations) are amenable to an analysis. This also means that it is possible to assess the runtime of a computation *before* it happens because the analysis is based on the algorithm's description.

Another assumption for runtime complexity is that one step in the algorithm generally corresponds to several steps that are executed by the performer of the algorithm. This is obvious in the example. The pebbles are probably not placed one footstep apart, so it will take Hansel and Gretel several footsteps to get from one pebble to the next. However, each algorithm step must not cause an arbitrarily large number of computer steps. This number must be constant and relatively small compared to the number of steps taken by the algorithm. Otherwise the information about the runtime of the algorithm would become meaningless: the number of algorithm steps would not be an accurate measure for the actual runtime. A related aspect is that different computers have different performance characteristics. In the example, Hansel may have longer legs than Gretel and thus may need fewer footsteps to move between pebbles, but Gretel might be a faster walker than Hansel and thus take a specific number of footsteps in less time. All these factors can be ignored by focusing on the runtime of algorithms.

## Cost Growth

Since information about runtime complexity for an algorithm is given as a function, it can capture the differences in runtime for different computations. This approach reflects the fact that algorithms typically require more time for bigger inputs.

The complexity of Hansel and Gretel's algorithm can be characterized by the rule "The runtime is proportional to the number of pebbles," which means that the ratio of the number of footsteps to pebbles is constant. In other words, if a path were doubled in length and thus had twice as many pebbles, the runtime would double as well. Note that this does not mean that the number of footsteps is *identical* to the number of pebbles, only that it increases and decreases in the same way as the input.

This relationship is called *linear*, and it presents itself as a straight line in a graph that plots the number of footsteps needed for any number of pebbles. In cases like this we say that the algorithm has *linear* runtime complexity. We also sometimes say, for short, the algorithm *is linear*.

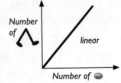

Linear algorithms are very good, and in many cases the best one can hope for. To see an example of a different runtime complexity, consider the algorithm that Hansel executes when dropping the pebbles. In the original version of the story he has all the pebbles in his pocket and thus can drop them as they go into the forest. This is clearly a linear algorithm (with respect to the number of pebbles), since Hansel only takes a constant number of footsteps to reach the location for dropping the next pebble.

But now suppose that Hansel has no way of storing and concealing the pebbles. In that case, he has to go back home and fetch a new pebble for each pebble he wants to drop, which takes roughly twice the number of steps needed to get to that pebble. The total number of steps is then the sum of the steps required for each pebble. Since the distance from home increases with each dropped pebble, the total number of steps is proportional to the sum $1 + 2 + 3 + 4 + 5 + \cdots$, which is proportional to the square of the number of pebbles placed.

This relationship can be illustrated by considering the distance that Hansel must travel, measured in number of pebbles. For dropping two pebbles, Hansel has to get to the place where he can drop the first pebble, go back to fetch another pebble, and then go via the first pebble to the location where he can drop the second pebble. This causes him to travel a total distance of four pebbles. For dropping three pebbles, Hansel first needs to traverse the distance required for dropping two pebbles, which we already know to be four. Then he has to go back to fetch the third pebble, which means traveling a distance of two pebbles. To place the third pebble, he then needs to go the distance of another three pebbles, which yields a total distance corresponding to $4 + 2 + 3 = 9$ pebbles.

Let us consider one more case. For the fourth pebble, Hansel has traveled the distance to drop three pebbles, goes back (three pebbles), and then needs to go the distance of another four pebbles to get to the place for the fourth pebble, for a total distance of $9 + 3 + 4 = 16$ pebbles. In a similar fashion, we can compute the distance required for placing five pebbles ($16 + 4 + 5 = 25$), six pebbles ($25 + 5 + 6 = 36$), and so on.

We can clearly see a certain pattern emerging, namely, that the number of steps needed by Hansel is proportional to the square of the number of pebbles placed. Algorithms that have this complexity pattern are said to have *quadratic* runtime, or for short, to *be quadratic*. The runtime of a quadratic algorithm grows much faster than that of a linear algorithm. For example, while for ten pebbles 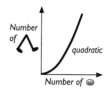 a linear algorithm takes ten steps, a quadratic algorithm needs 100. For 100 pebbles, the linear algorithm needs 100 steps, while the quadratic algorithm already needs 10,000.

Note that the actual number of steps may be higher. As mentioned, a linear algorithm may take any constant number of steps per pebble, say 2 or 3 or even 14. It may therefore take 20 or 30 or 140 steps, respectively, for a path of, say 10 pebbles. The same is true for a quadratic algorithm, whose number of steps may also need to be multiplied by a factor. This indicates that a linear algorithm is not necessarily faster than a quadratic algorithm in all cases. With a large constant factor it may take more steps than a quadratic algorithm with a small constant factor, at least for small enough inputs. For example, a linear algorithm that takes 14 steps per pebble takes 140 steps for an input of 10 pebbles, which is more than the 100 steps a quadratic algorithm with 1 step per pebble will take. However, we can also see that with larger and larger inputs, the impact of a constant factor fades and the growth of the quadratic algorithm takes over. For example, for 100 pebbles this linear algorithm takes 1,400 steps, whereas the quadratic one already takes 10,000.

In the story, the quadratic algorithm is prohibitive and wouldn't work. Think about the time it would take to place the last pebble. Hansel would have to walk all the way home and then back into the forest again, thus basically covering the distance into the forest three times. The parents were already impatient when he was placing pebbles using the linear algorithm.

> His father said: "Hansel, what are you looking at there and staying behind for? Pay attention, and do not forget how to use your legs."

They surely wouldn't have waited for Hansel to go back home every time he needed a new pebble. Thus an algorithm's runtime really matters. If the algorithm is too slow, it can become useless from a practical perspective (see chapter 7).

This example also illustrates that space and time efficiency are often interdependent. In this case one can improve the runtime efficiency of the algorithm from quadratic to linear at the expense of storage capacity, that is, using linear storage space, assuming that Hansel's pockets can store all the pebbles.

When two algorithms solve the same problem, but one has a lower runtime complexity than the other, then the faster algorithm is said to be *more efficient* (with respect to runtime). Similarly, when one algorithm uses less memory than the other, it is said to be *more space efficient*. In the example, the linear pebble-placing algorithm is more runtime efficient than the quadratic one, but less space efficient because it fills Hansel's pockets with pebbles.

# Further Exploration

The pebbles in the story of Hansel and Gretel were representations to be used by a way-finding algorithm. Marking a path can have different applications. On the one hand, it can help you find your way back when exploring an unknown territory. This is what happens in the story of Hansel and Gretel. On the other hand, it can help others follow you. This occurs, for example, in J.J.R. Tolkien's *The Lord of the Rings: The Two Towers* when Pippin, who was taken prisoner by the orcs with Merry, drops a brooch as a sign for Aragorn, Legolas, and Gimli. Similarly, in the movie *Indiana Jones and the Kingdom of the Crystal Skull*, Mac secretly drops radio beacons so that he can be followed.

In all three examples, the markers are placed on a more or less open terrain where movements can occur in almost any direction. In contrast, there are also situations when the movement is restricted to a fixed number of connections between junctions. This occurs in Mark Twain's *The Adventures of Tom Sawyer* when Tom and Becky explore a cave and place smoke marks on the walls to find their way back out. But they still get lost in the cave. When after several days Becky is too weak to go any further, Tom continues to explore the cave and uses, as a more reliable method, a thread from a kite to always find his way back to Becky. Probably the most famous (and oldest) example of using a thread to not get lost in a labyrinth can be found in the Greek myth of the Minotaur, in which Theseus uses a thread given to him by Ariadne to find his way out of the labyrinth. The same method is used by the Benedictine novice Adso in Umberto Eco's *The Name of the Rose* to find his way back through the labyrinth of the monastic library.

It is interesting to compare the different kind of markers used in the stories, and the implications for the corresponding way-finding algorithms. For example, the use of pebbles, brooch, or smoke marks still requires some search to get from one marker to the next, since they only appear at a few places. In contrast, a thread provides a continuous guide that can simply be followed without any search. Moreover, the use of a thread avoids the possibility of a dead-end situation, such as the one described in chapter 1, that can occur when using pebbles or other discrete markers.

Hansel and Gretel's method is used in modern user interfaces of file systems or query systems, where it is actually known as breadcrumb navigation. For example, browsers in a file system often show a list of the parent or enclosing folders of the current folder. Moreover, search interfaces for email programs or databases often show a list of search terms that apply to the currently shown selection. The action of going back to a parent folder or removing the last search term to get a wider selection corresponds to going to a pebble and picking it up.

# Representation and Data Structures

---◄○►---

*Sherlock Holmes*

# On Your Way

You are on your way to work. Whether you are driving your car, riding your bike, or walking, you will encounter traffic signs and traffic lights that regulate how you and your fellow commuters share the road. Some of the rules associated with traffic signs are algorithms. For example, a stop sign at a four-way stop street tells you to stop, wait for all other vehicles that have arrived before you to cross the intersection, and then cross the intersection yourself.[1] Following the rules associated with traffic signs amounts to executing the corresponding algorithms, which means that the resulting motions are examples of computation. Since many drivers and vehicles are engaged in this activity and since they share the road as a common resource, this is actually an example of distributed computing, but that is not the main point here.

It is remarkable that every day millions of people with completely different goals can effectively coordinate their actions and successfully navigate their ways around one another. Sure, traffic jams and accidents happen on a regular basis, but overall traffic works quite successfully. Even more remarkable is the fact that all this becomes possible through a small set of signs. Placing a red, hexagonally shaped sign containing the word "STOP" at all entries to an intersection enables the coordinated crossing of countless vehicles.

How is it possible that signs have such profound effects? The key observation is that signs carry *meaning*. For example, a direction sign provides information about the direction of a place of interest. The fact represented by such a sign supports the traveler in making decisions about which turns or exits to take. Other signs provide warnings (for example, of obstacles or curves), prohibit certain actions (such as limiting the maximum speed), and regulate access to shared traffic spaces (such as intersections). In chapter 1 I used the term *representation* for signs that stand for something else (such as the pebbles that represent locations). From this perspective, signs derive their power from the fact that they are representations.

The effect of a sign does not somehow appear magically by itself but needs to be extracted by some agent. This process is called *interpretation*, and different agents may interpret a sign in different ways. For example, while a typical traffic participant interprets traffic signs as information or instruction, traffic signs have also become collector's items. Interpretation is required to understand traffic signs and is also required for all representations used in computer science.

Signs are related to computation in several different ways, emphasizing their importance. First, signs can directly represent computation, as in the case of the stop sign, which designates a particular algorithm for traffic participants to execute. Even if the computation represented by an individual sign is trivial, a combination of such signs has the potential to produce a significant computation as an aggregate. Hansel and Gretel's pebbles provide an example of this. A single pebble triggers the simple action "Come here if you haven't visited me before," whereas all pebbles taken together affect the life-saving movement out of the forest.

Second, a systematic transformation of a sign is a computation.[2] For example, crossing out a sign suspends or negates its meaning; this is often done to prohibit actions, such as a bent arrow in a red circle with a red diagonal over it, which forbids a turn. Another example is a traffic light: when it changes from red to green, the meaning changes accordingly from "stop" to "go."

Finally, the process of interpreting a sign is a computation. This isn't obvious for simple signs such as pebbles and stop signs but becomes clear when looking at composite signs. One example is the crossed-out sign whose meaning is obtained from the original sign, to which then the meaning of crossing-out has to be applied. Other examples are food-exit signs, whose meanings are obtained as a combination of direction plus the meaning of the restaurant logos that indicate different kinds of food. Interpretation is discussed in chapters 9 and 13. The point here is that signs are entangled in computation in multiple ways. It is therefore a good idea to understand what they are, how they work, and what roles they play in computation. This is the subject of chapter 3.

# 3     The Mystery of Signs

As illustrated in the first two chapters, computation does its work by manipulating representations, which are symbols or signs that stand for meaningful things. We have seen how Hansel and Gretel employed pebbles as representations for locations in support of their way-finding algorithm. For that the pebbles had to fulfill a number of requirements that we took for granted. Taking a close look at these requirements will provide a better understanding of what a representation is and how it supports computation.

A representation consists of at least two parts, namely, something that represents and something that is represented. This fact is captured by the notion of a *sign*. The following are three aspects of signs to keep in mind: signs can operate on multiple levels; signs can be ambiguous (a single sign can represent different things); and one thing can be represented by different signs. This chapter also discusses how different mechanisms enable signs as representations.

## Signs of Representation

Do you have any doubt that 1 + 1 equals 2? Probably not, unless you are a time traveler from ancient Rome. In that case the number symbols would look funny to you, and you might instead agree that I + I equals II, that is, if somebody explained to you the meaning of the + symbol, which was not known to the Romans (it was first used in the fifteenth century). And if you could ask an electronic computer, whose number system is based on binary numbers, it would tell you that $1 + 1$ equals 10.[1] What's going on here?

This example illustrates that a conversation about even very simple facts of arithmetic requires an agreement about the symbols that represent quantities. This is of course also true for computations with quantities. Doubling 11 yields 22 in the decimal system, which is based on Hindu-Arabic numerals. In ancient Rome one would double II, which yields IV (not IIII),[2] and the result from an electronic computer would be 110, since 11 in binary notation represents the number 3, and 110 represents 6.[3]

What this shows is that the meaning of a computation depends on the meaning of the representation it transforms. For example, the computation that transforms 11 into 110 means doubling if the numbers are interpreted as binary numbers, whereas it means multiplying by 10 if the numbers are interpreted as decimal numbers. And the transformation is meaningless under Roman numeral interpretation because the Romans didn't have a representation for zero.

Since representation plays such a crucial role in computation, it is important to understand what it really is. And since the word representation is used in many different ways, it is important to be clear about its meaning in computer science. To this end, I solicit help from Sherlock Holmes, the famous detective whose crime-solving methods can reveal much about the way representations work in support of computation. It is typical of Sherlock Holmes to make keen observations of minute details and interpret them in surprising ways. Often these inferences help solve a crime, but sometimes they are just an entertaining way of revealing information for advancing the story. In either case, Sherlock Holmes's inferences are often based on interpreting representations.

Representations play an important part in one of the most popular and famous Sherlock Holmes adventures, *The Hound of the Baskervilles*. In typical Sherlock Holmes style, the story begins with a number of observations about a walking stick left behind by a visitor, Dr. Mortimer. Holmes and Watson interpret the engraving on the walking stick, which reads as follows: "To James Mortimer, MRCS, from his friends of the CCH." Living in England, Holmes and Watson know that "MRCS" stands for, or *represents*, Member of the Royal College of Surgeons, and from that and with the help of a medical directory, Holmes deduces that "CCH" must stand for Charing Cross Hospital, since Dr. Mortimer has worked there for some time. He also infers that the walking stick must have been given to Dr. Mortimer in appreciation of his service when he left the hospital to become a country practitioner, although it turns out later that this inference is incorrect and that Dr. Mortimer was given the walking stick on the occasion of his wedding anniversary.

The engraving contains three immediately recognizable representations: the two abbreviations and the inscription as a whole that represents the event of Dr. Mortimer's wedding anniversary. Each of these representations is captured in the form of a *sign*, a concept introduced by the Swiss linguist Ferdinand de Saussure. A sign consists of two parts, the *signifier* and the *signified*. The signifier is what is perceived or presented, whereas the signified is the concept or idea that the signifier stands for. To relate this notion of sign to the idea of representation, we can say that the signifier *represents* the signified. Since I use the word represent always in the sense of "to stand for," we can also say that a signifier *stands for* the signified.

The idea of a sign is important because it succinctly captures the idea of representations. Specifically, the relationship between a signifier and what it represents produces meaning for us—in the case of the walking stick, a part of Dr. Mortimer's professional history. The signified is often mistakenly assumed to be some physical object in the world, but that is not what Saussure meant by it. For example, the word "tree" does not signify an actual tree but the concept of a tree that we have in our minds.

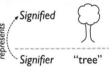

This aspect makes it quite tricky to write about signs because, on the one hand, text and diagrams that are used to write about signs are signs themselves and, on the other hand, abstract concepts or ideas in the mind can never be shown directly but have to be ultimately represented by signs as well. In the literature about semiotics, the theory of signs and their meaning, the idea of a sign is often illustrated by a diagram containing the word "tree" as an example of a signifier and a drawing of a tree as the thing signified by "tree." However, the drawing is itself a sign for the concept of a tree, and therefore the diagram can be misleading, since "tree" is not a signifier of the drawing but of what the drawing signifies, which is the concept of a tree.

Since we are bound to using language to talk about language and representation, there is no way out of this dilemma, and we can never present ideas or concepts other than through some linguistic means. Whether we want to talk about a signifier or a signified, we always have to use signifiers to do that. Fortunately, we can get around this problem most of the time by putting quote marks around a word or phrase that is used as a signifier or by typesetting it in a special form such as italics. The quote marks have the effect of referring to the word or phrase as such, without interpreting it. In contrast, a word or phrase used without quote marks is interpreted as what it stands for, that is, a signified concept.

Thus "tree" refers to the four-letter word, whereas the word without the quote marks refers to the concept of a tree. The distinction between a quoted word standing for itself and its unquoted use standing for what it means is referred to as the *use-*

*mention distinction* in analytic philosophy. The unquoted word is actually *used* and denotes what it represents, while the quoted word is only *mentioned* and does not refer to what it stands for. Quoting stops interpretation from acting on the quoted part and thus allows us to clearly distinguish between talk about a word and its meaning. For example, we can say that "tree" has four letters, whereas a tree does not have letters but branches and leaves.

The seemingly simple concept of a sign contains a lot of flexibility. For example, signs can operate on multiple levels, signs can have multiple meanings, and the link between signifier and signified can be established in different ways. I describe these three aspects in the following sections.

## Signs All the Way Down

In addition to the three signs on the walking stick that I have already identified—"MRCS" signifying Member of the Royal College of Surgeons, "CCH" signifying Charing Cross Hospital, and the whole inscription signifying Dr. Mortimer's wedding anniversary—there are actually a few more signs at work here. First, "Member of the Royal College of Surgeons" signifies membership in a professional society, and similarly, "Charing Cross Hospital" signifies a specific hospital in London (the concept, not the building). But that is not all. In addition, "MRCS" also signifies the surgeon society membership, and "CCH" also signifies the London hospital.

Thus an abbreviation has two possible meanings and can have two different signifieds, since it extends to the signified of its signified. What does that mean? Since the signified of "CCH" is the phrase "Charing Cross Hospital," which is itself a signifier for a London hospital, "CCH" can represent the London hospital by combining two representations in which the signified of the first is the signifier for the second. In a similar way, "MRCS" combines two levels of represen-

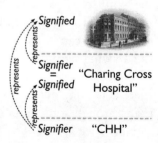

tation into one, since it represents the surgeon society membership by referring to the signified of "Member of the Royal College of Surgeons."

Why does this matter, and what does this have to do with computer science? Recall the two forms of representation distinguished in chapter 1: problem representation and computation representation. The fact that a sign can combine two levels of representation into one makes it possible to add meaning to computations that are otherwise purely symbolic. I explain this idea with an example that uses the number representation discussed earlier.

Viewed as a binary number, the signifier "1" represents the number one on the level of computation representation. This number can represent different facts in different contexts and thus has different problem representations. If you are playing roulette, this could be, for example, the amount of money you bet on black. The transformation that appends a 0 to the 1 means, on the level of computation representation, to double the number one to two. In the context of the problem representation the transformation can also mean that black did come up and that you won your bet and now have twice the amount of money available.

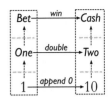

Similarly, the pebbles in the forest are signifiers that represent locations for Hansel and Gretel and belong to the computation representation. In addition, the individual locations represent positions of danger in the problem representation. To distinguish between different locations, one could further quantify the degree of danger by the distance of a location from Hansel and Gretel's home. Moving from pebble to pebble means simply a change of location in the computation representation but also means a decrease in danger in the problem representation if the location moved to is closer to home. The transitivity of signs is the reason "He worked at CHH" means that he worked at Charing Cross Hospital, *not* that he worked at "Charing Cross Hospital," which would not make any sense, since one cannot work at the name of a hospital.

## Making Sense of Signifiers

A sign that works across different representation levels provides an example of a signifier that is bound to multiple signifieds. The sign "1" in the roulette example signifies the number one and a bet; the pebbles used by Hansel and Gretel represent locations as well as danger; and the collection of pebbles represents a path as well as a way from danger to safety. Thus any abbreviation represents the name it stands for as well as the concept the name stands for.

However, one signifier can also represent different, unrelated concepts, and it is also possible for one concept to be represented by different, unrelated signifiers. For example, "10" signifies the number ten in the decimal representation and the number two in the binary representation. Moreover, the number two is represented by the signifier "2" in the decimal representation and by the signifier "10" in the binary representation. Of course, multiple representations exist also on the level of problem representation. Clearly, the number one can be used to represent other things than a bet on black at the roulette table.

These two phenomena are well known in linguistics. A word is said to be a *homonym* if it stands for two or more different signified concepts. For example, the word "trunk" can stand for the upright part of a tree, the nose of an elephant, or the luggage compartment of a car. In contrast, two words are said to be *synonyms* if they both represent the same concept. Examples are "bike" and "bicycle" or "hound" and "dog." In the context of computation, homonyms raise several important questions.

For example, if one signifier can represent different signifieds, which of the representations is actually active when the signifier is used? Not surprisingly, the representation that a signifier invokes depends on the context in which it is used. For example, when we ask the question, What does "CCH" stand for?, we are inquiring about the meaning of the abbreviation, which is the name "Charing Cross Hospital." In contrast, a question such as, Have you ever been to "CCH"? makes use of the fact that it refers to a hospital and thus picks out the second representation. Moreover, the signifier "10" represents ten or two, depending on whether one uses the decimal or the binary representation. The story of Hansel and Gretel also illustrates that usage context matters for a sign to play a particular representational role. For example, when the pebbles were lying in front of Hansel and Gretel's house, they didn't represent anything in particular. In contrast, once they were deliberately placed in the forest, they represented locations used for finding a path.

The same signifier can also have different meanings for different agents interpreting a sign. For example, the breadcrumbs used by Hansel and Gretel during the second night signified locations for Hansel and Gretel. However, the birds of the forest interpreted them as food. Both interpretations of the breadcrumbs make sense and work, from either Hansel and Gretel's or the birds' point of view. It doesn't require much imagination to see that homonyms can cause problems in algorithms, since they essentially present an ambiguity that has to be resolved somehow. Why would anyone want or even need one name representing different values in an algorithm? See chapter 13, where I also explain how to resolve the apparently resulting ambiguities.

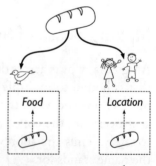

Finally, it is also possible to be mistaken about a representation and to associate an incorrect signified with a signifier. An example is Sherlock Holmes's inference that the inscription on Dr. Mortimer's walking stick represents his retirement, whereas it actually represents Dr. Mortimer's wedding anniversary (see figure 3.1). This particular misrepresentation is discussed and resolved as part of the story *The Hound of the Baskervilles* itself.

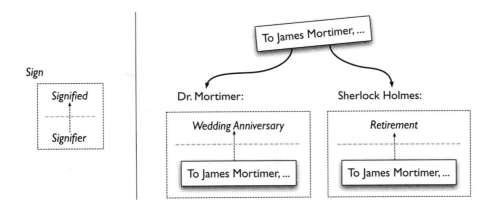

**Figure 3.1**  Signs are the basis for representation. A sign consists of a signifier that represents some concept, called the signified. One signifier can stand for different concepts.

The correctness of representation is crucial for computation because if a computation receives an incorrect representation as input, it will produce incorrect results. This fact is sometimes referred to as "garbage in, garbage out." Unsurprisingly, computations based on incorrect input that lead to incorrect results can have devastating consequences. If the pebbles represented a path farther into the forest, no correct path-finding algorithm could help find Hansel and Gretel their way home, and they would die in the forest.

A stark reminder of the importance of carefully choosing representations is the loss of the Mars Climate Orbiter, an unmanned spacecraft that was launched in 1998 by NASA to explore the climate and atmosphere of Mars. During a maneuver to correct its trajectory, the spacecraft came too close to the surface and disintegrated. The reason for the failed maneuver was the use of two different representations of numbers by the control software and the spacecraft. The software computed thrusts in English units while the thrust controller expected numbers in metric units. This failure of representation came with a heavy price tag of $655 million. I discuss methods to avoid these kind of mistakes in chapter 14.

## Three Ways to Signify

Given the importance of accurate representations, how is the relationship between a sign and what it signifies established? This can happen in several different ways, and signs can be classified accordingly. The logician, scientist, and philosopher Charles Sanders Peirce identified three different kinds of signs.

First, an *icon* represents an object based on its similarity or likeness to the object. An example is a drawing of a person that represents the person by highlighting specific features. An obvious example of an iconic representation in *The Hound of the Baskervilles* is the portrait of Sir Hugo Baskerville, which represents him through likeness. The portrait also looks similar to the murderer and is thus another example of a signifier that can stand for different signifieds. The fact that the portrait is effectively two signs helps Sherlock Holmes solve the case. Further examples are the abbreviations CCH and MRCS when they are used to represent the phrases they stand for. Here the likeness is established by the characters that a phrase and its abbreviation have in common. Finally, Sherlock Holmes employs a map of the Devonshire moor to understand the location where the murder has happened. A map is iconic, since the features it contains (paths, rivers, forest, etc.) resemble, mostly in shape and position, the objects they represent.

Second, an *index* represents an object through some lawlike relationship that lets the viewer of the index infer the object through this relationship. An example is a weather vane from whose direction the wind direction can be inferred. Other examples are all kinds of gauges that have been engineered as indexes for different physical phenomena (temperature, pressure, speed, etc.). The saying "Where there is smoke, there is fire" is based on smoke being an index for fire. An index sign is determined by the object it signifies through the lawlike relationship between them. Other important index signs in *The Hound of the Baskervilles* (and in other Sherlock Holmes stories) are footprints. For example, the dog footprints found near the deceased Charles Baskerville signify a gigantic hound. Moreover, the fact that the footprints stop at some distance from Sir Charles is interpreted by Sherlock Holmes to indicate that the hound did not have physical contact with him. The special form of Sir Charles's footprints indicates that he was fleeing the hound. Another index is the amount of ashes from Sir Charles's cigar found at the crime scene, indicating the time he was waiting at the location of his death. Incidentally, Peirce himself used the example of a murderer and his victim as an example of an index. Applied to the story, this means the dead Sir Charles is an index for his murderer.

Third, a *symbol* represents an object by convention only; no likeness or lawlike connection is involved in the representation. Since the link between the signifier and the signified is completely arbitrary, the creator and the user of the sign must agree on the definition and interpretation of the sign for it to work. Most modern languages are symbolic. The fact that the word "tree" stands for a tree cannot be inferred but is a fact that has to be learned. Similarly, that "11" is a symbol for eleven as well as three and that the pebbles are symbols for locations are conventions. Of the signs we have mentioned from *The Hound of the Baskervilles*, the abbreviations MRCS and CCH are symbols if used to represent the surgeon society membership and the hospital, respectively, because they bear no resemblance nor do they result from any lawlike relationship. Also, the symbol 2704 represents a cab that Holmes and Watson follow to identify a person suspected to be threatening the Baskerville heir Sir Henry.

## Using Representations Systematically

Having distinguished icon, index, and symbol, we can now look at how these different forms of representation are used in computation. Since computation works through transforming representations, the different representation mechanisms of icon, index, and symbol lead to different forms of computation.

For example, since icons represent through likeness, they can be transformed to reveal or hide specific aspects of the represented object. Photo editing tools offer numerous effects to alter pictures in a systematic way, for example, by changing colors or distorting image proportions. The computation effectively changes the likeness of the icon. Another method of computing with iconic representations that is relevant to the profession of Sherlock Holmes is the creation of drawings of suspects, facial composites, according to descriptions of eyewitnesses. The eye witness reports features about the face, such as the size and shape of the nose, or the color and length of the hair, which are interpreted by a police sketch artist as drawing instructions to produce a drawing of the suspect. The computation of a suspect drawing is the result of an algorithm that is given by the eye witness and executed by the police sketch artist. Given its algorithmic nature, it is not surprising that this method has been automated.

The method is due to Alphonse Bertillon, whose ideas about anthropometry, the measurement of people's body parts, were adopted by the Paris police in 1883 as a method for the identification of criminals. He created a classification system for facial features that was originally used to find specific suspects in a large collection of mug shots of criminals. This method is an example of a computation that uses sketches for searching, an important algorithmic problem (see chapter 5). Sherlock Holmes is an admirer of Bertillon's work, even though he does not speak too highly of him in *The Hound of the Baskervilles*. Another computation with sketches is the process of inferring the identity of suspects from facial composites. This computation is effectively establishing a sign where the signifier is the sketch and the suspect is the signified. A sign is also established when a suspect is recognized with the help of a sketch or picture.

This happens when Sherlock Holmes recognizes the murderer in the portrait of Sir Hugo Baskerville.

As an example of a computation with an index sign, recall the map of the Devonshire moor. To find the location where a particular road crosses a river, Sherlock Holmes could compute the intersection of the two lines that represent the river and the road, respectively. In fact, the map representation has the point effectively computed already, so that it could be simply read off the map. Assuming that the map is accurate, the resulting point then would represent the sought location.[4] Sherlock Holmes could also compute the length of a path on the map and, using the scale of the map, determine the length of the path in the moor and also the time needed to traverse it. Again, this works if the map is drawn to scale. Index computations exploit the lawlike relationship between sign and signified to move from one signified to another via a transformation of the index.

Computations with symbols are probably the most common in computer science, because symbols enable the representation of arbitrary problems. The most obvious symbol-based computations involve numbers and arithmetic, and we can find such an example in Sherlock Holmes's first adventure, *A Study in Scarlet*,[5] where he computes the height of a suspect from the length of the suspect's stride. This is a very simple computation, consisting of only one multiplication, and the corresponding algorithm consists of simply one step.

More interesting from a computational perspective are Sherlock Holmes's attempts to decode encrypted messages. In *The Valley of Fear* he tries to understand a message sent to him that starts as follows: 534 C2 13 127 36 . . .. This code signifies a message. The first task for Sherlock Holmes is to figure out the algorithm that was used to generate the code, since this allows him to decode the message. He concludes that 534 must be a page number of some book, that C2 means "second column," and that the following numbers represent words in that column.

But is the code really a symbolic sign? Since the code is generated by an algorithm from a given message, it seems that the encoding algorithm establishes a lawlike relationship between the message and its code. Therefore, the code is not a symbol but an index. This illustrates another way in which computation is involved with signs. Whereas interpretation produces the signified for a given signifier, an algorithm for generating index values operates in the opposite direction and generates a signifier from a given signified.

The bottom line is this: Representation is the basis for computation. Its nature and basic properties can be understood through the lens of signs. And much like works of art can be based on many different materials (clay, marble, paint, etc.), computation can be based on different representations. The importance of representation was emphasized in chapter 1: No computation without representation.

# In Your Office

You have arrived at your office and face the task of working through a collection of documents. Before you can start the actual work, you have to decide on the order in which to process the documents and how to manage the document collection to ensure that order. These questions are also relevant in other contexts. Think, for example, of a car mechanic who has to repair several different cars or a physician who has to treat a number of patients in the waiting room.

The order in which the elements of a collection (documents or cars or people) are to be processed is often determined by a policy, such as first come, first serve, which means that the elements are dealt with in the order in which they arrive. Such a policy requires that the maintenance of a collection follow a particular pattern that defines the interplay between adding, accessing, and removing elements. In computer science a collection with a specific access pattern is called a *data type*, and the data type that captures the first come, first serve principle is called a *queue*.

While queues are widely used to determine the order in which the elements of a collection are to be processed, there are also other strategies. For example, if elements are processed according to some priority instead of in the order they arrive, the collection is a *priority queue* data type. Some of the documents in your office might be of that type, for example, an urgent inquiry that has to be answered immediately, a memo that you have to respond to by lunch time, or an offer that must go out today. Other examples are patients in the emergency room, who are treated in order of the severity of their symptoms, or travelers who can board an airplane according to their frequent flier status.

Another pattern is the processing of requests in the opposite order of their appearance. While this may seem odd at first, this situation arises quite frequently. For example, imagine you are working on your tax return. You may start with the main tax form, but when one of the fields asks for your deductions, this requires you to fill out another form first. To do this, you have to retrieve the corresponding receipts and add the amounts. You finish dealing with the three kinds of documents in the opposite order in which they became relevant: You first enter the amounts from the receipts and put them away. Then you can complete the deductions form, and finally you go back to working on the main tax form. A collection whose elements are processed in this order is referred to as a *stack* data type, since it behaves like a stack of pancakes: the pancake that ended up last on the stack will be eaten first, and the bottom-most pancake, which is the first element put on the stack, gets eaten last. The pattern described by a stack data type occurs in a variety of tasks, ranging from baking to assembling furniture. For example, the egg whites have to be whisked before being added to the batter, and the drawer has to be screwed together before being inserted into the cupboard.

Knowing the access pattern for processing the elements of a collection leads to the second question of how to arrange the elements to best support that pattern. Such an arrangement of elements is called a *data structure*. Let's take the queue data type as an example and see how it can be implemented in different ways. If you have enough desk space (which may be too optimistic an assumption), you can line up the documents, add them at one end and remove them from the other. Every now and then you shift all documents to move the empty space at the front of the queue to its end. This is similar to how people line up one after another at a coffee shop. Each person enters the line at one end and makes their way to the front after all other people in front of them have left the line. A different method, employed in many government offices, is for everybody to pull a number and then wait to be called for their turn. You can also use this system for the documents in your office by attaching sticky notes with consecutive numbers to them.

The sequence of documents on your desk and the line in a coffee shop is called a *list* data structure. Here the physical arrangement of the people in line ensures the ordering required for a queue. In contrast, the method for assigning consecutive numbers doesn't require you to physically maintain the order of people or documents; they can be placed anywhere, since the numbers capture the correct ordering. This arrangement of assigning elements to numbered slots is called an *array* data structure. In addition to the numbered slots (realized by people carrying the numbers they have pulled), one also has to maintain two counters, one for the next available slot and one for the next number to be served.

By representing collections as data structures they become accessible to computation. The choice of data structure is important for the efficiency of algorithms and is sometimes influenced by other considerations, such as the available space. When Sherlock Holmes maintains information about a case, such as a collection of suspects, he is essentially using data types and data structures. I therefore continue using the story of *The Hound of the Baskervilles* to motivate and explain these concepts.

# Detective's Notebook: Accessory after the Fact

Computation is particularly useful when we have to deal with large amounts of data that cannot be handled in a few individual steps. In such cases an appropriate algorithm can ensure that all data are processed systematically and, in many cases, also efficiently.

Signs, discussed in chapter 3, illustrate how representation works for individual pieces of information and how this representation becomes part of computation. For example, Hansel and Gretel's movements from pebble to pebble mean that they are in danger until they make the move from the last pebble to their home. But even though collections of signs are signs themselves, it is not clear how to compute with such collections. In the case of Hansel and Gretel, an individual pebble is a signifier for one location, and the collection of all pebbles signifies a path from danger to safety, but how is such a collection built and used systematically? The maintenance of a collection of data raises two questions.

First, in which order will data be inserted into, looked up in, and removed from a collection? The answer depends, of course, on the computational task that the collection is involved in, but we can observe that specific patterns of accessing the elements in a collection reoccur. Such a data access pattern is called a *data type*. For example, the pebbles employed by Hansel and Gretel are visited in the opposite order in which they were placed; such an access pattern is called a *stack*.

Second, how can a collection be stored so that the access pattern, or data type, is supported most efficiently? Here the answer depends on a wide variety of factors. For example, how many elements have to be stored? Is this number known in advance?

How much space does each element require for storage? Do all elements have the same size? Any particular way of storing a collection is called a *data structure*. A data structure makes a collection amenable to computation. One data type can be implemented by different data structures, which means that a particular access pattern can be implemented through different ways of storing data. The difference between data structures lies in how efficiently they support specific operations on the collection. Moreover, one data structure can implement different data types.

This chapter discusses several data types, the data structures to implement them, and how they are used as part of computations.

## The Usual Suspects

When the perpetrator of a crime is known (maybe there are eye witnesses and a confession), we don't require the skills of a Sherlock Holmes. But when there are several suspects, we need to keep track of their motives, alibis, and other relevant information to investigate the case in detail.

In *The Hound of the Baskervilles* the suspects include Dr. Mortimer, Jack Stapleton and his presumed sister Beryl (who is really his wife), the escaped convict Selden, Mr. Frankland, and the Barrymore couple, the servants of the late Sir Charles Baskerville. Before Watson leaves to visit Baskerville Hall, Sherlock Holmes instructs Watson to report all relevant facts but to exclude Mr. James Desmond from the suspects. When Watson suggests to Holmes to also exclude the Barrymore couple, Sherlock Holmes responds:

> *No, no, we will preserve them upon our list of suspects.*[1]

This short exchange demonstrates two things.

First, even though Sherlock Holmes doesn't know anything about data structures, he is using one, since he seems to have kept a list of suspects. A *list* is a simple data structure for storing data items by linking them together. A list provides a distinctive form of accessing and manipulating these data items. Second, the list of suspects is not a static entity; it grows and shrinks as new suspects are added or when suspects are cleared. Adding, removing, or otherwise changing items in a data structure requires algorithms that generally take more than one step, and it is the runtime of these algorithms that determines how well a specific data structure is suited for a particular task.

Because of their simplicity and versatility, lists are probably the most widely used data structure in computer science and beyond. We all use lists on a regular basis in the form of to-do lists, shopping lists, reading lists, wish lists, and all kinds of rankings.

The order of the elements in a list matters, and the elements are typically accessed one by one, starting at one end and proceeding to the other. Lists are often written down vertically, one element per line, with the first element at the top. Computer scientists, however, write lists horizontally, presenting the elements from left to right, connected by arrows to indicate the order of the elements.[2] Using this notation, Sherlock Holmes can write down his list of suspects as follows:

Mortimer → Jack → Beryl → Selden → . . .

The arrows are called *pointers* and make the connection between list elements explicit, which becomes important when one considers how lists are updated. Assume Sherlock Holmes's suspect list is Mortimer → Beryl and that he wants to add Jack between the two.

If the elements are written down as a vertical list of items without any empty space between them, he has to resort to some extra notation to make the position of the new element clear. The alternative is to simply write down a fresh copy of the complete new list. That would be, however, a huge waste of time and space. It would require time and space that is in the worst case quadratic in the size of the final list.

Pointers give us the flexibility to write down new elements wherever we find space and still place them at the proper position in the list by connecting them to their neighboring list elements. For example, we can place Jack at the end of the list, redirect the outgoing pointer from Mortimer to Jack, and add a pointer from Jack to Beryl.

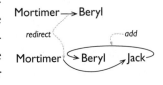

In the context of the story, the order of the suspects in this list is arbitrary and has no meaning, but we can see that the creation of a list forces us to pick some order for its elements. It is a defining characteristic of a list that its elements are kept in a specific order.

The inspection of the list's elements happens in the particular order given by the list. Thus to find out whether Selden is a suspect, we have to start at the beginning of the list and check the elements one by one by following the pointers. While it seems we can spot the element Selden directly in the list, this works only for relatively small lists. Since our visual field is limited, we cannot immediately recognize a specific element in a long list and thus have to resort to the one-element-at-a-time traversal of the list.

A physical analogy for a list is a ring binder that contains a sheet of paper for each element. To find a particular element in a ring binder one has to look at individual pages one by one, and one can insert new pages anywhere between other pages.

A salient property of lists is that the time it takes to find an element depends on where the element is located in the list. In this example, Selden would be found in the fourth step. In general, finding an element may require the traversal of the whole list, since the element could be last. In the discussion about runtime complexity in chapter 2, such an algorithm was called *linear*, since the time complexity is directly proportional to the number of elements in the list.

As mentioned, it is not clear that Sherlock Holmes's list actually contains the suspects in the particular order shown, and the fact that Selden comes after Beryl does not mean anything, since the purpose of the list is only to remember who is among the suspects. All that matters is whether a person is on the list.[3] Does that mean that a list is not an adequate representation to remember suspects? Not at all; it just means that a list may contain information (such as the ordering of elements) that is not needed for a particular task. This observation suggests that a list is just one possible data structure for representing data about suspects and that there might be other representations that could be used for the same purpose—as long as they support the same operations for adding, removing, and finding elements. These operations express requirements for what has to be done with the data.

Such requirements for data, expressed through a collection of operations, is called a *data type* in computer science. The requirements for the suspect data are the ability to add, remove, and find elements. This data type is called a *set*.

Sets are widely applicable, since they correspond to predicates related to a problem or algorithm. For example, the set of suspects corresponds to the predicate "is a suspect," which applies to people and which can be used to affirm or reject statements such as "Selden is a suspect," depending on whether the person to which the predicate is applied is a member of the set. The pebble-tracing algorithm used by Hansel and Gretel also uses a predicate when it instructs, "Find a shining pebble that was not visited before." The predicate here is "not visited before"; it applies to pebbles and can be represented by a set that is initially empty and to which pebbles are added after they have been visited.

While a data type describes requirements of what to do with data, a data structure provides a concrete representation to support these requirements. You can think of a data type as a description of a data management task and of a data structure as a solution for that task. (The following mnemonic may help with remem-

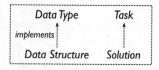

bering the meaning of the two terms: A data type describes a task; a data structure describes a solution.) A data type is a more abstract description of data management than a data structure and has the advantage that some details can be left unspecified and thus can lead to succinct and general descriptions. In *The Hound of the Baskervilles* the set data type reflects the task of maintaining a collection of suspects without having to say in detail how to implement it. In the Hansel and Gretel story a set data type to remember visited pebbles is enough to describe the algorithm. However, to actually execute the operations stipulated by a data type, a computer needs to employ a concrete data structure that defines how the operations operate on the representation offered by the data structure. Also, only when a concrete data structure is selected for an algorithm can we determine the algorithm's runtime complexity.

Since one data type can be implemented by different data structures, the question is which data structure one should choose. One would want the data structure that implements the data type operations with the best possible runtime so that the algorithm using the data structure runs as fast as possible. However, this is not always an easy decision because a data structure may support some operations well but not others. Moreover, data structures also have different space requirements. The situation is similar to choosing a vehicle for a particular transportation task. A bike is environmentally friendly, and you can't beat the mileage it gets per gallon. But it is comparatively slow, can only transport one or two people, and has a limited range. You may need a van or even a bus for traveling with many people over longer distances. You pick a truck to transport large items, a sedan for traveling comfortably, and maybe a sports car when you're a male in your fifties.

Coming back to the question of how to implement the set data type, two popular alternatives to using lists are the *array* and the *binary search tree* data structures. Binary search trees are discussed in detail in chapter 5; here I focus on arrays.

If a list is like a ring binder, an array is like a notebook, which has a fixed number of pages that are each uniquely identified. An individual field in an array data structure is called a *cell*, and a cell's identifier is also called its *index*. Identifying (or indexing) cells is usually done using numbers, but we can also use letters or names as identifiers as long as we can directly open a particular page using the identifier.[4] The importance of an array data structure lies in the fast access it provides to each individual cell. No matter how many cells the array contains, it takes just one step to access a cell. Any such operation that requires only one or a few steps, irrespective of the size of the data structure, is said to run in *constant time*.

To represent a set with a notebook, we assume that each page has
a tab that is labeled by one of the possible members of the set. Thus
to represent the suspects in *The Hound of the Baskervilles* we label
the pages with *all* potential suspects' names, that is, Mortimer, Jack,
and so on. The notebook also contain pages for Desmond and other
people that could in principle be suspects. This is different from the
ring binder, which contains only actual suspects. Then to add, say, Selden, as a suspect
we open the page labeled "Selden" and place some mark on it (for example, we write +
or "yes" on it). To remove a suspect, we also open that person's page, but remove the
mark (or write − or "no" on it). To find out whether somebody is a suspect, we go to
their page and check the mark. An array works in the same way. We directly access its
cells using an index and read or modify the information stored in it.

| + | − | + | + | + | . . . |
|---|---|---|---|---|-------|
| Mortimer | Desmond | Jack | Beryl | Selden | . . . |

The important difference between arrays and lists is that one can locate individual cells
immediately in an array, whereas one has to scan the elements of a list from the beginning to find the element (or reach the end of the list in case the element is not in the
list).

Since we can directly open a particular page in the notebook (or access a cell in an
array), all three operations—adding, removing, and finding suspects—can be performed
in constant time, which is optimal: we cannot possibly do any of this faster. Since the
list data structure requires linear time for checking and removing suspects, the array
data structure seems to be the winner hands down. So why are we even talking about
lists?

The problem with arrays is their fixed size, that is, a notebook has a specific number
of pages and cannot grow over time. This has two important implications. First, the
notebook has to be chosen big enough to contain all possible suspects right from the
beginning, even if many of them never become suspects. Thus we may waste a lot
of space, and we may be carrying around a huge book with pages for hundreds or
thousands of potential suspects, whereas in reality the set of suspects may be very small;
it may very well contain fewer than ten suspects at any given time. This also means that
the preparation of the notebook's thumb index at the start can take a long time because
it requires writing the name of each potential suspect on a different page. Second—
and this is an even more serious problem—it might not be clear at the beginning of
the mystery who all the potential suspects are. In particular, new potential suspects

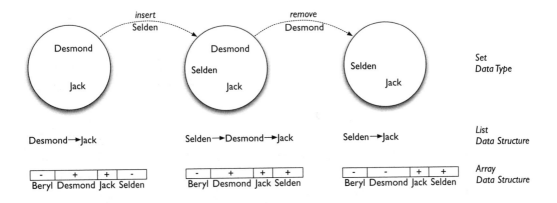

**Figure 4.1**   A data type can be implemented by different data structures. Inserting an element into a list can be done by simply adding it to the front of the list, but removal requires traversing the list to find it. With an array, insertion and removal are done by directly accessing the array cell indexed by an element and changing the mark accordingly. Arrays allow faster implementation, but lists are more space efficient.

may become known as the story unfolds, which is certainly the case in *The Hound of the Baskervilles*. This lack of information prohibits the use of a notebook, since its initialization is impossible.

This weakness of the bulky array is the strength of the nimble list, which can grow and shrink over time as needed and which never stores more elements than necessary. In choosing a data structure for implementing a set data type we have to be mindful of the following trade-off. An array provides a very fast implementation of the set operations but potentially wastes space and might not work in all situations. A list is more space efficient than an array and works under all circumstances, but it implements some operations less efficiently. The situation is summarized in figure 4.1.

# Information Gathering

Identifying suspects is only one step in solving a murder mystery. To narrow down the set of suspects Sherlock Holmes and Dr. Watson need to gather specific information about them, such as motive or potential alibi. In the case of Selden, for example, this information includes the fact that he is an escaped convict. All this additional information should be stored together with each corresponding suspect. When using a notebook,

Sherlock Holmes would add information about a person on the page reserved for that person.

The operations of the set data type cannot do that, but a few small changes to the operations for adding and finding elements are sufficient to make it happen. First, the operation for inserting elements takes two pieces of information: a *key* for identifying the information plus the additional information associated with the key. The key for information about a suspect is his or her name. Second, the operations for finding and removing suspects will only take the key as input. In the case of removing, a person's name and all the additional information stored with it will be removed. In the case of finding a person, the information stored for that name will be returned as a result.

This minor but important extension of the set data type is called a *dictionary* because like a real dictionary it allows us to look up information based on a keyword, as when Sherlock Holmes uses a medical directory to find out about Dr. Mortimer's professional history at the beginning of *The Hound of the Baskervilles*. A dictionary can be viewed as a collection of signs, and each key is a signifier for the information stored with it. The dictionary data type differs in two ways from a traditional printed dictionary. First, the content of a printed dictionary is fixed, whereas a dictionary data type can change— new definitions can be added, obsolete ones can be deleted, and existing ones can be updated. Second, the entries in a printed dictionary are alphabetically sorted by keys, whereas that is not required for a dictionary data type. The ordering of entries in a printed dictionary is necessary because the large number of entries makes direct access to particular pages impossible. Since a thumb index with access to each page would contain too many entries and would have to be too tiny to be of practical use, the sorted keys enable a user of the dictionary to find the entry using a search algorithm (see chapter 5).

Both restrictions of physical dictionaries, the need for sorted keys and the fixed size and content, do not apply to electronic dictionaries. A widely used dynamic dictionary is Wikipedia,[5] which not only lets you use it but also extend and update information in it. In fact, Wikipedia's content has been assembled by its users, a remarkable success of crowdsourcing and a testimony to the power of collaboration. If Sherlock Holmes and Watson were working on the *The Hound of the Baskervilles* case these days, they might very well, instead of sending letters back and forth, use a wiki[6] for maintaining information about the suspects and the case.

The dynamic nature of the dictionary is not limited to only inserting and removing information about suspects; it also allows updating that information. For example, the fact that the escaped convict, Selden, is Eliza Barrymore's brother is not known when Selden becomes a suspect and has to be added later to an already existing dictionary entry for him. But how can this be done? Since we have only three operations for adding, removing, and finding entries in a dictionary, how can we update information once it is stored with a key in the dictionary? We can achieve this by combining operations: find the entry using the key, take the returned information, modify it as needed, remove the entry from the dictionary, and finally add it back with the updated information.

We can add new operations to the set data type in a similar fashion. For example, if Sherlock Holmes maintains a set of people who benefit from Sir Charles's death, he might want to add a motive for some of the suspects. To do that he could compute the intersection of the set of beneficiaries with the set of suspects. Or perhaps he wants to identify new suspects by determining the beneficiaries who are not in the set of suspects. To do that he could compute the set difference between the two sets. Assuming that the set data type has an operation for reporting all elements in a set, an algorithm for computing the intersection or set difference of two sets can simply go through all elements of one set and for each element check whether it is in the second set. If it is, it reports the element as a result of set intersection. If it is not, it reports the element as a result of set difference. Such computations are quite common, since they correspond to the combination of predicates. For example, the intersection of the suspect and beneficiary sets corresponds to the predicate "is a suspect *and* a beneficiary," and the difference between beneficiaries and suspects corresponds to the predicate "is a beneficiary *and not* a suspect."

Finally, we need a data structure to implement dictionaries so that we can actually compute with them. Since the dictionary data type differs from the set data type only by associating additional information with elements, most data structures for sets, including arrays and lists, can be extended to also implement dictionaries. This is the case for all those data structures that explicitly represent each element of the set, because in that case we can simply add the additional information to the key. This also means that any data structure for implementing a dictionary could be used to implement a set; one can simply store an empty or meaningless piece of information together with the key.

## When Order Matters

As mentioned in chapter 3, a computation can only be as good as the representation it is working with. Thus Sherlock Holmes and Watson would like the set of suspects to accurately reflect the state of their investigation. In particular, they want the set to be as small as possible (to avoid wasting effort on false leads)[7] but also as large as needed (to avoid having the murderer go undetected). But otherwise the order in which suspects are added to or removed from the set doesn't really matter to them.

For other tasks the order of items in a data representation does matter. Consider, for example, the heirs of the deceased Sir Charles. The difference between the first and second in line is the entitlement to a heritage worth one million pounds. This information is not only important for determining who gets rich and who doesn't but also provides Holmes and Watson with clues about potential motives of their suspects. In fact, the murderer Stapleton is second in line and tries to kill the first heir, Sir Henry. While the succession of heirs matters, the ordering of heirs is not determined by the time people enter the collection of heirs. For example, when a child is born to the bequeather, it does not become the last in line but takes precedence in the ordering over, say, nephews. A data type in which the ordering of elements is not determined by the time of entry but by some other criterion is called a *priority queue*. The name indicates that the position of the element in the queue is governed by some priority, such as the relationship to the bequeather in the case of heirs, or the severity of the injury of patients in an emergency room.

In contrast, if the time of entry does determine the position in a collection, the data type is called a *queue* if the elements are removed in the order they were added or a *stack* if they are removed in reverse order. A queue is what you go through in a supermarket, a coffee shop, or a security check at the airport. You enter at one end and come out at the other. People are served (and then leave the queue) in the order they entered. A queue data type therefore establishes a first come, first serve policy. The order in which elements enter and leave a queue is also called FIFO for first in, first out.

In a stack, on the other hand, elements leave in the opposite order in which they were added. A good example is a stack of books on your desk. The topmost book, which was placed on the stack last, has to be removed before any other book can be accessed. When you have a window seat in an airplane, you are effectively on the bottom of a stack when it comes to going to the bathroom. The person in the middle seat who sat down after you has to leave the row before you can, and they have to wait for the person in the aisle seat, who sat down last and is on top of the stack, to get out first. Another example is the order in which Hansel and Gretel place and visit the pebbles. The pebble that is placed last is the one they visit first. And if they use the improved algorithm for avoiding loops, the last-placed pebble is the first they pick up.

At first, using a stack data type seems like a strange way of processing data, but stacks are really good for staying organized. For Hansel and Gretel the stack of pebbles allows them to systematically go to the place where they have been before, which ultimately leads all the way back to their home. In a similar way, Theseus escaped the Minotaur's labyrinth with the help of a thread given to him by Ariadne: unraveling the thread amounts to adding it inch by inch to a stack, and coming out of the labyrinth by rewinding the thread amounts to removing the thread from the stack. If in our daily lives we are interrupted in one task by, say, a phone call, which is then interrupted by, say, someone knocking at the door, we mentally keep those tasks on a stack, and we finish the last one first and then go back and pick up where we left the previous one. The order in which elements enter and leave a stack is therefore also called LIFO for last in, first out. And to complete the mnemonics, we could call the order in which elements enter and leave a priority queue HIFO for highest (priority) in, first out.

As for the set and dictionary data types, we would like to know which data structures can be used to implement the (priority) queue and stack data types. It is easy to see that a stack can be well implemented by a list: by simply adding and removing elements always at the front of a list we implement the LIFO ordering, and this takes only constant time. Similarly, by adding elements at the end of a list and removing them at the front, we obtain the FIFO behavior of a queue. It is also possible to implement queues and stacks with arrays.

Queues and stacks preserve the ordering of the elements during their stay in the data structure and thus exhibit a predictable pattern of elements leaving them. Waiting in the security line at an airport is usually rather boring. Things get more exciting when people cut into line or when special lanes for priority customers exist. This behavior is reflected in the priority queue data type.

## It Runs in the Family

The heirs of Sir Charles Baskerville provide a nice example of a priority queue. The priority criterion that defines each heir's position in the queue is the distance to the deceased Sir Charles. But how is this distance to be determined? A typical simple inheritance rule says that the children of the deceased are first in line to inherit in order of their age. Assuming the wealth of the deceased is itself inherited, this rule implies that if the deceased has no children, his or her oldest siblings will continue the succession, followed by their children. And if there are no siblings, the succession continues with the oldest aunts and uncles and their children, and so on.

This rule can be illustrated algorithmically: all family members are represented in a *tree* data structure that reflects their ancestor/descendant relationships. Then an algorithm for traversing the tree constructs a list of the family members in which the position of a person defines their priority for inheriting. This priority would then also be the criterion used in a priority queue of heirs. But if we have a complete list of heirs that is correctly sorted, why do we need a priority queue? The answer is, we don't. We need the priority queue only if the complete family tree is not known at first, or when it changes, for example, when children are born. In that case the family tree would change, and the list computed from the old tree would not reflect the correct inheritance ordering.

The information provided in *The Hound of the Baskervilles* indicates that the old Hugo Baskerville had four children. Charles was the oldest child and inherited from Hugo. The next-oldest brother, John, had one son named Henry, and the youngest brother, Rodger, had a son who is Stapleton. The story mentions that Hugo Baskerville had a daughter, Elizabeth, who I assume to be the youngest child. The names in the tree are called *nodes*, and as in a family tree, when a node B (such as John) is connected to node A above it (such as Hugo), B is called A's *child*, and A is called B's *parent*. The topmost node in a tree, which has no parent, is called its *root*, and nodes that don't have any children are called *leaves*.

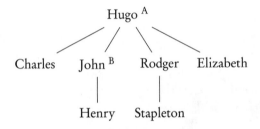

The inheritance rule applied to the Baskerville family tree says that Charles, John, Rodger, and Elizabeth should inherit from Hugo, in that particular order. Since the rule also says that children should inherit before siblings, this means that Henry is in line before Rodger, and Stapleton precedes Elizabeth. In other words, the ordered list of heirs should be as follows:

Hugo → Charles → John → Henry → Rodger → Stapleton → Elizabeth

This inheritance list can be computed by traversing the tree in a particular order, which visits each node before its children. The traversal also visits the grandchildren of older children before visiting younger children (and their grandchildren). The algorithm for computing an inheritance list for a node in a tree can be described as follows:

> To compute the inheritance list for a node $N$, compute and append the inheritance lists for all of its children (oldest to youngest), and place the node $N$ at the beginning of the result.

This description implies that the inheritance list for a node that does not have children simply consists of that node alone, so the inheritance list for that tree is obtained by computing the inheritance list for its root. It might seem peculiar that the algorithm refers to itself in its own description. Such a description is called *recursive* (see chapters 12 and 13).

The following illustrates how the algorithm works by executing it on an example tree, one with a few more members. Assume Henry had two children, Jack and Jill, and a younger sister, Mary:

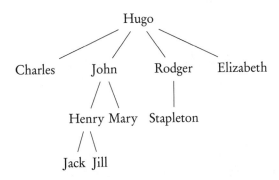

If we execute the algorithm on this tree, starting with Hugo, we have to compute the inheritance list for each of Hugo's children. Beginning with the oldest child, the inheritance list for Charles consists of only himself, since he has no children. The situation is more interesting for John. To compute his inheritance list, we need to compute the inheritance lists for Henry and Mary and append them. Henry's inheritance list consists of his children plus himself, and since Mary has no children, her inheritance list contains only herself. So far we have computed the following inheritance lists:

| Node | Inheritance List |
|---|---|
| Charles | Charles |
| John | John $\rightarrow$ Henry $\rightarrow$ Jack $\rightarrow$ Jill $\rightarrow$ Mary |
| Henry | Henry $\rightarrow$ Jack $\rightarrow$ Jill |
| Mary | Mary |
| Jack | Jack |
| Jill | Jill |

The inheritance list for a node always starts with that node itself, and the inheritance list for a node without children is a list that only contains that node. Moreover, the inheritance lists for Henry and John demonstrate how the inheritance lists for nodes with children are obtained by appending their children's inheritance lists. The inheritance lists for Rodger and Elizabeth are computed in a similar way, and if we append the inheritance lists for Hugo's four children, adding him at the front, we obtain the following ordered list of heirs:

Hugo → Charles → John → Henry → Jack → Jill → Mary → Rodger → Stapleton → Elizabeth

The inheritance algorithm is an example of a *tree traversal*, an algorithm that systematically visits all the nodes of a tree. Since it proceeds top-down, from the root to the leaves, and visits nodes before their children, it is called a *preorder traversal*. Think of a squirrel that scours a tree for nuts. In order not to let any nut go undetected, the squirrel has to visit every branch of the tree. It can do that by employing different strategies. One possibility is to ascend the tree in levels (of height) and visit all branches on one level before visiting any branch on the next level. A different approach is to follow each branch to the end, no matter how high, before switching to another branch. Both strategies ensure that every branch will be visited and every nut will be found; the difference is the order in which branches are visited. This difference doesn't really matter for the squirrel, since it will collect all nuts either way, but the order of visiting the nodes in a family tree does matter as far as inheritance is concerned, since the first person encountered will get it all. The preorder traversal of the inheritance algorithm is a tree traversal of the second kind, that is, following a branch until the end before switching.

A major use of data types and their implementation through data structures is to gather data at one point in a computation and use it later on. Since searching for an individual item in a collection is such an important and frequently used operation, computer scientists have spent considerable effort on investigating data structures that support this operation efficiently. This topic is explored in depth in chapter 5.

# Further Exploration

The examples in *The Hound of the Baskervilles* have illustrated how signs work as representations and how data types and data structures organize collections of data.

Many Sherlock Holmes stories are replete with signs and their interpretation, including the analysis of fingerprints, footprints, and handwriting. Even in *The Hound of the Baskervilles*, there are several additional signs that were not discussed. For example, Dr. Mortimer's stick contains scratches that indicate its use as a walking stick, and it also has bite marks indicating that Dr. Mortimer has a pet dog. Or, examining the anonymous message sent to Sir Henry, Sherlock Holmes concludes that based on their typeface, the letters used must have been cut out from the *Times* newspaper. He also concludes from the size of the cut marks that a small pair of scissors must have been used. For a detective, the conclusions to be drawn can differ when signs have multiple interpretations or when some signs are ignored. This is illustrated in Pierre Bayard's *Sherlock Holmes Was Wrong*, where he argues that Sherlock Holmes identified the wrong person as a murderer in *The Hound of the Baskervilles*. Of course, many other detective stories, movies, and popular TV series, such as *Columbo* or *CSI*, provide examples of signs and representations and demonstrate how they are used in computing conclusions about unsolved crimes.

Umberto Eco's *The Name of the Rose* is the story of a murder mystery that takes place in a monastery in the fourteenth century. It embeds semiotics into a detective story. The protagonist William of Baskerville (the last name is actually a signifier for the Sherlock Holmes story), who is in charge of the murder investigation, is open-minded in his interpretation of signs and thus encourages the reader to play an active role in analyzing the events in the story. More recently, Dan Brown employed many signs in the popular novels *The Da Vinci Code* and *The Lost Symbol*.

In *Gulliver's Travels*, by Jonathan Swift, we are told about a project in the grand academy of Lagado that aims at avoiding the use of words, and thus signs, because they only stand for things. Instead of uttering words, it is suggested that people carry objects that they produce whenever they need to talk about them. Swift's satire illustrates the importance of signs in contributing to the meaning of languages. Similarly, Lewis Carroll's books *Alice's Adventures in Wonderland* and *Through the Looking-Glass* contain examples of clever wordplay that sometimes challenge the traditional role of words as signs.

A stack data type can be used to reverse the elements in a list by first placing them on the stack and then retrieving them in the reverse order (last in, first out). One application is finding a way back, which is, of course, what Hansel and Gretel do, what Theseus did to find his way out of the labyrinth in the Greek myth of *Theseus and the Minotaur*, and what Adso did in *The Name of the Rose* to find his way back through the labyrinth of the library. Another application is understanding the movie *Memento*, which is mostly told in reverse chronological order. By pushing the scenes of the movie onto a mental stack and then taking them off in the reverse order they were presented, one obtains the events of the story in the proper order.

Using a tree to represent family relationships like those in *The Hound of the Baskervilles* might not seem necessary, but there are stories in which the families get so big that it becomes very hard to track the relationships without a corresponding representation. For example, George R. R. Martin's series of novels *A Song of Ice and Fire*, also known through the TV series *Game of Thrones*, contains three large family trees, House Stark, House Lannister, and House Targaryen. The gods from Greek and Norse mythology provide further examples of large family trees.

# Problem Solving and Its Limitations

*Indiana Jones*

# Lost and Found

Where is that note you created a few months ago? You know you wrote it on a sheet of paper that was related to the project that just came up again. You searched all the places where that sheet of paper could possibly be—at least you think you did. Yet, you can't find it. You observe yourself searching some of the places repeatedly—maybe you didn't look carefully enough the first time. You also find notes you were looking for desperately and unsuccessfully some time ago. Darn it.

Does that scenario sound familiar? I certainly have experienced it, and not just once. Without doubt, finding something can be difficult, and an unsuccessful search can be quite frustrating. Even in the days of the seemingly all-powerful Google search engine, finding the right information on the internet can be difficult if you don't know the right keywords or if the keywords are too general and match too many sources.

Fortunately, we are not doomed to be helpless victims of data deluge. The challenge of finding something efficiently can be met by organizing the space in which to search. After all, your mother was right when she told you to clean up your room.[1] An effective organization of the search space involves one or both of the following principles: (1) partition the space into disjoint areas and place the searchable items into these areas, and (2) arrange the searchable items in some order (within their areas).

For example, the partitioning principle may lead to placing all books on a shelf, all papers into a file drawer, and all notes into a ring binder. If you then have to find a note, you know that you only have to search in the ring binder and not in the file drawer or on the bookshelf. Partitioning is important because it allows you to effectively limit the search space to a more manageable size. This principle can also be applied on multiple levels to make a search even more focused. For example, books can be further grouped according to their subject, or papers can be grouped by the year in which they were written.

Of course, partitioning works only under two important conditions. First, the categories used for subdividing the search space must be discernible for the item you are looking for. Suppose, for example, you are looking for Franz Kafka's *The Metamorpho-*

*sis*. Did you place it under "Fiction" or under "Philosophy"? Or maybe you placed it with your other entomology books, or with comics about transforming superheroes, such as The Hulk or some of the X-Men. Second, this strategy can work only if the search partition is maintained correctly at all times. For example, if you take a note out of the ring binder, and instead of putting it back immediately after using it, keep it on your desk or stuff it in the bookshelf, you won't be able to find it in the binder the next time you're looking for it.

Maintaining an order, the second principle to support searching, finds applications in many different situations, from using printed dictionaries to holding a hand of playing cards. The order among the searchable items makes it easier and faster to find items. The method we employ effortlessly in searching a sorted collection is called *binary search*. We pick an item somewhere in the middle of the collection and then continue searching to the left or right, depending on whether the item we're looking for is smaller or larger, respectively. It is also possible to combine the partitioning and ordering principles, which often provides some helpful flexibility. For example, while we can keep the books on the shelf ordered by author name, we can order the papers by date or the notes by their main subject.

A closer look at the two principles reveals that they are related. Specifically, the idea of keeping things in order implies the idea of partitioning the search space, applied rigorously and recursively. Each element divides the collection space into two areas containing all smaller and larger elements, and each of those areas is again organized in the same way. Maintaining an ordered arrangement requires real effort. The interesting question from a computing perspective is whether the payoff of faster search justifies the effort of maintaining order. The answer depends on how large the collection is and how often one has to search it.

The need for searching arises not only in an office. Other environments, such as kitchens, garages, or hobby rooms, are subject to the same challenges, frustrations, and corresponding solutions. Searching is also called for in situations not usually perceived as such. In chapter 5, Indiana Jones's quest for the Holy Grail in *The Last Crusade* provides several obvious and not-so-obvious examples of searching.

# 5

# The Search for the Perfect Data Structure

Data types discussed in chapter 4 capture specific access patterns to collections of data. Since collections can grow very large, an important practical consideration is how to manage them efficiently. We have already seen that different data structures can support the efficiency of specific operations and that they have different space requirements. While building and transforming collections are important tasks, finding items in a collection is probably the most frequently needed operation.

We are searching for things all the time. Often this happens unconsciously, but sometimes we are made painfully aware of it, such as when a mundane activity like getting your car keys can turn into an agonizing search. The more places we have to search and the more items we have to go through, the more difficult it is to find what we're looking for. And we tend to accumulate lots of artifacts over the years—after all, we are descendants of hunters and gatherers. In addition to collector's items such as stamps, coins, or sports cards, we also hoard lots of books, pictures, or clothes over time. Sometimes this happens as a side effect of some hobby or passion—I know several home improvement aficionados who have amassed an impressive collection of tools.

If your bookshelf is organized alphabetically or by topic, or if your picture collection is electronic and has location and time tags, finding a particular book or picture might be easy, but if the number of items is large and lacks any form of organization, such a search can become arduous.

The situation gets much worse when it comes to electronically stored data. Since we have access to basically unlimited storage space, the size of stored data grows rapidly.

For example, according to YouTube, 300 hours of video are uploaded to its site every minute.[1]

Searching is a prevalent problem in real life, and it is also an important topic in computer science. Algorithms and data structures can speed up the search process considerably. And what works with data can sometimes help with storing and retrieving physical artifacts. There is indeed a very simple method that relieves you from ever having to search for your car keys again—if you follow the method meticulously, that is.

## The Key to Fast Search

In the story *The Last Crusade*, Indiana Jones embarks on two major searches. First, he tries to find his father, Henry Jones, Sr., and then both of them together try to find the Holy Grail. As an archaeology professor, Indiana Jones knows a thing or two about searching. In one of his lectures he actually explains to his students,

> *Archaeology is the search for facts.*

How does a search for an archaeological artifact—or a person for that matter—work? If the location of the sought object is known, no search is of course required. Simply go there and find it. Otherwise, the search process depends on two things: the *search space* and potential *clues* or *keys* that can narrow down the search space.

In *The Last Crusade*, Indiana Jones receives his father's notebook containing information about the Holy Grail by mail from Venice, which causes him to start his search there. The notebook's origin is a clue for Indiana Jones that narrows down the initial search space considerably—from all of earth to one city. In this example the search space is literally the two-dimensional geometric space, but in general the term search space means something more abstract. For example, any data structure for representing a collection of items can be viewed as a search space in which one can search for particular items. Sherlock Holmes's list of suspects is such a search space in which one can look for a particular name.

How well are lists suited for searching? As I have discussed in chapter 4, in the worst case we have to inspect all elements in the list before we find the desired element or learn that the element is not contained in the list. This means that searching through a list makes no effective use of clues for narrowing down the search space.

To understand why a list is not a good data structure for searching, it is instructive to take a closer look at how clues actually work. In the two-dimensional space a clue provides a boundary that separates an "outside," which is known to *not* contain the element, from an "inside," which may contain it.[2] 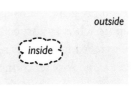 Similarly, for a data structure to make use of clues it must provide a notion of boundary that can separate different parts of the data structure and thus restrict the search to one of these parts. Moreover, a clue or a key is a piece of information that is connected to the object that is sought. The key must be able to identify the boundary between elements that are relevant for the current search and those that aren't.

In a list each element is a boundary that separates the elements preceding it from those that follow it. However, since we never directly access elements in the middle of a list and instead always traverse a list from one end to another, list elements are effectively unable to separate an outside from an inside. Consider the first element in a list. It does not rule out any element from the search except itself, because if it is not the element we are looking for, we have to continue the search through all the remaining elements of the list. But then, when we inspect the second list element, we're faced with the same situation. If the second element is not what we are looking for, we again have to continue the search through all the still remaining elements. Of course, the second element defines as outside the first element of the list, which we do not have to check, but since we have looked at it already, this does not mean any savings in search effort. And the same is true for each list element: the outside it defines has to be inspected to reach the element.

After he has arrived in Venice, Indiana Jones's search continues in a library. Searching for a book in a library provides a nice practical illustration for the notions of boundary and key. When book titles are placed on shelves grouped by the last name of the author, each shelf is often labeled with the names of the authors of the first and last book on the shelf. The two names define the range of authors whose books can be found on the shelf. These two names effectively define a boundary that separates the books from authors within the range from all other books. Suppose we are trying to find *The Hound of the Baskervilles*, by Arthur Conan Doyle, in a library. We can use the author's last name as a key to first identify the shelf whose name range contains it. Once we have found that, we continue searching for the book on that shelf. This search happens in two phases, one for finding the shelf and another to find the book on the shelf. This strategy works well, since it divides the search space into a number of small, nonoverlapping areas (the shelves) using author name boundaries.

The search through the shelves can be carried out in different ways. One simple approach is to inspect the shelves one by one until the shelf with the range containing Doyle is found. This approach treats the shelves effectively as a list and consequently has the same shortcomings. In the case of Doyle, the search might not take too long, but if we are looking for a book by Yeats, it will take much longer. Few people would actually start their search for Yeats at the *A* shelf but instead begin closer to the *Z* shelf and thus find the correct shelf more quickly. This approach is based on the assumption that all shelves are ordered by the names of authors whose books they carry and that if there were 26 shelves (and assuming one shelf per letter), one would start looking for Yeats on the twenty-fifth shelf and for Doyle on the fourth. In other words, one would treat the shelves as an array that is indexed by letters and whose cells are shelves. Of course, it is unlikely that the library contains exactly 26 shelves, but the approach scales to any number of shelves; one would simply start the search for Yeats in the last one-thirteenth of the shelves. A problem with this approach is that the number of authors whose names start with the same letter varies greatly (there are more authors whose names start with an *S* than with an *X*). In other words, the distribution of books is not uniform across all shelves, and thus this strategy is not exact. Therefore, one generally has to go back and forth to locate the target shelf. Exploiting knowledge about the distribution of author names, one could increase the precision of this method substantially, but even the simple strategy works well in practice and is effective in excluding as "outside" a large number of shelves that need not be considered at all.

The search for the book within one shelf can proceed again in different ways. One can scan the books one by one or apply a similar strategy to the one for locating shelves by estimating the location of the book based on the clue's position in the range of authors for that particular shelf. Overall, the two-phase method works pretty well and is much faster than the naive approach of looking at all books one by one. I performed an experiment and searched for *The Hound of the Baskervilles* in the Corvallis Public Library. I was able to locate the correct shelf in five steps and the book on the shelf in another seven steps. This is quite an improvement over the naive method, given that at the time the library carried in its adult fiction section 44,679 books on 36 shelves.

The decision by Indiana Jones to travel to Venice in search of his father is based on a similar strategy. In this case the world is viewed as an array whose cells correspond to geographic regions that are indexed by city names. The return address on the mail containing Henry Jones, Sr.'s notebook serves as a clue that picks out the cell indexed by "Venice" to continue the search. In Venice, the search leads Indiana Jones to a library, where he is looking not for a book but for the tomb of Sir Richard, one of the knights of the first crusade. He finds the tomb after crushing a floor tile marked with an X, which is not without irony, given his earlier proclamation to his students,

*X never, ever marks the spot.*

The key to a fast search is to have a structure that allows the search space to be effectively narrowed down quickly. The smaller the "inside" identified by a key, the better, because it allows the search to converge faster. In the case of the book search there are two search phases separated by one major narrowing-down step.

# Survival by Boggle

Search often comes in disguise and in the most unexpected circumstances. Toward the end of *The Last Crusade*, Indiana Jones arrives in the Temple of the Sun, where he has to overcome three challenges before he can finally enter the room that contains the Holy Grail. The second challenge requires him to cross a tiled floor over an abyss. The problem is that only some of the tiles are safe while others crumble and lead to a gruesome death when stepped on. The floor consists of 50 or so tiles, arranged in a nonregular grid, each marked with a letter of the alphabet. Life as an archaeologist is tricky: one day you have to crush a floor tile to make progress; on other days you have to avoid it at all costs.

Finding those tiles that are safe to step on is not an easy task, since without any further restrictions the number of possibilities is huge: more than one thousand trillion—1 followed by 15 zeros. The clue to finding a viable sequence of tiles that leads safely to the other side of the floor is that the tiles should spell the name *Iehova*. Although this information basically solves the puzzle, the identification of the correct sequence of tiles still requires some work. Surprisingly, it involves a *search* that systematically narrows down the space of possibilities.

This task is similar to playing Boggle, where the goal is to find strings of connected letters on a grid that form words.[3] Indiana Jones's task seems to be much easier because he knows the word already. However, in Boggle, consecutive characters must be on adjacent tiles, which is not a constraint for the tile floor challenge and thus leaves more possibilities for Indiana Jones to consider and makes it harder again.

To illustrate the search problem to be solved, let us assume for simplicity that the tile floor consists of six rows, each containing eight different letters, which yields a grid of 48 tiles. If the correct path consists of one tile in each row, there are $8 \times 8 \times 8 \times 8 \times 8 \times 8 =$

262,144 possible paths through all possible combination of tiles in the six rows. Of these, only one is viable.

How does Indiana Jones now find the path? Guided by the clue word, he finds the tile that contains the letter $I$ in the first row and steps on it. This identification is itself a search process that involves multiple steps. If the letters on the tiles do not appear in alphabetical order, Indiana Jones has to look at them one by one until he finds the tile with the letter $I$. He then steps on it, and continues searching for the tile with the letter $e$ in the second row of tiles, and so forth.

If the one-by-one search reminds you of the search for an element in a list, you are correct. This is exactly what's happening here. The difference is that the list search is applied repeatedly for each row, that is, for each character of the clue word. And therein lies the power of this method. Consider what happens to the search space, that is, the set of all 262,144 possible paths across the tile grid. Each tile in the first row identifies a different starting point that can be continued in $8 \times 8 \times 8 \times 8 \times 8 = 32,768$ different ways by selecting the different combination of letters from the five remaining rows. When Indiana Jones looks at the first tile, which is labeled, say, $K$, he will of course not step on it, since it doesn't match the required $I$. This single decision has removed in one fell swoop a total of 32,768 paths from the search space, namely, all those paths that can be formed by starting with the $K$ tile. And the same reduction happens with each further rejected tile in the first row.

Once Indiana Jones reaches the correct tile, the reduction of the search space is even more dramatic, because as soon as he steps on the tile, the decision process for the first row is completed, and the search space is immediately reduced to the 32,768 paths that can be formed with the remaining five rows. All in all, with at most seven decisions (which are required when the $I$ tile comes last) Indiana Jones has reduced the search space by a factor of eight. And so he continues with the second row of tiles and the letter $e$. Again, the search space is reduced by a factor of eight to 4,096 with at most seven decisions. Once Indiana Jones has reached the last row, only eight possible paths are left, and again with no more than seven decisions he can complete the path. In the worst case this search requires $6 \times 7 = 42$ "steps" (only six literal steps)—a remarkably efficient way of finding one path among 262,144.

It might not be obvious, but the challenge mastered by Indiana Jones bears some similarity to Hansel and Gretel's. In both cases the protagonists have to find a path to safety, and in both cases the path consists of a sequence of locations that are marked—in the case of Hansel and Gretel by pebbles, in the case of Indiana Jones by letters. The search for the next location in the paths is different, though: Hansel and Gretel just have to find any pebble (although they have to make sure not to revisit pebbles), whereas Indiana Jones has to find a specific letter. Both examples again emphasize the role of representation in computation. Indiana Jones's challenge specifically illustrates that the sequence of signifiers (letters) for individual tiles is itself another signifier (the word *Iehova*) for a path. Moreover, the fact that the word *Iehova* stands for a path illustrates how a computation that simply searches for a word becomes meaningful and important in the world.

The way in which Indiana Jones finds the clue word on the grid is exactly how one can search efficiently for a word in a dictionary: first narrow down the group of pages that contain words that start with the same letter as the clue word, then narrow down the group of pages further to those that match the first and second letters, and so on, until the word is found.

To better understand the data structure that lurks behind the tile grid and that makes Indiana Jones's search so efficient, we look at another way of representing words and dictionaries that uses trees to organize the search space.

## Counting with a Dictionary

Chapter 4 described the tree data structure. I used a family tree to demonstrate how to compute a list of heirs in order of their inheritance priority. The computation traversed the whole tree and had to visit every node in the tree. Trees are also an excellent data structure to support the search within a collection. In this case the search uses nodes in the tree to direct the search down one path to find the desired element.

Let's reconsider Indiana Jones's tile floor challenge. In the movie, his first step turns into a dramatic scene where he almost gets killed by stepping onto an unsafe tile. He uses the spelling *Jehova* and steps onto a *J* tile, which crumbles under his feet. This shows that the challenge is actually more tricky than it seemed at first because Indiana Jones can't really be so sure about the correct (spelling of the) clue word. In addition to the spellings with *I* and *J* there is another one that starts with *Y*. Moreover, other possible names that could in principle work are, for example, *Yahweh* and *God*. Let us assume that these are all the possibilities and that Indiana Jones and his father are certain that one of these words indeed indicates a safe path across the tile floor.

Now what would be a good strategy to decide which tiles to step on? If all the words are equally likely, he could improve his odds by picking a letter that occurs in more than one name. To illustrate, assume he picks *J* (as he actually does). Since the *J* occurs only in one of the five names, there is only a one in five (that is, 20%) chance that the tile will hold. On the other hand, stepping onto a *v* tile is 60% secure, since the *v* occurs in three of the names. If any of these three words is correct, the *v* tile will be safe, and since all words are considered to be equally likely correct, the chance of survival increases to three out of five for the *v* tile.[4]

Therefore, a good strategy is to first compute the frequency of letters among the five words and then try to step on tiles with the highest occurrence rate. Such a mapping of letters to frequencies is called
a *histogram*. To compute a letter histogram, Indiana Jones needs to
maintain a frequency counter for each letter. By scanning through all
the words he can increment the counter for each encountered letter.
Maintaining counters for different letters is a task that is solved by the

dictionary data type (see chapter 4). For this application the keys are individual letters,
and the information stored with each key is the letter frequency.

We could use an array with letters as indices as a data structure to implement this
dictionary, but this would waste over 50% of the array's space, since we have only a
total of eleven different letters to count. Alternatively, we could also use a list. But that
wouldn't be very efficient. To see this, let's suppose we scan the words in alphabetical
order. Thus we start with the word *God* and add each of its letters into the list, together
with the initial count of 1. We obtain the following list:

$$G{:}1 \rightarrow o{:}1 \rightarrow d{:}1$$

Note that the insertion of *G* took one step, the insertion of *o* took two because we had
to add it after the *G*, and the insertion of *d* took three steps because we had to add it
after both *G* and *o*. But couldn't we instead insert the new letters at the front of the
list? Unfortunately, that wouldn't work because we have to make sure a letter is not in
the list before we add it, and so we have to look at all existing letters in the list before
we can add a new one. If a letter is already contained in the list, we instead increment
its counter. Thus we have spent already $1 + 2 + 3 = 6$ steps on the first word.

For the next word *Iehova* we need 4, 5, and 6 steps to insert *I*, *e*, and *h*, respectively,
which brings us to a total of 21 steps. The next letter is an *o*, which already exists. We
only need 2 steps to find it and update its count to 2. Letters *v* and *a* are new and need
an additional $7 + 8 = 15$ steps to be inserted at the end of the list. At this point our list
has taken 38 steps to build and looks as follows:

$$G{:}1 \rightarrow o{:}2 \rightarrow d{:}1 \rightarrow I{:}1 \rightarrow e{:}1 \rightarrow h{:}1 \rightarrow v{:}1 \rightarrow a{:}1$$

Updating the dictionary with the counts from the word *Jehova* then takes 9 steps for
adding the *J* and 5, 6, 2, 7, and 8 steps for incrementing the counts for the remaining
letters that are already present in the list, which brings the total number of steps to
75. After processing the last two words, *Yahweh* and *Yehova*, using 40 and 38 steps,

respectively, we finally end up with the following list, which took a total of 153 steps to construct:

$$G{:}1 \rightarrow o{:}4 \rightarrow d{:}1 \rightarrow I{:}1 \rightarrow e{:}4 \rightarrow h{:}4 \rightarrow v{:}3 \rightarrow a{:}4 \rightarrow J{:}1 \rightarrow Y{:}2 \rightarrow w{:}1$$

Note that we must not add the second *h* in *Yahweh*, since counting it twice for one word would increase, incorrectly, the odds of the letter (in this case from 80% to 100%).[5] A final scan of the list shows that the letters *o*, *e*, *h*, and *a* are the safest to begin with, all having a probability of 80% of being contained in the correct word.

## Lean Is Not Always Better

The main drawback of the list data structure implementation of a dictionary is the high cost for repeatedly accessing items that are located toward the end of the list.

The *binary search tree* data structure tries to avoid this problem by partitioning the search space more evenly to support faster search. A *binary* tree is a tree in which each node has at most two children. As mentioned, nodes without any children are called *leaves*. The nodes with children are called *internal nodes*. Also, the node that has no parent is called the *root* of the tree.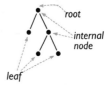

Let's look at some binary tree examples shown in figure 5.1. The left one is a tree of a single node—the simplest tree one can imagine. The root, which is also a leaf, consists of the letter *G*. This tree doesn't really look much like a tree, similar to a list of one element that doesn't look like a list. The middle tree has one more node, a child *o*, added to the root. In the right tree a child *d* itself has children *a* and *e*. This example illustrates that if we cut the link to its parent, a node becomes the root of a separate tree, which is called a *subtree* of its parent. In this case the tree with root *d* and two children *a* and *e* is a subtree of the node *G*, as is the single-node tree with root *o*. This suggests that a tree is inherently a recursive data structure and can be defined in the following way. A tree is either a single node, or it is a node that has one or two subtrees (whose roots are the children of the node). This recursive structure of trees was indicated chapter 4, which presented a recursive algorithm to traverse a family tree.

The idea of a binary *search* tree is to use internal nodes as boundaries that separate all its descendant nodes into two classes: those nodes with a smaller value than the boundary node are contained in the left subtree, and those with a larger value are contained in the right subtree.

This arrangement can be exploited for searching as follows. If we are looking for a particular value in a tree, we compare it with the root of the tree. If they match, we

**Figure 5.1**    Three example binary trees. *Left:* A tree of only one node. *Middle:* A tree whose root has a right subtree of a single node. *Right:* A tree whose root has two subtrees. All three trees have the binary search property, which says that nodes in left subtrees are smaller than the root, and nodes in right subtrees are larger than the root.

have found the value and the search is over. Otherwise, in case the value is smaller than the root, we can limit the further search exclusively to the left subtree. We do not have to look at any of the nodes in the right subtrees because all the nodes are known to be larger than the root and thus larger than the sought value. In each case, the internal node defines a boundary that separates the "inside" (given by the left subtree) from the "outside" given by the right subtree just as the return address of the Grail diary defines the "inside" of the next step of Indiana Jones's search for his father.

The three trees shown in figure 5.1 are all binary search trees. They store letters as values that can be compared according to their position in the alphabet. To find a value in such a tree works by repeatedly comparing the sought value to the values in nodes in the tree and correspondingly descending into the right or left subtrees.

Suppose we want to find out whether *e* is contained in the right tree. We start at the root of the tree and compare *e* with *G*. Since *e* precedes *G* in the alphabet and is thus "smaller" than *G*, we continue the search in the left subtree, which contains all values smaller than *G* that are stored in this tree. Comparing *e* with the root of the left subtree, *d*, we find that *e* is larger and therefore continue the search in the right subtree, which is a tree of only one node. Comparing *e* with that node finishes the search successfully. Had we searched for, say, *f* instead, the search would have led to the same node *e*, but since *e* does not have a right subtree, the search would have ended there with the conclusion that *f* is not contained in the tree.

Any search proceeds along a path in the tree, and so the time it takes to find an element or to conclude that it does not exist in the tree never takes longer than the longest path from the root to a leaf in the tree. We can see that the right tree in figure 5.1, which stores five elements, contains paths to leaves that have a length of 2 or 3 only.

This means we can find any element in at most three steps. Compare this with a list of five elements, where a search for the last element of the list always takes five steps.

We are now ready to follow the computation of the letter histogram using a binary search tree to represent a dictionary. Again, we start with the word *God* and add each of its letters into the tree, together with the initial count of 1. We obtain the following tree, which reflects the order of the letters where they appear in the tree:

In this case the insertion of *G* took one step, as it did for the list, but the insertion of *o* and *d* both took only two steps, since they are both children of *G*. Thus we have saved one step for the first word ($1+2+2 = 5$ steps for the tree versus $1+2+3 = 6$ for the list).

Inserting the next word, *Iehova*, requires three steps for each of the letters, except for *o* and *h*, which require two and four steps, respectively. As with lists, processing the *o* does not create a new element but increments the count of the existing element by 1. Processing this word therefore takes 18 steps and brings the total to 24 steps, compared to 38 steps that were needed for the list data structure. The word *Jehova* changes the tree structure only slightly by adding a node for *J*, which takes four steps. With $3+4+2+3+3 = 15$ more steps the counts for the existing letters are updated, leading to a total of 39 steps, compared to 75 for the list:

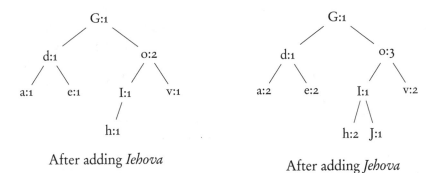

After adding *Iehova*                    After adding *Jehova*

Finally, adding *Yahwe(h)* and *Yehova*, each requiring 19 steps, we obtain the following tree, which took a total of 76 steps to construct. This is half of the 153 steps that were needed for the list data structure.

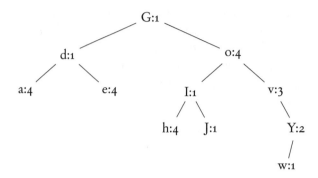

This binary search tree represents the same dictionary as the list, but in a form that supports searching and updating faster—in general, at least. The spatial shapes of lists and trees explain some of the differences in their efficiency. The long and narrow structure of the list often forces the search to go long distances and to look at elements that are not relevant. In contrast, the wide and shallow form of the tree directs the search effectively and limits the elements to be considered and the distance traversed. However, a fair comparison between lists and binary search trees requires us to consider a few additional aspects.

## Efficiency Hangs in the Balance

In computer science we usually do not compare different data structures by counting the exact number of steps for specific lists or trees, since this can give a misleading impression, specifically for small data structures. Moreover, even in this simple analysis we compared operations that are not of exactly the same complexity and take different amounts of time to execute. For example, to perform a comparison in a list we only have to test whether two elements are equal, whereas in a binary search tree we also have to determine which element is larger in order to direct the search into the corresponding subtree. This means that many of the 153 list operations are simpler and faster to perform than some of the 76 tree operations and that we shouldn't read too much into the direct comparison of the two numbers.

Instead we consider the increase in runtime of operations as the data structures get bigger and more complicated. Chapter 2 showed examples. For lists we know that the runtime for inserting new and searching for existing elements is linear, that is, the time for inserting or finding is proportional to the length of the list in the worst case. This isn't too bad, but if such an operation is executed repeatedly, the accumulated runtime becomes quadratic, which can be prohibitive. Recall the strategy that had Hansel go all the way back home for fetching each new pebble.

What, in comparison, is the runtime for inserting an element into a tree and searching for an element in a tree? The final search tree contains 11 elements, and searching and inserting takes between three and five steps. In fact, the time to find or insert an element is bounded by the height of the tree, which is often much smaller than the number of its elements. In a *balanced* tree, that is, a tree in which all paths from the root to a leaf have the same length (±1), the height of a tree is *logarithmic* in size, which means the height grows by 1 only whenever the number of nodes in the tree doubles. For example, a balanced tree with 15 nodes has a height of 4, a balanced tree with 1,000 nodes has height 10, and 1,000,000 nodes fit comfortably into a balanced tree of height 20. Logarithmic runtime is much better than linear runtime, and as the size of a dictionary gets really large, the tree data structure gets better and better compared to the list data structure.

This analysis is based on *balanced* binary search trees. Can we actually guarantee that constructed trees are balanced, and if not, what is the runtime in the case of unbalanced search trees? The final tree in this example is *not* balanced, since the path to leaf *e* is of length 3 while the path to leaf *w* is of length 5. The order in which the letters are inserted into the tree matters and can lead to different trees. For example, if we insert the letters in the order given by the word *doG*, we obtain the following binary search tree, which is not balanced at all:

This tree is extremely *un*balanced—it is not really different from a list. And this is not some quirky exception. Of the six possible sequences of the three letters, two lead to a balanced tree (*God* and *Gdo*) and the other four lead to lists. Fortunately, there are techniques to balance search trees that get out of shape after insertions, but these add to the cost of insertion operations, although the cost can still be kept logarithmic.

Finally, binary search trees work only for those kind of elements that can always be ordered, that is, for any two elements where we can say which is larger and which is smaller. Such a comparison is required to decide in which direction to move in a tree to find or store an element. However, for some kinds of data, such comparisons are not possible. Suppose, for example, you are keeping notes on quilting patterns. For each pattern you want to record what fabrics and tools you need, how difficult it is to make, and how much time it takes. To store information about those patterns in a binary search tree, how could you decide whether one pattern is smaller or larger than another? Since patterns differ in the number of pieces they contain, as well as the shapes and colors of the pieces, it's not obvious how to define an order among those patterns. This is not an impossible task—one could decompose a pattern into its constituting parts and describe it by a list of its features (for example, the number of pieces or their colors and shapes) and then compare patterns by comparing their lists of features, but this requires effort, and it may not be very practical. Thus a binary search tree might not be well suited for storing a quilting pattern dictionary. However, you could still use a list, since all you need to do for a list is to decide whether two patterns are the same, which is easier than ordering them.

To summarize: Binary search trees exploit a strategy employed naturally and effortlessly by people to decompose search problems into smaller ones. In fact, binary search trees have systematized and perfected the idea. As a consequence, binary search trees can be much more efficient than lists in representing dictionaries. However, they require more effort to guarantee the balancing, and they do not work for every kind of data. And this should match your experience with searching your desk, office, kitchen, or garage. If you regularly devote effort to keeping things in order, for example, by placing documents or tools back after their use, you have a much easier time finding objects than by having to search through a pile of unorganized stuff.

## Try a Trie

Binary search trees are an efficient alternative to lists when it comes to computing a histogram of letter frequencies in words. But this is only one of the computations that help Indiana Jones solve the tile floor challenge. The other computation is to identify a sequence of tiles that spell a particular word and lead safely across the tile floor.

We have already determined that a grid consisting of six rows, each with eight letters, contains 262,144 different six-tile paths. Since each path corresponds to one word, we could represent the association of words to paths with a dictionary. A list would be an inefficient representation, since the clue word *Iehova* might be located near the end of the list and thus might take quite some time to locate. A balanced binary search tree would be much better because its height would be 18, ensuring the clue word can be found relatively quickly. But we don't have such a balanced search tree available, and constructing it is a time-consuming endeavor. As with the search tree containing the letters, we have to insert each element separately, and to do so we have to repeatedly traverse paths in the tree from the root to the leaves. Without analyzing this process in detail, it should be clear that building the tree takes more than linear time.[6]

Still, we can identify the sequence of tiles quite efficiently (with no more than 42 steps) without any additional data structure. How is this possible? The answer is that the tile floor with the letters on the tiles is itself a data structure that supports particularly well the kind of search Indiana Jones has to perform. It is called a *trie*,[7] a data structure that is somewhat similar to a binary search tree but also different in an important way.

Recall how Indiana Jones with each step on a tile reduces the search space by a factor of eight. This is similar to what happens when by descending into a balanced binary search tree the search space is cut in half: by taking one of two tree branches, half the nodes in the tree are excluded from the search. Similarly, by not taking a tile, the search space is reduced by one-eighth, and by selecting a tile, the search space is reduced to one-eighth of its previous size, because selecting one tile means not selecting seven others and thus reducing the search space by seven-eighth.

But something else happens here as well that is different from how a binary search tree works. In a binary search tree each element is stored in a separate node. By contrast, a trie stores only single letters in each node and represents words as paths connecting different letters. To understand the difference between a binary search tree and a trie, consider the following example. Suppose we want to represent the set of words *bat*, *bag*, *beg*, *bet*, *mag*, *mat*, *meg*, and *met*. A balanced binary search tree containing these words looks as follows:

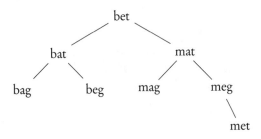

To find the word *bag* in this tree, we compare it with the root *bet*, which tells us to continue the search in the left subtree. This comparison takes two steps for comparing the first two characters of both words. Next we compare *bag* with the root of the left subtree, *bat*, which tells us again to continue the search in the left subtree. This comparison takes three steps, since we have to compare all three characters of the two words. Finally, we compare *bat* with the leftmost node in the tree, which results in the successful completion of the search. This last comparison also takes three steps, and the whole search requires 8 comparisons altogether.

We can represent the same collection of words by a 2-by-3 tile floor, where each row contains tiles for the letters that can occur at the corresponding position in any of the words. For example, since each word begins with either *b* or *m*, the first row needs two tiles for these two letters. Similarly, the second row needs two tiles for *a* and *e*, and the third row needs tiles for *g* and *t*.

| b | m |
|---|---|
| a | e |
| g | t |

Finding a word on the tile floor works by systematically traversing the tile floor row-by-row. For each letter of the word the corresponding tile row is traversed from left to right until the letter is found. For example, to find the word *bag* on this tile floor, we start searching for the first letter, *b*, in the first row. We find the tile in one step. Next we search for the second letter *a* in the second row, which again takes one step. Finally, we can complete the search successfully by finding *g* in the third row, which also takes only one step. Altogether this search takes 3 comparisons.

The search on the tile floor requires fewer steps than the binary search tree because we have to compare each letter only once, whereas the search in the binary tree causes repeated comparisons of initial parts of the word. The word *bag* represents the best case scenario for the tile floor, since each letter can be found on the first tile. By contrast, the word *met* requires six steps, since each of its letters is contained on the last tile in a row. But it cannot get worse than this because we have to check each tile at most once. (For comparison, finding *met* in the binary search tree requires 2+3+3+3 = 11 steps.) The best case for the binary search tree is finding the word *bet*, which requires only three steps. However, with growing distance from the root, binary search leads to more and more comparisons. Since most words are located toward the leaves of the tree, at a greater distance from the root,[8] we generally have to repeatedly perform comparisons of initial parts of the word, which indicates that in most cases search in a trie is faster than in a binary search tree.

The tile floor analogy suggests that a trie can be represented as a table, but this is not always the case. The example works out nicely because all words have the same length and each position in a word can contain the same letters. However, suppose we want to also represent the words *bit* and *big*. In this case, the second row needs an additional tile for the letter *i*, which breaks the rectangular shape. Adding the two words reveals another regularity in the example that does not exist in general. The example words are chosen so that different prefixes of the same length have the same possible suffixes, which allows the sharing of information. For example, *ba* and *be* can both be completed by adding either *g* or *t*, which means that the possible continuations of both prefixes can be described by a single tile row containing the letters *g* and *t*. However, this is not true anymore when we add the words *bit* and *big*. While *b* can be continued with 3 possible letters, namely, *a*, *e*, and *i*, *m* can be continued only with *a* and *e*, which means that we need two different continuations.

Therefore, a trie is typically represented as a special kind of binary tree in which nodes carry single letters, left subtrees represent word continuations, and right subtrees represent letter alternatives (plus their continuations). For example, the trie for the words *bat*, *bag*, *beg*, and *bet* looks as follows:

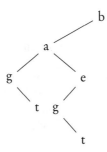

Since the root has no right edge, all words start with *b*. The left edge from *b* to the subtree with root *a* leads to the possible continuations, which start with either *a* or *e*, the alternative to *a* pointed to by the right edge from *a*. The fact that *ba* and *be* can be continued by either *g* or *t* is represented by a left edge from *a* to a subtree with root *g*, which has a right child *t*. The fact that the left subtrees of *a* and *e* are identical means that they can be shared, which is exploited in the tile floor representation by having a single tile row. Because of this sharing, a trie typically requires less storage than a binary search tree.

Whereas in the binary search tree each key is completely contained in a separate node, the keys stored in a trie are distributed over the trie's nodes. Any sequence of nodes from the root of a trie is a prefix of some key in the trie, and in the case of the tile floor, the selected tiles are a prefix of the final path. This is why a trie is also called a *prefix tree*. The trie data structure representing the tile floor facing Indiana Jones is illustrated in figure 5.2.

Like binary search trees and lists, tries have their advantages and their problems. For example, they work only for keys that can be decomposed into sequences of items. As with Indiana Jones, who in the end was not able to hold on to the Holy Grail, there

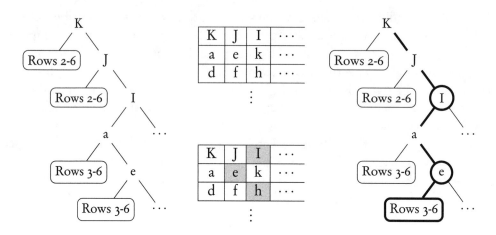

**Figure 5.2**    A trie data structure and how to search it. *Left:* A trie representation where left subtrees represent possible word continuations of the letter in the parent node (represented by the rounded rectangles) and right subtrees represent alternatives to the parent node. *Middle top:* The tile floor representation of the trie on the left in which the common subtrees are shared through single tile rows. *Middle bottom:* Three selected tiles that spell the beginning of the word *Iehova*. *Right:* A path through the trie marked by bold edges for the selected tiles. The circled nodes correspond to selected tiles.

is no Holy Grail of data structures. The best choice of a data structure always depends on the details of the application.

When we watch the movie scene, we consider the real challenge to be finding the clue word or jumping precisely onto the target tiles, but hardly the identification of the tiles according to the letters of the clue word. This seems so obvious that we don't think about it at all, which again demonstrates how natural the execution of efficient algorithms is to us. As with Hansel and Gretel and Sherlock Holmes, Indiana Jones's adventures and his survival are based on core computing principles.

And finally, if you're still wondering about the method to never lose your car keys again, it is very simple: When you come home, always place them at one particular location. This location is the key to the keys. But you probably knew that already.

# Getting Your Ducks in a Row

If you are a teacher, a significant part of your job is to grade essays or exams for the students in your classes. The task involves more than just reading and grading individual exams. For example, before deciding on the final grades you may want to get a sense of the grade distribution and potentially curve the grades. Moreover, once the grades are fixed, you have to enter them into the class roster, and finally, you have to hand the exams back to the students. In some cases each of these tasks can be performed more efficiently by employing some form of sorting.

Let's first consider entering grades into a roster. Even for this simple task one can identify three different algorithms with different runtime performances. First, you can go through the pile of graded exams and enter each grade into the roster. Each exam is obtained in constant time from the pile, but it takes logarithmic time to find the student's name in the roster, assuming it is sorted by names and you use binary search to find it. For entering all grades into the roster this adds up to *linearithmic* runtime,[1] which is much better than quadratic but not quite as good as linear.

Second, you can go through the roster name by name and find for each student her or his exam in the pile. Again, getting to the next name in the roster takes constant time, but finding the exam for a particular student in the list requires, on average, traversing half the list, resulting in quadratic runtime.[2] Thus this algorithm should not be used.

Third, you could sort the exams by name and then go through the roster and the sorted pile in parallel. Since the sorted pile and the roster are aligned, entering each grade takes only constant time. Altogether this leads to linear time plus the time it takes to sort the list of exams, which can be done in linearithmic time. The total runtime for this method is dominated by the linearithimc time required for sorting. Therefore, the total runtime of this last algorithm is also linearithmic. But that's not better than the first approach, so why go to the extra trouble of sorting the exams in the first place? Since there are situations in which we can actually sort faster than linearithmic time, the third method can in these cases improve the performance and be the most efficient approach.

The second task, curving the exam grades, requires creating a point distribution, that is, a map with point scores and the number of students who have obtained that score. This task is similar to Indiana Jones's task of computing a histogram of letters. A grade distribution is also a histogram. Computing a histogram using a list takes quadratic runtime while using a binary search tree takes linearithmic runtime, which suggests using the latter. You could also compute a histogram by first sorting the pile of exams by points, followed by a simple scan of the sorted pile where you count how often each point score repeats. This works, since in a sorted list all the exams with the same points will follow one another. As in the case of entering the grades into the class roster, sorting does not increase the runtime but can potentially shorten it. However, the situation is different if the point range is small. In that case, updating an array of point scores is probably the fastest method.

Finally, handing back exams in a classroom can become an embarrassingly slow endeavor. Imagine standing in front of a student and trying to find her or his exam in a large pile. Even using binary search this takes too long. Repeating the search for a large number of students makes this an inconveniently slow process (even though it gets faster with each step as the pile of exam gets smaller). An alternative is to sort the exams by position of students in the class. If seats are numbered and you have a seating chart (or just happen to know where students sit), you can sort the exams by seat numbers. Handing back the exams then becomes a linear algorithm where, similarly to entering the grades into the class roster, you can traverse the seats and the pile of exams in parallel and hand back each exam in one step. In this case, even if the sorting takes linearithmic time, it is worth the effort, since it saves precious class time. This is an example of *precomputing*, where some data needed for an algorithm is computed before the algorithm is executed. It is what the mail carrier does before delivering mail or what you do when arranging your shopping list according to how items are placed in the aisles at the grocery store.

Sorting is a more general activity than one might think. In addition to sorting collections of items, we regularly have to sort tasks based on their dependencies. Consider the algorithm for getting dressed: you have to figure out to put on socks before shoes and underpants before pants. Assembling furniture, repairing or maintaining machines, filling out paperwork—most of these activities require us to perform some actions in the correct order. Even preschoolers are given problems to sort pictures into a coherent story.

# 6 Sorting out Sorting

Sorting is a major example of a computation. In addition to having many applications, sorting helps to explain some fundamental concepts of computer science. First, different sorting algorithms with different runtime and space requirements illustrate the impact of efficiency in deciding how to solve a problem computationally. Second, sorting is a problem for which a minimal complexity is known. In other words, we know a *lower bound* on the number of steps that any sorting algorithm must take. Sorting thus illustrates that computer science as a field has identified principal limitations on the speed of computation. Knowledge about limits is empowering because it helps us direct research efforts more productively. Third, the distinction between the complexity of a problem and the complexity of its solutions helps us understand the notion of an *optimal solution*. Finally, several sorting algorithms are examples of *divide-and-conquer* algorithms. Such an algorithm splits its input into smaller parts, which are processed recursively and whose solutions are reassembled into a solution for the original problem. The elegance of the divide-and-conquer principle stems from its recursive nature and its relationship to its close cousin, mathematical induction. It is a very effective approach to problem solving and illustrates the power of problem decomposition.

As mentioned in chapter 5, one of the applications of sorting is to support and speed up search. For example, finding an element in an unsorted array or list takes linear time, whereas in a sorted array this can be achieved in logarithmic time through binary search. Thus computation (here, sorting) expended at one time can be preserved (in the form of a sorted array) to be used at a later time to speed up other computations (for example, searching). More generally, computation is a resource that can be saved and reused through data structures. This interplay between data structures and algorithms shows how closely related the two are.

## First Things First

For his day job, Indiana Jones works as a college professor, which means that he faces issues related to grading exams. Thus sorting is relevant for him. Moreover, as an archaeologist he has to keep collections of physical artifacts and organize notes and observations made over the course of his excursions. Like the documents in an office these can benefit greatly from being sorted because order makes the search for particular items more efficient. Indiana Jones's adventures illustrate another application of sorting, which arises whenever he makes a plan of how to accomplish a complex task. A plan is the arrangement of a set of actions in the right order.

Indiana Jones's task in *Raiders of the Lost Ark* is to find the ark containing the Ten Commandments. The ark is rumored to be buried inside a secret chamber in the ancient city of Tanis. To find the ark, Indiana Jones has to find this secret chamber, called Well of Souls. The chamber's location can be discovered in a model of Tanis, itself located in a map room. By placing a special golden disc at a particular location in the map room, sunlight will be focused on the location of the Well of Souls in the model of Tanis, thus revealing the place where the Well of Souls can be found. The golden disc was originally in possession of Indiana Jones's former teacher and mentor Professor Ravenwood but was later given to his daughter, Marion Ravenwood. Thus to find the ark Indiana Jones has to perform several tasks, including the following:

- Locate the Well of Souls (Well).
- Find the map room (Map).
- Obtain the golden disc (Disc).
- Use the disc to focus the sunbeam (Sunbeam).
- Find the possessor of the golden disc (Marion).

In addition to performing these tasks, Indiana Jones has to travel between different places: to Nepal to find Marion Ravenwood and to the city of Tanis in Egypt, where the ark is hidden in the Well of Souls.

It is not difficult to find the correct ordering for this particular set of tasks. The interesting question, from a computing perspective, is what different algorithms exist for solving the problem and what the runtimes of these algorithms are. There are two approaches that most people will probably apply when asked to order the sequence.

# Libraries NI

Holywood Library
Sullivan Building
86-88 High Street
Holywood
Down
BT18 9AE
Ph. 028 9042 4232

## Borrowed Items 03/11/2017 13:58
### XXXXXX0188

| m Title | Due Date |
|---|---|
| nce upon an algorithm : | 24/11/2017 |
| w stories explain |  |
| mputir |  |

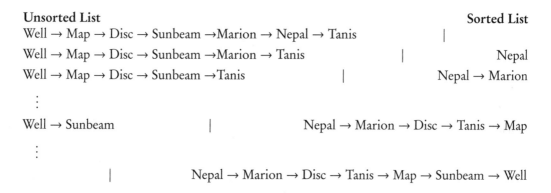

**Figure 6.1**   Selection sort repeatedly finds the smallest element in an unsorted list (*left of vertical bar*) and appends it to the sorted list (*right*). Elements are not sorted by name but according to the dependency of tasks they represent.

Both methods start with an unsorted list and repeatedly move elements around until the list is sorted. The difference between the two methods can be best illustrated by describing how to move elements from an unsorted list into a sorted list.

The first method, illustrated in figure 6.1, is to repeatedly find the smallest element in the unsorted list and append it to the sorted list. To compare actions, one action is considered to be smaller than another if it can come before. Consequently, the smallest action is one that does not have to be preceded by any other action. At the beginning all elements are still to be processed, and the sorted list is empty. Since the first task is to travel to Nepal, this means Nepal is the smallest element and is thus the first element to be selected and appended to the sorted list. The next step is to find the possessor of the disc, that is, to find Marion. Next Indiana Jones has to obtain the disc, travel to Tanis, and uncover the map room, which is reflected in the second-to-last line in figure 6.1. Finally, Indiana Jones has to focus the sunbeam using the disc to reveal the location of the Well of Souls, where he can then find the ark. The resulting sorted list represents the plan for Indiana Jones's adventure.

As the figure illustrates, the algorithm is finished when the list of unsorted elements becomes empty, since in that case all elements have been moved to the sorted list. This sorting algorithm is called *selection sort* because it is based on repeatedly selecting an element from an unsorted list. Note that the method works just as well the other way around, that is, by repeatedly finding the *largest* element and adding it to the *beginning* of the sorted list.

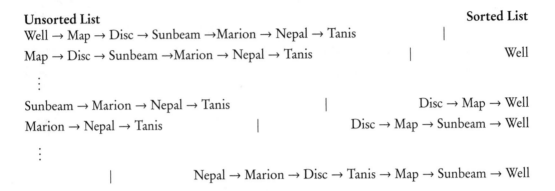

**Unsorted List**                                                                                           **Sorted List**

Well → Map → Disc → Sunbeam →Marion → Nepal → Tanis      |

Map → Disc → Sunbeam →Marion → Nepal → Tanis             |          Well

⋮

Sunbeam → Marion → Nepal → Tanis          |          Disc → Map → Well

Marion → Nepal → Tanis          |          Disc → Map → Sunbeam → Well

⋮

     |      Nepal → Marion → Disc → Tanis → Map → Sunbeam → Well

**Figure 6.2** Insertion sort repeatedly inserts the next element from the unsorted list (*left of the vertical bar*) into the sorted list (*right*).

It may seem obvious, but how can we actually find the smallest element in a list? A simple method is to remember the value of the first element and compare it with the second, third, and so on, until we find an element that is smaller. In that case, we take the value of that element and continue comparing and remembering the currently smallest element until we reach the end of the list. This method takes linear time in the length of the list in the worst case, since the smallest element can be at the end of the list.

Most of the effort in selection sort is expended on finding the smallest element in an unsorted list. Even though the unsorted list shrinks by one element in each step, the overall runtime of the sorting algorithm is still quadratic, since we have to traverse, on average, a list that contains half the elements. We saw the same pattern when analyzing Hansel's algorithm in chapter 2 for fetching the next pebble from home: the sum of the first $n$ numbers is proportional to the square of $n$.[1]

The other popular method for sorting takes an arbitrary element (usually the first) from the unsorted list and places it at the correct position in the sorted list. The element is inserted *after* the largest element in the sorted list that is *smaller* than the element to be inserted. In other words, the insertion step traverses the sorted list to find the last element that has to precede the element to be inserted.

The effort in this method is spent on the insertion of elements, not their selection, which gives the method the name *insertion sort* (see figure 6.2). Insertion sort is the preferred sorting method of many people who play cards. Having a pile of dealt cards in front of them, they pick up one after the other and insert it into an already sorted hand.

The difference between insertion sort and selection sort can best be seen when the Sunbeam element is moved from the unsorted list into the sorted list. As figure 6.2 shows, the element is simply removed from the unsorted list, without the need for any search, and is inserted into the sorted list by traversing it until its proper position between Map and Well is found.

This example also demonstrates a subtle difference in the runtime of both algorithms. While selection sort has to traverse one of the two lists completely for every selected element, insertion sort has to do this only when the element to be inserted is larger than all elements currently in the sorted list. In the worst case, when the list to be sorted is already sorted to begin with, every element will be inserted at the end of the sorted list. In this case insertion sort has the same runtime as selection sort. In contrast, when the list is inversely sorted, that is, from the largest to smallest element, every element will be inserted at the front of the sorted list, which leads to a linear runtime for insertion sort. One can show that on average insertion sort still has quadratic runtime. Insertion sort can be much faster than selection sort in some cases and never does worse.

Why does insertion sort have a better runtime in some cases than selection sort, even though they both operate similarly? The key difference is that insertion sort makes use of the result of its own computation. Since new elements are inserted into an already sorted list, insertions do not always have to traverse the whole list. In contrast, selection sort always appends to the sorted list, and since the selection process cannot exploit the sorting, it always has to scan the whole unsorted list. This comparison illustrates the important computer science design principle of *reuse*.

Apart from efficiency, do the two sorting methods differ in how well they are suited for the problem of arranging actions into a plan? Neither method is ideal, because a particular difficulty in this example problem is not the process of sorting but the decision about which actions precede other actions. If there is uncertainty about the exact ordering of elements, selection sort seems least attractive, since in the very first step one already has to decide how a tentative smallest element compares to all other elements. Insertion sort is better, since one can pick an arbitrary element in the first step without the need to perform any comparisons and thus already obtains a sorted one-element list. However, in the steps that follow, each selected element has to be compared to more and more elements in the growing sorted list to find its correct position. While in the beginning the number of difficult comparisons might be smaller for insertion sort than for selection sort, the algorithm might force decisions that one might not be able to make yet. Is there a method that gives a sorter more control over which elements to compare?

## Split as You Please

Preferably, a sorting method would allow one to delay difficult decisions and start with those that are easy. In the case of Indiana Jones's plan for locating the Lost Ark, for example, it is clear that the Well of Souls and the map room are in Tanis, so every action connected to those two locations must come after the step of traveling to Tanis, and everything else must come before.

By dividing the list elements into those that come before and after a separating element, which is called a *pivot*, we have split one unsorted list into two unsorted lists. What have we gained from doing this? Even though nothing is sorted yet, we have accomplished two important goals. First, we have decomposed the problem of sorting one long list into that of sorting two shorter lists. Problem simplification is often a crucial step toward solving a problem. Second, once the two subproblems are solved, that is, after the two unsorted lists are sorted, we can simply append them to get one sorted list. In other words, the decomposition into subproblems facilitates constructing the solution for the overall problem from the two subproblems.

This is a consequence of how the two unsorted lists are formed. Let's label by $S$ the list of elements that are smaller than Tanis, and by $L$ the list of those that are larger than Tanis. We then know that all elements in $S$ are smaller than all elements in $L$ (but $S$ and $L$ are not sorted yet). Once the lists $S$ and $L$ have been sorted, the list that results from appending $S$, Tanis, and $L$ will also be sorted. Therefore, the last task is to sort the lists $S$ and $L$. Once this is done, we can simply append the results. How are these smaller lists to be sorted? We can choose any method we like. We can recursively apply the method of splitting and joining, or if the lists are small enough, we can employ a simple method, such as selection sort or insertion sort.

In 1960 the British computer scientist Tony Hoare (formally, Sir Charles Antony Richard Hoare) invented this sorting method, which is called *quicksort*. Figure 6.3 illustrates how quicksort works in generating Indiana Jones's plan for locating the Lost Ark. In the first step, the unsorted list is split into two lists, separated by the pivot element, Tanis. In the next step, the two unsorted lists have to be sorted. Since each of them contains only three elements, this can be easily done using any algorithm.

For illustration, let's sort the sublist of elements smaller than Tanis using quicksort. If we pick Nepal as the separating element, we obtain the unsorted list Disc → Marion when gathering the elements that are larger than Nepal. Correspondingly, the list of

Well → Map → Disc → Sunbeam →Marion → Nepal → Tanis

Disc → Marion → Nepal        |        Tanis        |        Well → Map → Sunbeam

Nepal → Marion → Disc        |        Tanis        |        Map → Sunbeam → Well

Nepal → Marion → Disc → Tanis → Map → Sunbeam → Well

**Figure 6.3**   Quicksort splits a list into two sublists of elements that are smaller and larger, respectively, than a chosen pivot element. Then those two lists are sorted, and the results are appended together with the pivot element to form the resulting sorted list.

elements smaller than Tanis is empty, which is trivially sorted already. To sort this two-element list, we simply have to compare the two elements and invert their position, which yields the sorted list Marion → Disc. Then we append the empty list, Nepal, and Marion → Disc and obtain the sorted sublist Nepal → Marion → Disc. The sorting works similarly if we pick any of the other elements as pivots. If we pick Disc, we again obtain an empty list and a two-element list that needs to be sorted, and if we pick Marion, we obtain two single-element lists that are both already sorted. Sorting the sublist of elements larger than Tanis is analogous.

Once the sublists are sorted, we can append them with Tanis in the middle and obtain the final result. As figure 6.3 shows, quicksort converges surprisingly quickly. But is this always the case? What is the runtime of quicksort in general? It seems we got lucky by picking Tanis as the pivot in the first step, since Tanis divides the list into two lists of equal size. If we can always pick a pivot with that property, the sublists will always be cut in half, which means that the number of division levels will be proportional to the logarithm of the original list's length. What does this mean for the overall runtime of quicksort in this and the general case?

The first iteration, in which we split one list into two, takes linear time, since we have to inspect all the elements in the list. In the next iteration we have to split two sublists, which again takes altogether linear time because the total number of elements in both lists is 1 less than the original list,[2] no matter where we split and how long each of the two sublists are. And this schema continues: each level has no more elements than the previous one and thus takes linear time to split. Altogether we accumulate linear time for each level, which means that the runtime of quicksort depends on the number of levels needed for splitting sublists. Once the original list has been completely decomposed into single elements, the splitting process ensures that all these elements are in the correct order and can simply be concatenated into a sorted result list. This takes,

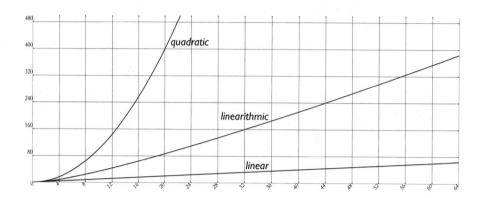

**Figure 6.4**    Comparison of linearithmic, linear, and quadratic runtimes.

once more, linear effort, so the total runtime for quicksort is given by the sum of the linear times for all levels.

In the best case, when we can split each sublist roughly in half, we obtain a logarithmic number of levels. For example, a list with 100 elements leads to seven levels, a list with 1,000 elements leads to ten levels, and a list with 1,000,000 can be completely decomposed in only 20 levels.[3] For the total runtime this means that in the case of 1,000,000 elements, we have to spend the linear effort of scanning a list of 1,000,000 elements only 20 times. This leads to a runtime on the order of tens of millions of steps, which is much better than a quadratic runtime, which means hundreds of billions to trillions of steps. This runtime behavior, where the runtime grows proportionally to the size of the input times the logarithm of the size is called *linearithmic*. It is not quite as good as linear runtime, but it is much better than quadratic runtime (see figure 6.4).

Quicksort has linearithmic runtime in the best case. However, if we pick the pivots unwisely, the situation is quite different. For example, if we choose Nepal instead of Tanis as the first pivot, the sublist of smaller elements will be empty, and the sublist of larger elements will contain all elements except Nepal. If we next choose Marion as the pivot of that sublist, we run into the same situation where one list is empty and the other is only one element shorter than the sublist that is split. We can see that in this situation quicksort effectively behaves just like selection sort, which also repeatedly removes the smallest element from the unsorted list. And like selection sort, quicksort will in this case also have quadratic runtime. The efficiency of quicksort depends on the selection of the pivot: if we can always find an element in the middle, the splitting process returns evenly divided lists. But how can we find a good pivot? While it is not easy to guarantee good pivots, it turns out that picking a random element or the median of the first, middle, and last element works well on average.

The importance and impact of the pivot is closely related to the notion of boundary that was used in chapter 5 to explain the essence of effective search. In the case of searching, the purpose of the boundary is to divide the search space into an outside and an inside so that the inside is as small as possible to make the remainder of the search easier. In the case of sorting, the boundary should divide the sorting space into equal parts so that the sorting of each part is sufficiently simplified through the decomposition. Therefore, if the pivot is not chosen well, quicksort's runtime deteriorates. But while quicksort has quadratic runtime in the worst case, it has linearithmic runtime on average, and it performs well in practice.

## The Best Is Yet to Come

Are there even faster sorting methods than quicksort, for example, an algorithm with linearithmic or better runtime in the worst case? Yes. One such algorithm is *mergesort*, which was invented by the Hungarian-American mathematician John von Neumann in 1945.[4] Mergesort splits the unsorted list into two and thus works by decomposing the problem into smaller parts similarly to quicksort. However, mergesort does not compare elements in this step; it just divides the list into two equal parts. Once these two sublists are sorted, they can be merged into one sorted list by traversing them in parallel and comparing the elements from the two sublists one by one. This works by repeatedly comparing the first elements of the two sublists and taking the smaller one. Since both those sublists are sorted, this ensures that the merged list is sorted, too. But how can the two sublists that result from the splitting step be sorted? This is done by recursively applying mergesort to both lists. Mergesort is illustrated in figure 6.5.

While quicksort and mergesort are great algorithms to program an electronic computer with, they are not so easy for the unaided human memory to use, because they require a fair amount of bookkeeping. In particular, for larger lists, both algorithms have to maintain a potentially large collection of small lists; in the case of quicksort, those lists also have to be kept in the right order. Thus, Indiana Jones, like the rest of us, would probably stick to some form of insertion sort, perhaps augmented by a smart selection of elements, unless the size of the list to be sorted demands a more efficient algorithm. For example, whenever I teach a large undergraduate class, I use a variant of *bucket sort* for sorting exams by name. I place exams into different piles (called *buckets*) according to the first letter of the student's last name and keep each bucket sorted by

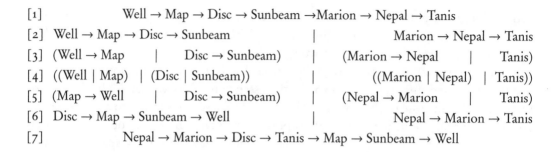

**Figure 6.5**  Mergesort splits a list into two sublists of equal size, sorts them, and merges the sorted results into one sorted list. The parentheses indicate the order in which lists must be merged. In line 4 the decomposition is complete when only single-element lists are obtained. In line 5 three pairs of single-element lists have been merged into three sorted two-element lists, and in line 6 those lists are merged again into one four-element and one three-element list, which are merged in the last step to produce the final result.

using insertion sort. After all exams have been placed into their buckets, the buckets are appended in alphabetical order to produce an ordered list. Bucket sort is similar to counting sort (discussed later).

On the face of it, mergesort looks more complicated than quicksort, but this may be due to the fact that some steps were skipped in the description of quicksort. But still it seems that the repeated merging of longer and longer lists is inefficient. However, this intuition is deceptive. Since the decomposition is systematic and halves the size of lists in every step, the overall runtime performance is quite good: in the worst case the runtime of mergesort is linearithmic. This can be seen as follows. First, since we always split lists in half, the number of times lists need to be split is logarithmic. Second, the merging on each level takes only linear time because we have to process each element once (see figure 6.5). Finally, since merging happens on each level once, we altogether obtain linearithmic runtime.

Mergesort bears some similarity to quicksort. In particular, both algorithms have a phase for splitting lists, followed by a recursive sorting step for each of the smaller lists, and finally a phase for combining the sorted sublists into longer sorted lists. In fact, both quicksort and mergesort are examples of divide-and-conquer algorithms, which all are instances of the following general schema:

If the problem is trivial, solve it directly.

Otherwise

(1) Decompose the problem into subproblems.

(2) Solve the subproblems.

(3) Combine the solutions for the subproblems into a solution for the problem.

The case for solving a nontrivial problem shows how divide-and-conquer works. The first step is the *divide* step; it reduces the problem's complexity. The second step is the recursive application of the method to the subproblems. If the subproblems thus obtained are small enough, they can be solved directly. Otherwise, they will be decomposed further until they are small enough to be solved directly. The third step is the *merge* step; it is assembling a solution for the problem from the solutions of the subproblems.

Quicksort does most of its work in the divide step, where all the element comparisons happen: by ensuring that the elements in the two lists are separated by the pivot, it allows the merge step to be a simple concatenation of lists. In contrast, mergesort's divide step is very simple and does not contain any element comparisons. Most of mergesort's work happens in the merge step, where the sorted lists are combined, similar to a zipper.

## The Quest Is Over: No Better Sorting Algorithm, Ever

Mergesort is the most efficient sorting method discussed so far, but is it possible to sort even faster? The answer is yes and no. Although we cannot sort faster in general, we can do better under certain assumptions about the elements to be sorted. For example, if we know the list to be sorted contains only numbers between 1 and 100, we can create an array of 100 cells, one for each potential number in the list. This approach is similar to bucket sort, where there is one pile for each letter of the alphabet. Here each array cell corresponds to a pile that contains a particular number. The array cells are indexed from 1 to 100. We use each cell with index $i$ to count how often $i$ occurs in the list. First, we store 0 in each array cell, since we don't know which numbers are in the list to be sorted. Then we traverse the list, and for each encountered element $i$, we increment the number stored in the array cell with index $i$. Finally, we traverse the array in order of increasing indices and put each index into the result list as many times as the cell's counter indicates. For example, if the list to be sorted is 4→2→5→4→2→6, we end up with the following array after traversing the list:

| 0 | 2 | 0 | 2 | 1 | 1 | 0 | · · · | *counter* |
|---|---|---|---|---|---|---|-------|-----------|
| 1 | 2 | 3 | 4 | 5 | 6 | 7 | · · · | *index*   |

By traversing the array we find that 1 does not occur in the list, since its counter is still 0. A 1 will therefore not be part of the sorted result list. In contrast, the 2 occurs twice and will therefore be put twice into the list, and so on. The resulting list will be 2→2→4→4→5→6. This method is called *counting sort*, since the array maintains a counter for how often an element occurs in the list to be sorted. The runtime of counting sort results from the combined cost of traversing the list and array. Since either step is linear in the size of the respective data structure (list and array), counting sort runs in linear time in the size of the list or array, whichever is larger.

The downside of counting sort is that it can waste a lot of space. In the example all cells with index 7 through 100 are never used. Moreover, it only works if the elements can be used to index an array and if the range of the elements of the list is known and is not too large. For example, we cannot sort a list of names using counting sort because names are sequences of characters and cannot be used to index arrays.[5] There are other specialized sorting algorithms for lists of strings. For example, the trie data structure (see chapter 5) can be used to sort lists of strings, but those methods make other assumptions about the elements to be sorted.

## As Good as It Gets

Without exploiting special properties of the data, we cannot sort faster than mergesort. While this fact may seem disappointing at first, it is also good news because it gives us the assurance that we have found the fastest algorithm possible. In other words, mergesort is the best possible solution for the problem of sorting. It is therefore an *optimal algorithm*. Computer science researchers can consider the problem solved and spend their time and energy on solving other problems.

The optimality of mergesort rests on two related but distinct facts. Mergesort has linearithmic runtime, and any sorting algorithm for the general case must have at least linearithmic runtime. It is this second part that justifies the conclusion about merge-sort's optimality and, for that matter, about the optimality of any other sorting algorithm that has linearithmic runtime in the worst case. The ultimate goal in designing algorithms and data structures is to find an optimal algorithm for a problem, that is, an algorithm whose worst-case runtime complexity matches the intrinsic complexity of the problem it solves. Any such algorithm could be considered the Holy Grail for that problem. And like Indiana Jones in *The Last Crusade*, John von Neumann found in mergesort the Holy Grail of sorting.[6]

It is important to distinguish between the runtime of an algorithm and the complexity of a problem. The latter says that a correct solution must take *at least* that many steps. In contrast, the runtime of an algorithm says that the particular algorithm takes *at most* that many steps. A statement about the minimal complexity of a problem is called the problem's *lower bound*. A lower bound provides an estimate of how much work a problem will need at minimum and thus characterizes the problem's inherent complexity. It is similar to the geometric distance between two points, which is a lower bound for any path connecting the points. Any such path may be longer than the distance because of obstacles, but it cannot be shorter than the distance. The possible disappointment one may feel about the lower bound of sorting and the related limitation of sorting algorithms should be offset by the deep insight that this knowledge provides about the problem of sorting. Compare this with similar results from other disciplines. For example, in physics we know that we cannot travel faster than light and that we cannot create energy out of nothing.

But how can we be so certain about the lower bound of sorting? Maybe there is an algorithm no one has thought of yet that actually does run faster than linearithmic time. Proving a negative is not easy, since it requires us to show that any algorithm, existing or yet to be invented, has to perform a certain minimum number of steps. The argument for the lower bound of sorting counts the number of possible lists of a specific length[7] and shows that the number of comparisons required to identify the sorted list is linearithmic.[8] Since every algorithm needs to perform this minimum number of comparisons, it follows that any algorithm requires at least a linearithmic number of steps, which proves the lower bound.

The reasoning about the runtime of algorithms and lower bounds makes assumptions about the capabilities of the computer that is executing algorithms. For example, a typical assumption is that the steps of an algorithm are carried out in sequence and that it takes one time unit to perform one computational step. These assumptions also underlie the analysis of the sorting algorithms discussed in this chapter. If we assume, however, that we can perform comparisons in parallel, the analysis changes, and we obtain different results for runtimes and lower bounds.

## Computation Preservation

It seems that Indiana Jones is pretty organized about going on an adventure: he always packs his hat and whip into his travel bag. But instead of making a comprehensive plan of all the steps, he could also approach an adventure by determining his next step just right before it is necessary to do so. Both approaches, planning ahead and living in the moment, have their respective advantages and disadvantages. A trip to the North Pole requires different clothing and equipment than one to the Amazon. Here planning ahead seems like a good idea. On the other hand, changing circumstances can make prior plans obsolete and render the planning effort useless. In particular, during an adventure the unexpected may happen, which often requires taking different actions than anticipated.

If Indiana Jones's strategy for finding the Lost Ark were to determine the next action whenever it is needed, he would essentially be performing a selection sort and would always search for the smallest element among the actions left to be performed, because *smallest* here means "has to come before all other actions." As discussed, this is not very efficient, since selection sort is a quadratic algorithm. Indiana can do significantly better if he creates a plan in advance by employing a linearithmic sorting algorithm such as mergesort. This strategy of computing information ahead of time is called *precomputation.* In the case of the plan for locating the Lost Ark the precomputed information is not the set of individual steps but the arrangement of the steps into the correct order.

The ordering information is kept in a sorted list. The crucial aspect of precomputation is that computational effort is expended at one time and the computed result is used at a later time. The precomputed result is preserved in a data structure—in this case a sorted list. This sorted list acts like a computational battery that can be charged through sorting. The runtime spent by an algorithm to establish the sorted list amounts to the energy used to charge the data structure battery. This energy can be used to power computation, such as finding the next smallest element. Here, to power means to speed up: without the sorted-list battery, it takes linear time to find the next smallest element; with the battery, it only takes constant time.

Some ways are more efficient than others in charging data structure batteries, which is reflected in the different runtimes of the different sorting algorithms. For example, insertion sort is less efficient than mergesort, and the fact that mergesort is an optimal sorting algorithm means that a most efficient method exists for charging the sorted-list battery. Unlike electrical batteries, whose energy can be spent only once, data structure batteries have the nice property that, once charged, they can be discharged repeatedly without ever having to recharge them. This feature is an important point in favor of precomputing. Situations in which one can expect to make use of a data structure repeatedly provide a strong incentive to expend the precomputing effort because the cost can be amortized over several uses. On the other hand, a data structure battery must be fully charged to work properly. An almost sorted list is not sufficient because it does not guarantee that the smallest element will be at the front and can therefore produce incorrect results. Essentially, this means that a data structure battery has two states: it is either completely charged and useful, or not.

Precomputation seems like a great idea—like the squirrel that gathers nuts to save them for the winter. There are many situations, however, when it's not clear whether the precomputation effort will pay off. We know many circumstances when acting early can be beneficial, but this isn't guaranteed and could actually turn out to be a disadvantage. If you buy a plane ticket early or book a hotel room at a nonreimbursable hotel rate, you may get a good deal, but if you fall ill and can't make the trip, you can lose your money and do worse than you would have by waiting with the purchase.

In cases like these, the value of acting early, or precomputating, is called into question by uncertainty about the future. Since the benefit of precomputation depends on a specific outcome of future events, it reflects a rather optimistic computation attitude with a confident outlook on the future. But what if you're skeptical about the future? You may think that people who file their tax returns early are masochists, and you always delay yours until April 14, because the IRS could be dissolved any day now, or you could die before. However, if, like Ben Franklin, you are certain that taxes are as certain as death, then precomputation may seem a prudent thing to do.

A skeptical attitude toward the future calls for a radically different strategy for scheduling computation, namely, a strategy that tries to delay costly operations as much as possible until they cannot be avoided anymore. The hope or expectation is that something might happen that makes the costly operation obsolete and thus saves its runtime (and potentially other resources). In real life this behavior would be called procrastination; in computer science it is called *lazy evaluation*. Lazy evaluation can save computation effort whenever the information that would have been obtained by the saved computation is not needed anymore. In the case of Indiana Jones's adventures, it happens quite often that an initial plan has to be changed or abandoned because of unforeseen events or complications. In such cases, all the effort that went into creating the plan is wasted and could have been saved by not making a plan in the first place.

Whereas the precomputing advocate's motto is "A stitch in time saves nine" or "The early bird catches the worm," the champion of lazy evaluation might respond with "Yes, but the second mouse gets the cheese." While lazy evaluation seems attractive in its promise to not waste effort, it is problematic when an action that becomes unavoidable takes longer than it would have under precomputing, or worse, longer than there is time available. In particular, when several delayed actions become due at the same time, this might present a serious resource problem. Therefore, an overall more sensible strategy is to distribute work evenly over time. While this might waste some effort on precomputing, it avoids crises that a lazy evaluation strategy might bring on.

# Getting Lunch

It's Wednesday, the day of the week when you and some of your colleagues go out to lunch together. You decide to try out the new Italian restaurant, but when you arrive you learn that their credit card reader is not working and they are accepting only cash today. Before you order, you determine how much cash your lunch party has. When it comes to ordering, you are faced with the problem of selecting a set of items (appetizers, entrées, side dishes, and drinks) that will feed all members of the lunch party and satisfy their preferences as much as possible but that also doesn't exceed the budget given by the amount of cash available. Of course, if you have enough money, the menu selection doesn't pose a problem, but that is not necessarily a safe assumption these days, as few people carry cash at all, expecting to be able to pay by debit or credit card or smartphone.

How do you go about selecting the menu items to order? You could start with everybody's preferred order. If that fits within the budget, then the problem is solved. But what if the total exceeds the available cash amount? In that case, people could offer to order cheaper alternatives or to not order appetizers or drinks until the total is within the limit. This approach depends on your ability to determine the overall value of each lunch order based on all participants' preferences. Here *value* means the combined satisfaction of the lunch party with a particular lunch selection.

This is probably not an easy task, but let's assume that we can determine the value of lunch orders. Now the goal is to find a lunch order of maximum satisfaction value whose total cost doesn't exceed the cash limit. Perhaps a good strategy for this is to gradually trade value for cost. However, this strategy isn't as simple as it looks. Even if it is better for Bob to refrain from ordering a drink than for Alice to not order an appetizer, it is not clear that going along with this selection yields the better overall value. This is because Alice's appetizer might be more expensive than Bob's drink and thus might save enough so that Carol could have her second entrée preference instead of her third. Now Bob's and Carol's preferences together might be more valuable to satisfy than Alice's. When it gets down to the details, it is not so clear which selections to change and in which order.

We encounter this problem of selecting a number of items on a limited budget in many other situations as well, including planning a vacation with more costly or less costly events, choosing different options for traveling, or selecting among the upgrades for a new car or some electronic gadget. It might not seem like it, but this problem is surprisingly difficult in general. All known algorithms to solve these problems have runtimes that are exponential in the number of items to select from. For instance, consider writing down all possible lunch selections on small napkins of size 10 cm by 10 cm that each fit ten selections. Assuming that each person selects between one and four items out of a menu of ten items (which gives 5,860 menu options for each person), the napkins needed for writing down all possibilities for a lunch party of five would be enough to cover the surface of the earth over 13 times.

The lunch selection problem has two characteristic features: (1) the number of possibilities to be considered grows very quickly, and (2) known algorithms work only if they examine all or most of these possibilities. Problems like these are called *intractable* because algorithms take too long to be of practical use for all but very simple cases.

But this doesn't stop us from ordering lunches, planning vacations, and making other selections we are often quite happy with. We employ *approximation algorithms*, which are efficient algorithms that do not necessarily compute an exact solution for the problem but a solution that is just good enough. For example, a very simple approximation for the lunch problem is to split the total budget among all members of the lunch party and have each person find a selection that fits.

The difficulty of finding optimal selections can also be exploited. Insurance companies can offer overwhelmingly many choices that make it difficult for customers to find the optimal choice and make more money for the company.

# 7

# Mission Intractable

The algorithms discussed in previous chapters exhibited a range of different runtimes. For example, finding the smallest element in an unsorted list takes linear time, while it takes only constant time in a sorted list. Similarly, it takes linear time to find a specific element in an unsorted list, whereas this can be done in logarithmic time in a sorted array or a balanced binary search tree. In both cases the precomputed sorted data structure makes a difference. But different algorithms can also have different runtimes for the same input. For example, selection sort is a quadratic algorithm, whereas mergesort has linearithmic runtime.

An algorithm with quadratic runtime might be too slow to be useful in practice. Consider the task of sorting the names of all 300 million residents of the United States. Executed on a computer that can perform a billion operations per second, selection sort would take about 90 million seconds, or about 2 years and 10 months, which is rather impractical. In contrast, the linearithmic mergesort finishes the same task in less than 10 seconds. But if we are dealing with inputs of moderate size, maybe we don't have to worry too much about runtime complexity, especially since computers get faster every year.

As an analogy consider the range of transportation solutions to different traveling problems. For example, to go to work, you may be able to ride a bike, take the bus, or drive a car. To cross the Atlantic, none of these solutions will do, and you have to take a cruise ship or an airplane. You could in principle also cross the Atlantic in a kayak, but the time (and other resources) it would take to actually do that makes it close to impossible in practice.

Similarly, there are computational problems that have solutions in principle but take too long to compute in practice. This chapter discusses examples of that sort. I present some problems that can be solved (so far) only by algorithms that have *exponential* runtime, that is, algorithms whose runtimes grow exponentially with the size of the input. Algorithms with exponential runtime are unusable in practice for all but very small inputs, which makes the question of lower bounds and whether faster algorithms exist particularly important. This question is at the core of the P = NP problem, a prominent problem in computer science that is still open.

As in the case of sorting, a result about the limits of computer science that looks at first like a disappointment doesn't have to be. Even if no efficient algorithms can be developed for a particular problem, that doesn't mean we have to give up on such problems altogether. In particular, we can devise *approximation algorithms* that compute not exact yet good enough solutions to such problems. Moreover, the fact that a particular problem cannot be solved in practice can sometimes be exploited for solutions to other problems.

While large inputs reveal the difference between a quadratic or a linearithmic algorithm, a quadratic algorithm may work fine for small inputs. For example, sorting a list of 10,000 elements with selection sort takes about one-tenth of a second on a computer that can perform a billion operations per second. While the runtime is barely noticeable in this case, an increase in the list's size by a factor of ten means an increase of the algorithm's runtime by a factor of one hundred. Thus, the runtime for sorting lists of 100,000 elements increases to about 10 seconds. This may not be acceptable anymore, in particular, in situations where users are interacting with a system and expect instant responses. However, the next generation of computers may remedy the situation, and the algorithm may again become usable. Technological advances may suffice to push the limit of a quadratic algorithm. Unfortunately, we cannot rely on this effect to make an algorithm with exponential runtime usable.

## Tipping the Scale

At the beginning of *Raiders of the Lost Ark*, Indiana Jones explores a cave in search of a precious golden idol, the target of his expedition. The idol rests on a scale that is designed to trigger a series of deadly traps in case the idol is removed. To circumvent the protective mechanism, Indiana Jones replaces the idol by a bag of sand that he hopes approximates the idol's weight. Alas, the bag is too heavy and triggers the traps, which leads to a spectacular escape from the deadly cave.

Had Indiana Jones known the exact weight of the idol, he could have filled the bag with the precise amount of sand, and his exit from the cave would have been much less dramatic. But since he was probably not carrying around a scale, he needed to gauge the weight in some other way. Fortunately, it is not too difficult to build a balance scale. Basically all you need is a stick; attach the sand bag to one end and the exact weight at the other, and then fill the sand bag with sand until the stick is balanced. Assuming that Indiana Jones doesn't have an object that has the exact same weight as the idol, he has to approximate the weight with a collection of objects. This doesn't seem like such a difficult problem. If the idol has an estimated weight of, say, 42 ounces (which is about 2.6 pounds or 1.2 kg) and Indiana Jones has six objects that weigh 5, 8, 9, 11, 13, and 15 ounces, respectively, then after trying several combinations he will find that the 5, 9, 13, and 15 ounce objects add up exactly to 42 ounces.

But how exactly does the approach of trying several combinations work, and how long does it take? In the example, the heaviest object weighs less than half of the idol, which means we need at least three objects to get to the idol's weight. However, it is not immediately clear which three objects to pick and whether we need a fourth or fifth object as well. Moreover, an algorithm must work for any possible situation and thus be able to handle as input different numbers of objects of different weights as well as arbitrary target weights.

A straightforward method for solving the weighing problem is to systematically form all combinations of objects and check for each combination whether the total weight is equal to the target weight. This strategy is also called *generate-and-test*, , since it consists of the repeated execution of the following two steps: (1) *generate* a potential solution, and (2) *test* whether the potential solution actually is a solution. In this case, the generating step produces a combination of objects, and the testing step adds the weights of the objects and compares the sum with the target weight. It is important that the generating step be repeated systematically and cover all cases because otherwise the algorithm could miss the solution.

The runtime of the generate-and-test method depends on how many combinations of objects can be formed. To understand how many combinations exist, let us consider how any one particular combination is formed from all the available objects. To this end, take an arbitrary combination such as 5, 9, and 11. For every available object we can ask whether it is contained in this particular combination. For example, 5 is contained in it, but 8 is not; 9 and 11 are elements of the combination, but the elements 13 and

15 are not. In other words, any possible combination is given by a decision for each element to either include or exclude it, and all these decisions are independent of each other.

We can compare the process of forming a combination with that of filling out a questionnaire that contains the available objects, each with a check box next to it. One combination corresponds to a questionnaire in which the boxes of the selected objects are checked. The number of combinations is then identical to the number of different ways the questionnaire can be filled out. And here we see that each box can be checked or not, independently of all the other boxes.

Therefore, the number of possible combinations is given by the product of the available choices, which is 2 for selecting or not selecting an object (or equivalently, checking or not checking a box). Since Indiana Jones has six objects to choose from, the number of combinations is 2 multiplied by itself six times, that is, $2 \times 2 \times 2 \times 2 \times 2 \times 2 = 2^6 = 64$.[1] Since the generate-and-test algorithm has to test each combination, its runtime grows at least at the same rate. In fact, it is even more time consuming, since testing one combination requires adding all the weights and comparing the sum with the target weight.

## When Runtime Explodes

While 64 combinations don't seem too bad, the important aspect about the algorithm's runtime is how fast it grows with larger input. As explained in chapter 2, the runtime of algorithms is measured as a growth rate rather than in absolute time, since this provides a more general characterization that is independent of specific problem examples and computer performance characteristics.

The latter aspect is sometimes given as an excuse for using algorithms with bad runtimes. The argument goes like this: "Yes, I know the algorithm takes several minutes to complete, but wait until we get the new, faster computer. That will resolve this issue." This argument has some validity to it. Moore's law says that the speed of computers doubles about every 18 months.[2]

When the runtime of a computer doubles, a quadratic algorithm can handle an input that is larger by a factor of about 1.4.[3] Now consider what happens with the runtime of an exponential algorithm in such a case. How much can the input be increased so that the runtime does not increase by more than a factor of two? Since the runtime of the algorithm doubles if the input is increased by 1, this means the algorithm can deal with only one additional element. In other words, we need to double the speed of a computer to be able to process input with only one more element.

**Table 7.1**   Approximate runtimes for different sizes of input on a computer that can perform a billion steps per second.

| Input Size | Runtime | | | |
|:---:|:---:|:---:|:---:|:---:|
| | Linear | Linearithmic | Quadratic | Exponential |
| 20 | | | | 0.001 second |
| 50 | | | | 13 days |
| 100 | | | | |
| 1,000 | | | | |
| 10,000 | | | 0.1 second | |
| 1 million | 0.001 second | 0.002 second | 16 minutes | |
| 1 billion | 1 second | 30 seconds | 32 years | |

*Note*: Blank cells indicate runtimes < 1 millisecond, too small to be meaningful for human perception of time, and thus of no practical significance. Gray cells indicate runtimes too immense to comprehend.

Since the runtime of the algorithm doubles so fast, technological improvements that increase computing power by some fixed factor are simply not sufficient to scale an exponential algorithm to cope with significantly larger inputs. Note that a larger factor for increasing the speed, say ten, does not make much of a difference. While this would allow a quadratic algorithm to handle input that is three times as large, an exponential algorithm would be able to deal with input that is increased by only 3, since this would increase the runtime by a factor of $2 \times 2 \times 2 = 2^3 = 8$.

Table 7.1 illustrates the huge gap between algorithms with nonexponential and exponential runtimes in handling different input sizes: Runtimes for nonexponential algorithms start to be noticeable only for inputs larger than 1,000, whereas exponential algorithms handle inputs of 20 and below quite well. But for inputs of 100, exponential algorithms take more than 400 billion centuries to run which is 2,900 times the age of our universe.

The overwhelming effect of exponential growth is analogous to the explosion of a nuclear bomb, whose effect is due to miniscule amounts of energy that are released when atoms are split.[4] The devastating destruction is caused by the fact that many of these fissions occur in a very short period of time—every split atom leads to two (or more) fissions in short succession—an exponential growth of fissions and correspondingly released energy.

Or consider the legend about the peasant who is said to have invented the game of chess. The king was so pleased that he granted the peasant any wish. The peasant asked for one grain of rice to be put on the first square, two on the second, four on the  third, and so on, until all the squares were covered. Not realizing the nature of exponential growth, the king thought this wish was easy to fulfill and promised to grant it. Of course, he couldn't keep his promise, since the number of rice grains needed to cover the board is larger than 18 trillion trillion, which is more than 500 times the rice production of the entire world in 2014.

The immense gap between the size of inputs that exponential and nonexponential algorithms can cope with justifies the distinction into practical algorithms (those that have less than exponential runtime) and impractical algorithms (those that have exponential runtime or worse). Algorithms with exponential runtime cannot be considered practical solutions to problems because they take too long to compute results for all but small inputs.

## Shared Destiny

The generate-and-test algorithm for solving the weighing problem works only for relatively small inputs (less than 30 or so), which is fine for the specific problem Indiana Jones faces. But because of the exponential growth of its runtime, the algorithm will never be able to deal with inputs of size 100 or larger. This particular algorithm's exponential runtime does not mean that there can't be other, more efficient algorithms with nonexponential runtimes. Currently, however, no such algorithm is known.

A problem that can only be solved by algorithms with exponential (or worse) runtime is called *intractable*. Since we only know algorithms with exponential runtime for the weighing problem, it may seem that it is intractable, but we don't really know for sure. Maybe there is a nonexponential algorithm that just hasn't been discovered yet. If we could prove that no such nonexponential algorithm can exist for the problem, then we would know the problem is intractable. A lower bound could provide us with certainty.

But why should we care about this? Maybe computer scientists should just let go of this problem and move on to investigate other questions. However, the weighing problem is very similar to a range of other problems that all share the following two intriguing properties. First, the only known algorithms for solving the problem have exponential runtime, and second, if a nonexponential algorithm were found for any one of the problems, it would immediately lead to nonexponential algorithms for all the others. Any problem that is a member of this exclusive club is called *NP-complete*.[5] The significance of NP-complete problems comes from the fact that many practical problems are indeed NP-complete and they all share the fate of potentially being intractable.

Toward the end of the adventure *The Kingdom of the Crystal Skull*, Indiana Jones's companion Mac collects treasure items in the temple of the crystal skull. He tries to carry as many items as he possibly can while maximizing their total value. This problem, the weighing problem, and the group lunch problem are all instances of the knapsack problem, which is named for the task of filling a knapsack of limited capacity with as many items as possible while maximizing some value or utility of the packed items. In the weighing problem the knapsack is the scale, its limit is the weight to be measured, the packing of items amounts to placing objects on the scale, and the optimization objective is to get as close as possible to the target weight. For Mac's selection problem the limit is what he can carry, packing means to select items, and the optimization is maximizing the items' total value. In the lunch problem the limit is the total amount of cash available to purchase items, the packing is the selection of items, and the optimization is maximizing the value of the menu selection.

Incidentally, Mac and Indiana Jones both fail: Mac spends too much time selecting the items and dies in the crumbling temple, and Indiana Jones's sandbag triggers the deadly traps, although he ultimately manages to escape them. It's unclear whether their failure is due to the NP-completeness of the problems they try to solve, but it is a nice reminder of intractability.

The knapsack problem with its applications is only one of many NP-complete problems. Another well-known example is the traveling salesman problem, which asks for a round trip connecting a number of cities that minimizes the length of the trip. A simple method is to generate all possible round trips and find the shortest one. The complexity of this algorithm is also exponential, but it is much worse than the weighing problem. For example, while the weighing algorithm can complete a problem of size 20 in 1 millisecond, computing a round trip for 20 cities would take 77 years. Finding round trips is not just useful for traveling salesmen but has many other applications, ranging from planning school bus routes to scheduling tours of cruise ships. Many other optimization problems are also NP-complete.

The intriguing property of NP-complete problems is that they all are either intractable or have algorithms with nonexponential runtimes as solutions. One way of showing that a problem is NP-complete is to demonstrate that a solution for the problem could be transformed (in nonexponential time) into a solution for another problem that is already known to be NP-complete. Such a transformation of a solution is called a *reduction*. Reductions are clever ways of problem solving by transforming a solution for one problem into a solution for another. Reductions occur quite frequently, and sometimes implicitly, as when Indiana Jones reduces the problem of finding safe tiles to the spelling of the name *Iehova*, or when Sherlock Holmes reduces the task of maintaining information about suspects to operations on a dictionary.

Reductions are themselves computations, and they make a handy addition to the repertoire of computational techniques, since they can be combined with other computations. For example, the problem of finding the smallest element in a list can be reduced to sorting the list and then taking the first element of the sorted list. Specifically, a reduction transforms the input (here, an unsorted list) into a specific form (here, a sorted list) on which another algorithm (here, taking the first element) can operate. Combining both computations, sorting followed by taking the first element, yields the computation that is a solution to the original problem of finding a minimum in an arbitrary list. However, it is important to take into account the runtime of reductions. For example, since the sorting step requires linearithmic time, the method obtained by this reduction does not have the same runtime as simply scanning the list for the minimum, which takes only linear time. This reduction is therefore not very useful because it leads to a less efficient algorithm.[6] Therefore, the reductions between NP-complete problems must be achieved by nonexponential algorithms because otherwise a nonexponential solution to one problem would become exponential because of the reduction's exponential runtime.

The nonexponential reduction between all NP-complete problems provides enormous leverage. Just like the wheel had to be invented by only one individual and could then be used by all humans, the solution to one NP-complete problem solves all others. And this fact leads to the question that is summarized by the famous equation:

$$P = NP\ ?$$

The problem was first brought up by the Austrian-American logician Kurt Gödel and was made precise in 1971 by the Canadian-American computer scientist Stephen Cook. The question is whether the class P of problems that can be *solved* in nonexponential (or, polynomial) time is equal to the class NP of problems that can be *verified* in polynomial time. Finding an exponential lower bound for NP-complete problems would provide "no" as the answer to the equation question. On the other hand, finding a nonexponential algorithm for any of the problems would yield "yes" as the answer.

The tractability of a huge number of practical problems depends on the answer to the P = NP question, which emphasizes its great importance. This problem has been vexing computer scientists for over four decades and is probably the most important open problem in computer science. Most computer scientists today believe that NP-complete problems are indeed intractable and that nonexponential algorithms do not exist for the problems, but no one really knows for sure.

## The Nirvana Fallacy

Prohibitive algorithmic runtime can certainly be frustrating. There is a solution for a problem, but it is too costly to be actually achieved—much like the fruits that are in front of Tantalus in the Greek myth, but are forever out of his reach. However, the discouraging facts about NP-complete problems are no reason to despair. In addition to methods to cope with the inefficiency of the algorithms, there is also a surprising upside to the limitation.

If it takes too long to find a solution to a problem, we can throw up our hands and give up, or we can try to make the best of the situation and try to find an approximate solution, one that might not be exact but good enough. For instance, if you are currently working to make a living, you are probably saving some portion of your income so that you will have enough money for your retirement. This sounds like a good plan. An arguably better plan is to win the lottery and retire right now. However, this plan rarely works out in practice and is thus not a practical alternative to the good plan you have in place.

An exponential algorithm that computes an exact solution to a problem is as impractical for large inputs as the lottery plan is for retirement. Therefore, as an alternative, one can try to find an efficient nonexponential algorithm that may not (always) compute a perfect solution but one that produces approximate results that are good enough for practical purposes—an approximation algorithm. One might consider working and saving to be an approximation to winning the lottery. It's probably not a very good approximation, though.

Some approximation algorithms compute results that are guaranteed to be within a certain factor of the exact solution. For example, Indiana Jones can find an approximate solution to his weighing problem in linearithmic time by adding objects in order of decreasing weight. With this method, the solution is guaranteed to be at most 50% worse than the optimal solution. This doesn't seem too promising because of the potentially low precision, but in many cases the solutions are actually much closer to the optimal solution, and they are cheap—you get what you pay for (in runtime).

In the weighing problem the simple algorithm initially has to sort the objects by weight. It then finds the first object that weighs less than the target weight and keeps adding objects until the target weight is reached. Start by adding 15, 13, and 11, which makes a total of 39. Adding the next weight, 9, would exceed the target weight, and thus we skip it and try the next one. But both 8 and 5 are also too heavy, and thus the approximate result obtained is 15, 13, and 11, which is only 3 off the optimal solution. In other words, the solution is within 7% of the optimal solution.

This strategy of repeatedly picking the largest possible value is called a *greedy algorithm*, since it always jumps at the first opportunity. Greedy algorithms are simple and work well for many problems, but for some problems they miss exact solutions, as in this case. It was the greedy action of taking the 11 instead of waiting for the 9 that made an optimal solution unachievable in this example. This greedy algorithm takes linearithmic runtime (caused by the initial sorting step) and is therefore quite efficient.

An important question for an approximation algorithm is how good an approximation it can produce in the worst case. For the greedy weighing algorithm one can show that it is always within 50% of the optimal solution.[7]

Approximations are solutions to problems that are good enough. They are not as good as an optimal solution but better than no solution at all. In *Indiana Jones and the Temple of Doom*, Indiana Jones and his two companions face the problem that their plane is about to crash into a mountain. The two pilots have abandoned the plane, drained the remaining fuel, and have not left any parachutes on board. Indiana Jones solves this problem by using an inflatable boat to sail the passengers to the ground, approximating the effect of a parachute. Having any approximation algorithm, no matter how crude, is often better than having no practical algorithm at all.

## Make Lemonade

Approximation algorithms can ameliorate the problem of inefficiency caused by exponential algorithms. That is good news, but there is more. The fact that solutions to a particular problem cannot be computed efficiently can actually be a good thing. For example, the generate-and-test algorithm for solving the weighing problem is similar to what we have to do when trying to unlock a number lock after having forgotten its combination: We have to go through all combinations, of which there are $10 \times 10 \times 10 = 1,000$ in the case of three single-digit dials. It is the fact that it takes a long time to try all 1,000 combinations that makes number locks somewhat effective in protecting access to bags and lockers. Of course, locks can be broken, but that is more like bypassing the problem, not solving it.

To check 1,000 combinations with an electronic computer is trivial, but for a slow human it takes long enough, which shows that efficiency is a relative notion and depends on the ability of the computer. But since algorithmic runtime is really about the growth of an algorithm's runtime in relation to its growing input, faster computers cannot make up for the immense increase in runtime of exponential algorithms that is caused by minor increases in the size of the input. This fact is exploited in cryptography to facilitate the secure exchange of messages. Whenever you access a website whose address starts with https://, the padlock in your web browser's address bar locks to indicate that a secure communication channel to the website has been established.

One approach to sending and receiving encrypted messages works by encoding and decoding messages with two related *keys*, one *public key* and one *private key*. Each participant in the communication has one such pair of keys. The public key is known to everybody, but each participant's private key is exclusively known by the participant. The two keys are related in such a way that a message encoded by the public key can be decoded only through the use of the corresponding private key. This makes it possible to send a secure message to someone by encoding it using that person's public key, which is publicly known. Since only the recipient of the message knows the private key, only the recipient can decode the message. For example, if you want to check the current balance of your bank account via the internet, your web browser transmits your public key to the bank's computer, which uses it to encrypt the amount and sends it back to your browser. Anyone who sees this message can't decipher it, since it is encrypted. Only you can decode it in your browser using your private key.

If we didn't have the internet and had to do this with postal mail, this would be similar to sending a box with an unlocked padlock (to which only you have the key) to your bank. The bank writes the amount on a piece of paper, puts it into the box, locks the box with the padlock, and sends the locked box back to you. When you receive the box, you can unlock the padlock with your key and see the amount. Since nobody else can unlock the box, the information is protected from unauthorized access during the transportation. In this example, the box with the open padlock corresponds to the public key, and the bank's action of putting the sheet with the amount into the box corresponds to the encryption of the message.

An encrypted message is practically safe from unauthorized access, since in order to decode it without knowing the private key one has to compute the prime factors of a large number. While it is not known whether the computation of prime factors is an NP-complete problem, nonexponential algorithms are not known at this time, and thus it takes too long in practice to solve. Thus the difficulty of solving a problem can be utilized for protecting the transmission of information from unauthorized access.

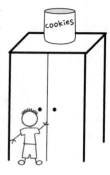

This is not really a new idea. Moats, fences, walls, and other protective mechanisms are all based on this principle. But many of these protections can be broken. Currently, sending and receiving encrypted messages can be considered safe because of the lack of a nonexponential algorithm for prime factorization. However, as soon as anyone finds a nonexponential algorithm, that safety evaporates in an instant. If, on the other hand, someone could establish an exponential lower bound on the problem, we would be certain that encrypted messages are safe. In the meantime, our ignorance about this question keeps the method working.

# Further Exploration

The adventures of Indiana Jones usually concern searches for artifacts, locations, and people. Sometimes a quest is guided by items or information gathered along the way. In these cases the path that is traveled is determined dynamically. In such stories the search leads to a list of places visited, and this list is a search path toward the final goal. Movies such as *National Treasure* or Dan Brown's *The Da Vinci Code* follow this pattern as well.

At other times, the basis for a search is a treasure map. In this case the path is clear right from the beginning, and the search is about locating landmarks shown on the map in the real world. The book *Treasure Island*, by Robert Louis Stevenson, has made treasure maps famous. A treasure map is an algorithm for finding a specific location, but the algorithm can be given in quite different ways. In some stories the treasure map does not contain direct instructions for locating the treasure but rather contains clues, codes, or riddles that need to be decoded or solved. Such treasure maps do not really describe algorithms but rather problems to be solved. This is the case, for example, in the movie *National Treasure*, where a treasure map is hidden on the back of the Declaration of Independence that contains a code for locating spectacles that reveal further clues on the map.

The movie *National Treasure* also contains a riddle similar to the tile challenge faced by Indiana Jones. Ben Gates, one of the protagonists, has to infer from the keys pressed on a keyboard the password that was typed in, which requires finding the right ordering of the letters. A word or phrase whose letters denote another phrase is called an anagram. Solving anagrams is not really about sorting but about finding among all possible letter orderings a particular one. Anagrams appear, for example, in the *Harry Potter* stories, where "I am Lord Voldemort" is an anagram of his birth name Tom Marvolo Riddle, and in the movie *Sneakers*, where "Setec Astronomy," a code name for a decrypting device, is an anagram of "too many secrets."

In the Brothers Grimm version of the fairy tale *Cinderella*—in German, *Aschenputtel*, the bad stepmother presents Aschenputtel with the challenge to sort out lentils from the ashes, which is a simple form of bucket sort. Sometimes the events of a story also require sorting when they are narrated in nonchronological order. One extreme is the movie *Memento*, which presents much of its story in reverse. Something similar happens in the movie *Eternal Sunshine of the Spotless Mind*, where a couple undergoes a procedure to erase their memories after a breakup. The memories of one of them are then presented in reverse order. The movie *Vantage Point* presents the events leading up to an attempt to assassinate the U.S. President from different perspectives. Each description is itself incomplete, but adds more details and facts, and the viewer must merge all accounts together to understand the story.

David Mitchell's book *Cloud Atlas* consists of several stories that are nested within one another. To obtain a completed version of the stories, one has to reorder different parts of the book. An interesting variation of the ordering challenge is presented in Julio Cortázar's *Hopscotch*, which contains two different sets of explicit instructions about the order in which to read the chapters of the book.

# Part II

# LANGUAGES

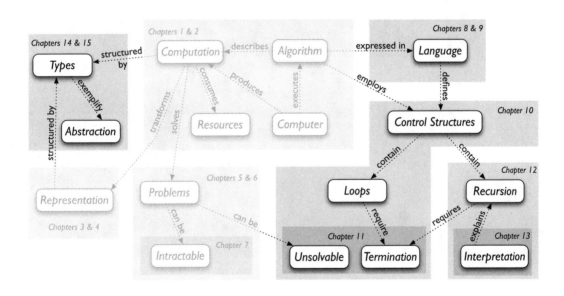

Chapters 14 & 15

Types

structured by

Chapters 1 & 2

Computation — describes — Algorithm — expressed in — Language

Chapters 8 & 9

exemplify

Abstraction

structured by

consumes

produces

transforms

solves

executes

employs

defines

Resources

Computer

Control Structures

Chapter 10

contain

contain

Representation

Problems

Chapters 5 & 6

Loops

Recursion

Chapter 12

Chapters 3 & 4

can be

can be

require

requires

explains

Intractable

Chapter 7

Chapter 11

Unsolvable

Termination

Interpretation

Chapter 13

# Language and Meaning

---◦○◦---

## *Over the Rainbow*

# Doctor's Orders

After lunch you have a doctor's appointment. Following the exam, the physician writes a prescription and fills out a form for ordering some blood tests. You take the form to the lab, get blood drawn, and then take the prescription to the pharmacy. At this point it should come as no surprise that the lab technician, in subjecting the blood to several tests, is executing an algorithm, as is the pharmacist in preparing the prescription according to the doctor's instructions. A noteworthy feature of this scenario is that the algorithm is defined by one person and executed by another.

This division of labor is possible only because the algorithm is written down in a *language*. Although the physician could also have called and instructed the pharmacist directly, this would have complicated the process, since it would have required the physician and the pharmacist to work simultaneously. The representation of the algorithm in a written form allows them to work independently of one another, and at different times. Moreover, once written, a prescription can be used multiple times.

The separation of algorithm definition and execution makes the need for a precise definition of a language evident. The physician and the pharmacist must agree on what a prescription is, what it may contain, and what it means. Your health as a patient depends on this. For example, a dosage must state its unit to avoid ambiguity. If physician and pharmacist interpret dosage in different units, ambiguity could cause the medication dosage to be ineffectively low or dangerously high. Similar agreements are required between the physician and the lab technician.

The pharmacist and lab technician are computers who have to execute the algorithms given to them by the physician. Only if they know how to read and interpret the physician's instructions can they successfully execute them to support the physician's goal of helping you, the patient.

The first step in executing a written algorithm is to parse it, which means to extract its underlying structure. This structure identifies the key components of an algorithm (in the case of a prescription, drug names, quantities, and frequency of intake) and how they are related (for example, whether the quantity refers to each intake or the total amount of the drug). Once the structure is identified, the meaning of the language in which the algorithm is expressed defines what exactly the pharmacist and lab technician have to do. The process of parsing is itself an algorithm for extracting the underlying structure of any given sentence.

The languages used for ordering blood work and for prescriptions are quite different. In addition to their content, they also have different external appearances. While a prescription typically consists of a sequence of words for drugs, amounts, frequency of intake, and so on, an order for blood work is routinely given by a form with several checked boxes. Often the particular format of a language is due to historical reasons, but it can also be the result of a conscious design decision to better support some of the language's goals. For example, a form with check boxes reflects the internal structure of the language and simplifies the task of writing and interpreting (and billing) orders. It can also avoid potential ambiguities. For example, the form can be designed to prevent the selection of redundant tests, such as ordering a basic and a comprehensive test.

Language plays a central role in computer science. Without language, we could not talk about computation, algorithms, or their properties. Many domains have developed specialized languages with their own terminology and notation. In addition to using languages, computer scientists study language itself, as linguists and philosophers of language do. In particular, computer scientists address questions of how languages can be precisely defined, what features languages (should) have, and how new languages can be designed. Computer scientists study formalisms for specifying, analyzing, and translating languages, and they develop algorithms to automate these tasks.

The philosopher Ludwig Wittgenstein famously wrote: "The limits of my language mean the limits of my world."[1] In chapter 8 I use the language of music to illustrate concepts of language relevant to computer science and to show that the application of language has few limits in this world.

# 8  The Prism of Language

We use language effortlessly every day, unaware of the complicated mechanisms involved when language does its work. It is similar to walking. Once it is learned, we can easily wade through water, plow through sand, climb up stairs, and step over obstacles. The complexity of the task becomes apparent when we try to build a robot that mimics the behavior. The same is true of languages. Once you try to instruct machines how to use language effectively, you realize how difficult this actually is. Did you ever get frustrated using Siri or failing to find what you were looking for on Google? The Turing test for machine intelligence reflects this state of affairs perfectly. According to this test, a machine is deemed intelligent if a user cannot distinguish it from a human being in a conversation. In other words, language competence is used as a benchmark for artificial intelligence.

The phenomenon of language has been studied in several disciplines, including philosophy, linguistics, and sociology, so there is no single agreed-upon definition of what a language is. From a computer science point of view, a language is a *precise and effective means to communicate meaning.* Chapter 3 showed how signs form the basis for representation and thus can give meaning to computations by linking symbols to the concepts they stand for. While signs can represent merely individual concepts, a language defines the meaningful combination of signs into sentences and represents relationships between such concepts. Signs and languages are both representations, but while signs are sufficient to represent objects of interest for a particular discourse, it takes a language to represent computations through algorithms.

This chapter explains what a language is and how languages can be defined. I begin by illustrating how languages enable the representation of algorithms and thus computation, which accounts for the importance of languages as a subject in computer science. I then show how languages can be defined through grammars. A language consists of sentences, and while a sentence is often considered to be simply a list of symbols or words, this is too narrow a view. It is like looking at the drawing of a scene and only recognizing the objects in it but ignoring their relationships. Imagine a drawing that shows a man, a dog, and a stick. It matters whether the dog is carrying the stick and is walking toward the man or whether the man is holding the stick and the dog is biting the man. Similarly, each sentence of a language has an internal structure that plays an important role in assembling its meaning. To illustrate this aspect, I demonstrate how a grammar not only defines the external appearance of sentences as sequences of words (*concrete syntax*) but also their internal structure (*abstract syntax*).

✳ ✳ ✳

This chapter is not about computation per se but about the description of computation, or rather about the description of the description of computation. What does that mean? An algorithm is a description of a computation, but this chapter is not about specific algorithms; it's about how to describe algorithms. It turns out that such a description amounts to a language.

When we have to explain what a car or a flower is, we do not talk just about a few specific cars or flowers but rather about what all cars or flowers have in common, the essence of cars or flowers, so to speak. Individual specimens of cars and flowers will likely be mentioned as examples, but to talk about all possible cars or flowers requires the development of a *model* of what a car or a flower is. A model defines the *type* of all cars or flowers (see chapter 14).

Templates, which consist of a fixed structure with some variable parts, can be effective models for cars and flowers, since much of their inherent structure is fixed. While templates work well to describe some kinds of algorithms, for example, spreadsheets or the forms for ordering blood work, a template-based model would be too rigid and not expressive enough for algorithms in general. The flexibility required for the description of arbitrary algorithms is provided by languages.

In the story accompanying this chapter, language itself plays a prominent role. I chose music as the domain in which to study the concepts of language because musical languages are simple and structured enough so that the concepts to be explained are easily appreciable. The domain of music is narrow enough to lend itself to a specialized notation, yet it is universally understood and thus can be taken for granted while the discussion focuses directly on musical languages.

Regarding music as a language is not a new idea. For example, using ideas that go back to Pythagoras, the astronomer Johannes Kepler employed musical concepts to explain the laws governing the orbiting frequencies of the planets. Francis Godwin describes in the novel *Man in the Moone* (1638) how the inhabitants of the moon use musical language to communicate. In the movie *Close Encounters of the Third Kind*, humans communicate with aliens using a five-tone scale. Since music is a highly structured yet concrete and culture-transcendent medium, it is well suited to explain the concepts of language.

## Take Note of the Melody

"Over the Rainbow" is one of the most popular songs of the twentieth century in the United States.[1] It was composed by Harold Arlen[2] for the movie *The Wizard of Oz*. At the beginning of the movie, Dorothy, played by Judy Garland, wonders whether there is a place without trouble, which leads to her singing the song.

If this were an audio book or a YouTube video, you could listen to the song right now. However, in the absence of an audio medium, how can I communicate the music to you? I can show you a representation of the music that can be interpreted to produce the melody. One such representation, widely used today, is the *standard music notation*, also called *staff notation*. Here is a small part of the song represented in this notation:

Some - where    o - ver    the    rain - bow    way    up    high

Don't worry if you don't know music notation. I explain the necessary concepts over the course of this chapter. At this point, it is sufficient to know that the balloon-shaped symbols represent individual notes of the melody, their vertical position determines the pitch of the note, and that the duration of a note is indicated by the kind of stem attached and whether the note oval is black or empty. Pitch and duration are the basic elements to form melodies. By singing or listening to the tune and following the score one can get a pretty good understanding of the meaning of the individual notes and the notation in general.

This score can be regarded as a sentence in the language of music notation. What's more, the score is the description of an algorithm to produce music. Anyone who

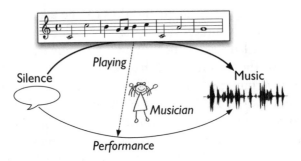

**Figure 8.1**   Playing (executing) a music score (an algorithm) generates a performance (a computation), which transforms silence into music. The performance is produced by a musician (a computer), for example, a person or a machine that can understand the music notation (language) in which the piece is written. See figure 2.1 on page 36.

understands this language can execute this sentence, which effectively turns the musician into a computer. The analogy with computing is depicted in figure 8.1. The generated computation produces representations of sounds, which can take quite different forms. A vocalist will exert movement of her vocal chords, and a pianist, guitarist, or violinist will start and stop string vibrations, using keys and hammers, fingers, or a bow.

The remarkable thing about music notation is that it facilitates the faithful reproduction of a melody, even by people who have never heard it before. The composer Harold Arlen, who invented the melody and then coded it by writing it down in music notation, could have simply sent the score to Judy Garland, and this would have been enough to ensure that she could sing the song properly. Without such a notation, the only way to share music would be through a recording or by hearsay (hearplay?), that is, to perform it in front of others who would then have to remember it to reproduce it. If you have ever played the telephone game, you know how unreliable such a process is.[3]

Pondering the design of the staff notation, one can notice how arbitrary it is. Even though a note is an indexical sign (see chapter 3) whose height reflects the pitch of the represented note, there seems to be no particular reason for having five staff lines, for the elliptical shape of notes, or for the particular length and direction of stems. This could all be done quite differently. In fact, it is sometimes done differently.

For example, the tablature notation for guitar is based on a very different representation. It shows how to interact directly with the strings of the guitar and thus avoids an abstract concept of notes. A number on a line indicates where (on which fret) to hold down the string while plucking it. One advantage of this notation lies in its directness: it allows beginners to quickly play tunes without first having to learn an abstract music notation. A disadvantage is that the notation does not precisely reflect the duration of notes. Moreover, it is limited to one kind of instrument.

The tablature notation reflects the physical structure of the guitar and is thus less arbitrary. For example, since a guitar usually has six strings, the design of the notation requires that it have six horizontal lines and that numbers appear only on those lines. By contrast, the number of five lines in the score notation is arbitrarily chosen and can be extended when needed. In fact, the very first note in the staff notation example does just that and employs an auxiliary line.

Tablature and staff notation are two different languages for representing the domain of music. Each language is defined by a set of rules that specify what kind of symbols can be used and how they can be combined. The rules define the *syntax* of the language; they are used to distinguish proper elements of the language, called *sentences*, from gibberish. A properly constructed music score or tablature is a sentence. Any notation that violates the rules cannot be properly executed as an algorithm. For example, it would make no sense to use negative numbers in tablature. A guitar player would not know how to interpret them and what to do. Similarly, if we had a note in the staff notation that was spread out over several staff lines, Judy Garland would not have known which note to sing.

A music performer can reproduce music only if the music notation is clear and unambiguous.[4] This is another way of saying that the music notation, like any other algorithmic notation, must represent effectively executable steps that can be interpreted unambiguously. Thus, to ensure the effectiveness of any musical (and other algorithmic) language we first need a precise definition of what counts as a sentence of that language.

## Grammar Rules

The syntax of a language can be defined with a *grammar*, which is understood as a set of rules for constructing sentences of the language. Using natural languages like Spanish or English to describe syntax is not a good alternative, because the descriptions tend to be long and imprecise. This is why math equations or physics laws are generally not expressed in prose but in some specialized notation. In fact, many scientific and technical fields have developed their own terminology and notation to enable effective communication about the ideas in their respective domains. And the same is true for the study of languages, whether it is in the field of linguistics or computer science, and one special notation to define languages is that of grammars.

One problem in describing a language is how to represent in a finite way a potentially infinite set of sentences. Science faces a similar challenge by having to describe an infinite set of facts through a small set of laws. Science's solution to this problem is helpful in explaining some concepts of grammars. Consider, for example, the famous physics equation $E = mc^2$, which relates the energy ($E$) that an object contains to its mass ($m$). The exact meaning of this equation is not really important here; what matters is that the equation contains a *constant c* and two *variables, m* and *E*, which can stand for arbitrary positive numbers. In particular, the two variables in this equation allow the computation of the energy content of any object, no matter how large or small, how simple or complicated. The use of variables enables the single equation to represent an infinite number of physical facts. A variable in an equation serves the same purpose as a parameter in an algorithm.

Similar to equations, a grammar also contains constants and variables. The constants are called *terminal symbols*, or *terminals* for short, and the variables are called *nonterminal symbols*, or *nonterminals* for short. The reason for these names will become clear shortly. A sentence of a language is given by a sequence of terminal symbols and does not contain any nonterminals, which play only an auxiliary role in constructing sentences. In the case of staff notation, terminals are, for example, individual notes appearing on staffs and bars that group notes into measures. Of course, the notation contains other terminal symbols, but notes and bars are sufficient to illustrate the grammar concepts needed to define simple melodies.

For example, the terminals that constitute the first measure of "Over the Rainbow" are the two note symbols ≡ and ≡, followed by a bar ≡. Similar to a constant in an equation, a terminal symbol represents a fixed, unchangeable part of a

Some - where    o

sentence, and a sentence corresponds to one particular scientific fact that results from an equation by substituting numbers for the variables.

In contrast, a nonterminal symbol acts like a variable in an equation that can take on different values. A nonterminal can be substituted by a sequence of other (terminal and nonterminal) symbols. However, substitution is not arbitrary. Instead, all the possible substitutions are defined by a set of rules. A nonterminal is like a placeholder and is typically used to represent a particular part of a language. The substitution rules define what those parts look like in terms of sequences of terminals. For example, in the definition of a simplified grammar for the staff notation we find a nonterminal *note* that can stand for an arbitrary note terminal symbol.[5]

**Table 1.1**

| Grammars | Equations | Algorithms |
|---|---|---|
| Nonterminal | Variable | Parameter |
| Terminal | Constant, operation | Value, instruction |
| Sentence | Fact | Algorithm with only values |
| Rule | | Instruction |

A grammar consists of several *rules*. Each such rule is given by a nonterminal to be substituted, an arrow to indicate the substitution, and a sequence of symbols to replace the nonterminal with. This replacement sequence is also called the rule's right-hand side (RHS). A simple example is the rule *note* → ♩. Here the RHS consists of just one terminal symbol. The correspondence between the components of grammars, equations, and algorithms is summarized in table 8.1. A grammar consists of rules, much like an algorithm is built out of individual instructions. For equations there are no corresponding components.

Since notes vary in pitch and duration, and since we have only one note nonterminal, we need a large number of rules for *note*, as illustrated in figure 8.2.[6] The nonterminal *note* represents the category of individual notes, and this category is defined through all the rules for *note*.

In general, the RHS of a rule can contain several symbols, and those symbols can be terminals as well as nonterminals. A sequence that consists only of terminal symbols cannot be changed, since rules can only substitute nonterminal symbols. This also explains the two names *terminals* and *nonterminals*. A finished sequence of terminals is a sentence of the language described by the grammar rules. On the other hand, a sequence that still contains nonterminal symbols is not finished yet and is also not a sentence of the language. Such a sequence is also called a *sentential form*, since it generally describes a whole class of sentences that can be obtained from it by further substitution of the nonterminals. A sentential form is similar to an equation in which some but not all variables have been substituted or an algorithm in which some but not all parameters have been replaced by input values.

Sentential forms can be seen in the rules that define a melody. The nonterminal *melody* stands for all melodies that can be formed by the grammar. In a first approach,

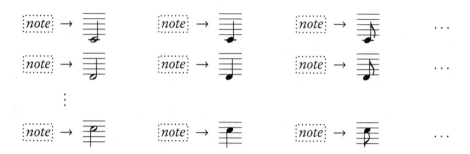

**Figure 8.2** Grammar rules defining the possible substitutions for the note nonterminal. Since an arbitrary note is represented by one nonterminal, a separate rule is required for each combination of pitch and duration. Each column shows the rules for notes for a particular duration: *left*, half notes (notes that last one half of a measure); *middle*, quarter notes; *right*, eighth notes.

we can define melodies by the following three rules. (Each rule is given a name for later reference.)

$$melody \rightarrow note\ melody \qquad (\text{NewNote})$$

$$melody \rightarrow note\ \mathsf{measure}\ melody \qquad (\text{NewMeasure})$$

$$melody \rightarrow note \qquad (\text{LastNote})$$

The first rule, NewNote, says that a melody starts with some note and is followed by another melody. This may seem strange at first, but if we consider that a melody is a sequence of notes, this rule says that a sequence of notes starts with a note and is followed by another sequence of notes. The form of the rule looks peculiar because it replaces a symbol by an RHS that contains that very symbol. Such a rule is said to be *recursive*. It seems that a recursive rule does not really achieve the substitution that it is supposed to accomplish. And if we had only recursive rules for *melody*, the grammar would indeed be problematic because we could never get rid of the nonterminal. However, in the example, the third rule, LastNote, is not recursive and can always be employed to replace a melody nonterminal by a note nonterminal, which could then be replaced by a terminal note symbol. Instead of the rule LastNote we could also employ the following alternative third rule that has an empty RHS:

$$melody \rightarrow \qquad (\text{EndMelody})$$

This rule says to replace :*melody*: by an empty sequence of symbols (that is, nothing). Such a rule can be used to effectively remove a melody nonterminal from a sentential form.

Recursive rules are typically used to generate some number of symbols through repeated applications.

The second rule, NewMeasure, is similar to the first and also allows the repeated generation of note nonterminals. In addition, however, it generates a bar terminal symbol 辵, which indicates the end of one measure and the beginning of a new one.

Starting with a nonterminal such as :*melody*:, we can generate sequences of symbols by repeatedly replacing nonterminals through the application of grammar rules. For example, the first measure of "Over the Rainbow" can be produced as follows:

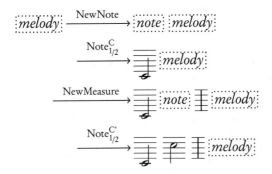

The labeled arrow in each line indicates which rule was applied. For example, first the rule NewNote is applied to generate the first note nonterminal. Then this nonterminal is immediately replaced by a terminal that represents the first note of the song. The specific rule from figure 8.2 that is used is indicated by the pitch and duration annotations of the rule $\text{Note}_{1/2}^{C}$ (C for the pitch and 1/2 for a note that lasts for one half of a whole measure). The process then continues by using the NewMeasure rule to generate another note nonterminal, followed by a bar terminal that ends the current measure. The new note nonterminal is then also substituted in the next step by a note terminal.

The decisions about which rules to use determine the melody that is generated. Notice that the order in which the rules are applied is flexible to some degree. For example, we could have swapped the application of the rules $\text{Note}_{1/2}^{C}$ and NewMeasure and still obtained the same sentential form:

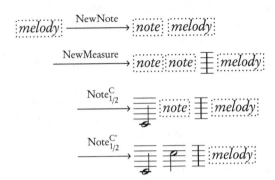

We could have also swapped the order in which the two note nonterminals have been substituted and obtained the same result.

We can terminate the series of rule applications by applying the third rule (either LastNote or EndMelody), which eliminates the remaining melody nonterminal. (If we use LastNote, we also have to apply one more Note rule to eliminate the resulting note nonterminal.) The produced sequence of terminals is a sentence of the language, and the sequence of sentential forms and rule applications, from the initial melody nonterminal to the final sentence, is called a *derivation*. A sequence of terminals is a sentence of the language only if such a derivation exists, and deciding a sentence's membership in a language boils down to finding a corresponding derivation. A derivation is proof that its resulting sequence of terminals is an element of the language.

One of the nonterminals of a grammar is designated as the *start symbol*, which represents the main category of sentences that are defined by the grammar. This nonterminal also gives the grammar its name. For example, since the purpose of this grammar is to define melodies, the start symbol of the grammar should be *melody*, and we can refer to the grammar as the melody grammar. The language defined by the melody grammar is the set of all sentences that can be derived from the *melody* start symbol.

## Structure Grows on Trees

Having more than one language for a particular domain (such as staff notation and tablature for music) may seem peculiar, and one may wonder whether there are good reasons for this. Perhaps it would be better to have only one language that could serve as a standard notation? We appreciate variety in food, clothing, vacation destinations, and so on, but having to work with different languages is often an annoying and costly business. It may require translation and clarification, and it can lead to misunderstandings and mistakes. In the story about the tower of Babel the existence of many languages is considered a punishment. Efforts to create universal languages such as Esperanto were an attempt to eliminate the problems caused by having too many languages. And language standardization committees find themselves in a constant struggle to keep the diversification of technical languages under control.

Why do we have so many different languages, despite all the costs? Often a new language is adopted because it serves a particular purpose. For example, languages such as HTML or JavaScript can help represent information on the internet, an extremely useful thing to do for many businesses and organizations. In the domain of music, the tablature notation works well for many guitar players, in particular, for those who do not know the staff notation. With the advent of programmable music machines (such as sequencers and drum machines) the language MIDI (Musical Instrument Digital Interface) was developed to encode control messages to tell synthesizers to produce sounds. Here is the beginning of the MIDI version of "Over the Rainbow":

4d54 6864 0000 0006 0001 0002 0180 4d54 . . .

However, while effective in controlling a synthesizer, this representation is not very user friendly. It is not clear what the numbers and letters mean and how they relate to the music they are supposed to represent. It is convenient to keep staff notation and tablature for people's use and to translate scores to MIDI if we want to feed the music to a synthesizer. We may also want to translate between staff notation and tablature. Of course, we want this translation between languages to be done automatically, using an algorithm, and we also want it to preserve the meaning of what is represented, that is, the music.

Translation between different notations is best accomplished via an intermediate representation, called *abstract syntax*. In contrast to *concrete syntax*, which defines the textual or visual *appearance* of a sentence, abstract syntax reveals the *structure* of a sentence in a hierarchical form. The concrete syntax of a music piece in staff notation is given by a sequence of note, bar, and other symbols, which is not adequate for capturing the hierarchical structure of a music piece. For that we can employ trees, which were used in chapters 4 and 5 to represent a family hierarchy and a dictionary. The abstract syntax is represented in an *abstract syntax tree*.

The transformation from concrete syntax into an abstract syntax tree can be achieved in two steps. First, the sequence of symbols in the concrete syntax is turned into a *parse tree*, which captures the hierarchical relationships between the symbols. Second, the parse tree is simplified into an abstract syntax tree. A parse tree can be constructed alongside the derivation of a sentence. Remember that in each step of a derivation a nonterminal is replaced with the RHS of a rule for that nonterminal. Now instead of replacing the nonterminal with the RHS, we simply add a node for each symbol of the RHS and connect it by an edge to the nonterminal. Thus, each derivation step extends the abstract syntax tree by adding new nodes to a nonterminal at the fringe of the tree. If we follow the previous derivation, we first obtain the following sequence of trees, which illustrates how the application of a rule extends a tree downwards:

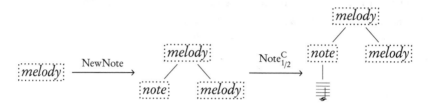

These two steps are simple and straightforward. The next two steps lead to a somewhat unexpected result because the parse tree does not reveal the structure of the song. The parse tree does not show how a melody consists of measures and how measures consist of notes:

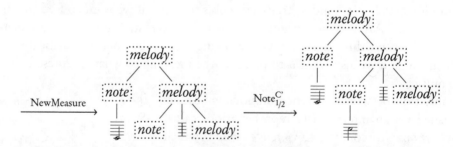

The lack of structure is a consequence of how the earlier grammar was defined: its rules expanded a melody simply into a sequence of notes. Therefore, it is not surprising that the parse tree does not mention any measures. By changing the grammar definition to account for measures, we can remedy the situation. Figure 8.3 shows parts of the parse and abstract syntax trees. In computer science trees are drawn upside down with the root at the top and the leaves at the bottom. Nonterminals are the locations of branching in the tree, and terminals occur as the leaves of the tree.

The parse tree in the figure is the immediate result of turning a derivation into a tree; it retains all the details of the derivation, even those parts that are not required for translating the tree into a different notation. In contrast, the abstract syntax tree ignores

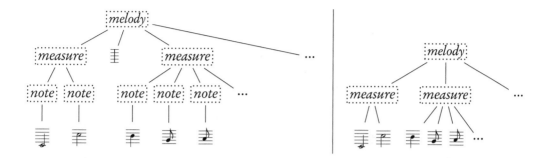

**Figure 8.3**   The structure of a melody represented by syntax trees. A syntax tree captures the structural result of a derivation but ignores details, such as which rules have been applied in which order. *Left:* A parse tree, which captures all the details of the derivation. *Right:* An abstract syntax tree, which omits unnecessary details and retains only the structurally relevant information.

terminals and nonterminals that are not essential for the structure of the sentence. For example, the bar terminals are redundant, since the grouping of notes into measures is already captured by measure nonterminals. The note nonterminals are not needed either, since each one of them is always expanded into exactly one note terminal. Adding the note terminals directly as children to the measure nonterminals captures the same structural information and thus justifies the removal of the note nonterminals. The parse tree and the abstract syntax tree share a common structure: both roots are given by the melody nonterminal, and all the leaves are terminal symbols. The abstract syntax tree reflects the structure of the sentence more directly and is the basis for analysis and translation; it also facilitates the definition of a sentence's meaning.

The process of constructing a parse tree or an abstract syntax tree for a given sentence is called *parsing*. The relationships between sentences, syntax trees, and parsing are illustrated in figure 8.4. Parsing is a computation for which several different algorithms exist. While a grammar provides a clear definition of which sentences belong to a language, parsing also needs a strategy for turning a given sentence into a syntax tree. The difficulty in parsing lies in deciding which grammar rules to select during the analysis of a sentence. There are different strategies for parsing sentences of a grammar. We have seen one, called *top-down parsing*, which begins with the start symbol of the grammar and repeatedly applies rules to gradually build a syntax tree by expanding nonterminals. This process is repeated until the sentence appears as the sequence of terminals in the leaves of the tree. In contrast, *bottom-up parsing* tries to match right

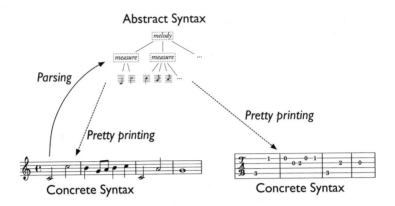

**Figure 8.4** Parsing is the process of identifying the structure of a sentence and representing it as a syntax tree. Pretty printing turns a syntax tree into a sentence. Since an abstract syntax tree may omit certain terminal symbols (for example, bars), pretty printing cannot just collect the terminals in the leaves of the syntax tree but must generally employ grammar rules to insert additional terminal symbols. The parsing arrow is missing for the tablature notation because it is an ambiguous notation and thus doesn't allow the construction of a unique abstract syntax tree.

sides of rules in the sentence and applies rules in reverse. The goal is to build the syntax tree by adding the nonterminals of the left side of matched rules as parents to the tree. This is repeated until a tree with a single root node is obtained.

The opposite process, turning a syntax tree into concrete syntax, is called *pretty printing*. This is a mostly straightforward computation, since the structure of the sentence is already given and provides guidance for the creation of the concrete representation.

With parsing and pretty printing we have the necessary tools to translate between languages. A translation between two languages that have the same abstract syntax is obtained by parsing a sentence in the first language and applying pretty printing for the second. For example, in figure 8.4 we can see how to get from staff notation to tablature by first parsing a sentence in the staff notation and then applying the tablature pretty printer to the resulting abstract syntax tree. To translate between languages that do not share the same abstract syntax requires an additional transformation between the abstract syntax trees.

Parsing is also the necessary first step in determining the meaning of a sentence, since it depends on the structure of the sentence, which is represented by its abstract syntax tree. This is a crucial observation that deserves repeating. To understand a sentence one has to first establish the structure of the sentence in the form of an abstract syntax tree.[7] This is also true for listening to music. To  understand the song "Over the Rainbow" one has to parse the sounds and identify different notes that give rise to the melody. Moreover, the grouping of notes into measures goes along with noticing emphasis on notes and making sense of phrases as part of the melody. Finally, the higher-level structuring of the song into chorus and verses provides a framework for recognizing repetitions and motifs.

Since syntax trees are a gateway to the meaning of sentences, the question arises whether parsing always succeeds and what happens to the understanding of a sentence if.[8] The previous (non)sentence was lacking a syntax tree and thus had no clear meaning. But what happens if we can construct *several* different syntax trees for one sentence? This question is considered in chapter 9.

# The Pharmacy Calls Back

You are at the pharmacy to pick up your medication, but there is a problem. The prescription lacks information about the dosage form—capsules or liquid? Since the prescription is ambiguous and lacks a precise meaning, it does not represent an algorithm. The prescription does not describe a set of effective steps that would allow the pharmacist to assemble a medication.

Ambiguities can occur for several reasons. In this case the lack of information is reflected in the abstract syntax tree by a nonterminal for the dosage form that is unexpanded. Since the pharmacist cannot execute the prescription provided by the physician, she has to call and ask for clarification. Once the ambiguity is resolved, she has an algorithm to execute and can successfully prepare your medication.

The separation of work between physician and pharmacist is successful because both use a shared language of prescriptions. But that alone is not enough. Both of them also have to understand the sentences of the language in the same way. This is not a trivial requirement, evidenced by the fact that abbreviations of drug names and dosing have actually led to dispensing mistakes. A naive idea for defining the meaning, or *semantics*, for a language is to explicitly assign a meaning for each possible sentence. This cannot work for languages that contain an infinite number of sentences, but even for finite languages such an approach is highly impractical.

Instead the semantics definition has to work in two related steps. First, it assigns semantics to individual words, and then it defines rules for how to derive the semantics for a sentence from the semantics of its parts. For example, in the form for ordering blood work, the semantics of an individual check box is to order one particular blood test. The semantics of a group of such check boxes is defined as a collection of orders, that is, to carry out all the orders that are obtained from the semantics of each individual check box in the group. This compositional approach requires the syntax definition of the language to make the structure of sentences available to the semantics definition, which it does in the form of abstract syntax trees.

The languages for blood work and prescriptions show that the semantics of a language can take different forms. For example, a prescription defines an algorithm for filling prescriptions, whereas the form for blood work provides instructions to draw blood and perform lab tests. The computers for executing the algorithms in these different languages need to understand the different semantics and consequently need different skill sets to do their work successfully. The form language for blood work also illustrates that even a single language can have different semantics, namely, instructions to draw a specific amount of blood and to perform different lab tests. Thus one sentence in one language can be executed differently, often by different computers (for instance, a phlebotomist and a lab technician) and produce completely unrelated results. This can be beneficial and supports the division of labor.

One important application of having different semantics for one language is the analysis of algorithms to detect and eliminate potential mistakes, which can help prevent the computation of incorrect results. Compare this with a document that can be read by different people to find typos or grammar mistakes, to judge the content, or to check for compliance with typesetting conventions. All of these tasks have different goals and can be performed before the document is published. Similarly, a pharmacist should double-check a prescription before filling it to prevent any unintended side effects for the patient.

Languages are everywhere. In addition to prescriptions, lab work, music, and numerous other specific domains, computer science itself is full of languages, not even counting the thousands of programming languages. We have already seen a language for describing grammars. There are also languages to define the semantics of languages, to define parsers and pretty printers, and many others. Languages are an essential computer science tool for representing data and computation. The effective use of languages depends on having a precise semantics, just as the health and safety of patients depends on a clear semantics for prescriptions. Based on the song "Over the Rainbow," I will illustrate in chapter 9 how the semantics of a language can be defined and some of the challenges involved in establishing such a definition.

# 9

# Finding the Right Tone: Sound Meaning

In chapter 8 we saw that the score for the song "Over the Rainbow" is an algorithm that can be executed by musicians to produce music. The algorithm was written (that is, invented and coded) by the composer Harold Arlen in the language of staff notation. The syntax of this language can be defined by a grammar, which defines the appearance of a sentence as a score and its internal structure as an abstract syntax tree.

We also saw that one language can be defined by different grammars, which may at first seem like an oddity. However, differences in grammars lead to differences in the abstract syntax and represent different views of music structure. These differences matter because when Judy Garland wants to perform "Over the Rainbow," she first has to parse the music notation to uncover the song's structure. In other words, the meaning of a language builds on its abstract syntax.

This is why ambiguity poses a problem for any language. If a sentence can have more than one abstract syntax tree, then it is not clear which structure to follow when applying the semantics definition. Consequently, an ambiguous sentence may have more than one potential meaning, which is how the word *ambiguous* is usually defined.

This chapter looks more closely at the problem of ambiguity and addresses the question of how sentences acquire meaning. A key insight is that a systematic definition of language meaning hinges on the concept of *compositionality*, which says that the semantics of a sentence is obtained by combining the semantics of its parts in a systematic way, as defined by the sentence's structure. This shows that the structure of a language plays a pivotal role in defining its meaning.

## That Doesn't Sound Right

The language for music notation can be defined by a fairly simple grammar. But even for such a simple language it is not clear which grammar rules to use. One problem that can plague a language is that of *ambiguity*, which means that one sentence can have more than one meaning. Ambiguity can creep into a sentence in two different ways. First, the basic words or signs of a language can be ambiguous, a phenomenon called *lexical ambiguity* (see chapter 3). Second, a particular combination of words in a sentence can be ambiguous, even though the individual words themselves are not. This is called *grammatical ambiguity*. Consider, for example, the sentence "Bob knows more girls than Alice." It could mean that Bob knows more than one girl, or it could mean that he knows more girls than Alice does.

A grammatical ambiguity occurs when a grammar can generate more than one syntax tree for a given sentence. To continue with the music example, consider the following part of "Over the Rainbow." Curiously, the score does *not* contain any bars, which causes this sentence to be ambiguous, since it is not clear which note, the first or the second, should be emphasized when playing it.

*Some - day    I'll    wish    u - pon    a    star    and*

If you know the song and try to sing the score, you notice that the emphasis should be on the second note. It will probably not be easy to sing the song by emphasizing the first note. Usually, however, it is the first note in each bar that is emphasized. This means if Judy Garland had been given the previous score instead of the original, she would probably have assumed, incorrectly, that the emphasis should be on the first note. These two different interpretations are reflected in two different abstract syntax trees, shown in figure 9.1. The first interpretation groups the first eight notes into the first measure and the last note into the second measure. The second interpretation groups the first note into the first measure and the remaining eight notes into the second measure.

Both these syntax trees can be derived if we modify the grammar to not include bar symbols. The difference in the two abstract syntax trees results from a different decision

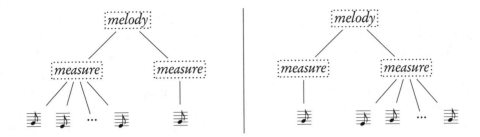

**Figure 9.1**    Ambiguity in a grammar can cause a sentence to have different abstract syntax trees. These trees present a different hierarchical structure for the same sentence. It is generally impossible to determine the meaning of such a sentence, since its structure affects its meaning.

on which rule to use to expand the first measure nonterminal. The tree on the left in the figure results when we expand it into eight note nonterminals, whereas the tree on the right results if we expand it into only one note nonterminal. Both trees represent the same sequence of notes, but their internal structures are different. The left-hand tree emphasizes "Some," whereas the right-hand tree emphasizes "day." This sequence of notes cannot actually be properly parsed, since the total time of the nine notes adds up to $1^{1}/_{8}$, which is more than fits into one measure.

To correctly express the sentence one has to place a bar somewhere to split the notes into two measures. The correct placement of the bar is after the first note. This will put the emphasis on the second note.

*The Wizard of Oz* contains another example of an ambiguity, in English, which occurs as the Wicked Witch skywrites "Surrender Dorothy" with her broom when Dorothy and her friends are in Emerald City. This message can mean either a call to the inhabitants of Emerald City to surrender Dorothy or a call to Dorothy to surrender herself. In the latter case, there should be a comma between "Surrender" and "Dorothy." Just as bars in music notation help to clarify the correct structure and emphasis of melodies, commas and periods serve this purpose in written natural languages. And punctuation symbols and keywords serve the same purpose in programming languages.

Sometimes languages offer constructs that leave some choice to the interpreter of the algorithm as to what steps to perform. For instance, the improvisation notation here provides the musician with a choice for the pitch of the second, third, and fourth notes. An algorithm that employs such constructs is called *nondeterministic*. In music notation this is sometimes used to provide room for improvisation, that is, to give musicians more freedom in their interpretation and performance of a music piece. But nondeterminism must not be confused with ambiguity. From an algorithmic point of view, a music score provides instructions for a musician to produce a sequence of sounds, each of a particular pitch and duration. In contrast, an ambiguous notation would leave the musician wondering what to do. Thus, while nondeterminism is a *feature* of a language, ambiguity is a *bug* in a language's syntax definition. It may come as a surprise, but algorithms that leave some choices open are quite common. For example, in Hansel and Gretel's simple way-finding algorithm, the next pebble to be chosen was not uniquely specified.

Ambiguity is a pervasive phenomenon in languages. It reminds us that a language is not just a collection of its well-formed sentences but also maps these sentences to their structure in the form of abstract syntax trees. Ambiguities can be fun; they are sometimes exploited in music to create clever effects, for example, by starting a melody that is interpreted by the listener in some way and then adding a different rhythm that creates a surprise and forces the listener to change the interpretation.

In our example you can simulate this as follows. (This is best done with two people. If you have a keyboard available, this can also be done by one person, but the effect is not as strong.) One person starts by humming or playing (but not singing—this is probably too difficult) the alternating G and E eighth notes with the (wrong) emphasis on the Gs. Then, after some time, the second person starts humming quarter notes (for example, C) that start together with each E hummed by the first person. After a few iterations, you will perceive a shift in the rhythm and the song will suddenly sound like the well-known part from "Over the Rainbow."

Ambiguities occur in other notations as well. You have probably seen the Necker cube. If you look long enough at the picture, your perception shifts between looking down on a cube from the right to looking up at a cube from the left. Again, there is one visual representation that has two different structural interpretations. This ambiguity matters. Suppose you want to touch the cube at its top right front corner; then the position you reach out to depends on your interpretation of the figure.

Related are figures like the Penrose triangle (inspired by M. C. Escher drawings). However, the issue with these figures is not ambiguity between different possible interpretations but rather the fact that *no* interpretation exists that is consistent with physical reality as experienced by people (see chapter 12).

Ambiguity is an intriguing concept and a great source for humor in natural languages, as in playing on the difference between "Let's eat, grandma" and "Let's eat grandma." However, ambiguity presents a serious problem for algorithmic languages, since it can prevent the clear representation of a sentence's intended meaning. There is a subtle interplay between the syntax of a language and its meaning. On the one hand, one needs to think carefully about the syntax of a language to be able to define its meaning. On the other hand, one has to understand the meaning before one can define the syntax properly.

## Take on Meaning

The ambiguity example demonstrates that without knowing the structure of a sentence it is impossible to understand its proper meaning. But what really is the meaning of a sentence?

Since natural languages such as English are used to talk about everything, it is very difficult to narrow down the domain of their meaning other than saying "everything that can be talked about." For music languages this is much easier: The meaning of a sentence, that is, a music piece, is the sound you can hear when the piece is performed. Before diving more deeply into questions about the meaning of a language and how to define it, I want to point out two different senses of the word *meaning*. On the one hand, we have the meaning of an individual sentence. On the other hand, we have the meaning of a language. To distinguish between the two, I mostly use the word *semantics* when talking about languages and the word *meaning* when referring to individual sentences.

An overview of how sentences, languages, and meaning are related is given in figure 9.2. In a nutshell, the semantics of a language is given by the meaning of all its sentences, and the meaning of an individual sentence is given by associating it with a value of the domain the language talks about.

The meaning of one particular sentence in a music language is the music you hear when somebody performs it. However, since different musicians will interpret the song differently—some will sing it, some will play it on an instrument, others will vary harmonization or speed—there doesn't seem to be one unique sound that can be defined to be the meaning of the song. This problem can be addressed either by postulating the performance with one particular instrument by one particular musician or by taking the performance by a MIDI synthesizer as the standard. Alternatively, we could say that the meaning of "Over the Rainbow" is given by the set of all possible sounds that result from proper performances of the song. Of course, this raises the further question of what counts as a proper performance. To avoid a full discussion of this

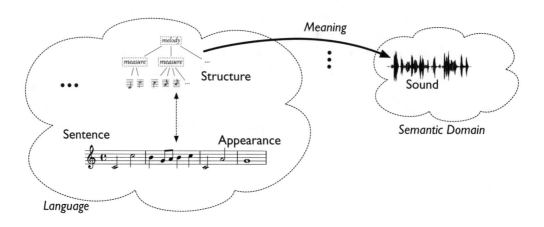

**Figure 9.2**   The semantics of a language is given by a mapping that associates each sentence's structure, represented by its abstract syntax tree, with an element of the semantic domain. This view of meaning is called *denotational semantics*, since it is based on assigning denotations to sentences of a language.

thorny philosophical issue, I refer to words of the former U.S. Supreme Court Justice Potter Stewart, who, when asked what his criterion for obscenity was, famously replied, "I know it when I see it." Thus, if you've heard the original version of "Over the Rainbow" in *The Wizard of Oz*, you can tell a proper performance if you hear one. After all, music is art, and we shouldn't be surprised or concerned that it can't be captured completely through formal definitions. The important point here is that the meaning of the "Over the Rainbow" score is a sound that somebody who knows the song well would recognize as its performance.

If we now take all the sounds that could result from performing any music score imaginable, we obtain a semantic domain. A *semantic domain* for a language such as staff notation or tablature is the set of all meanings that any sentence of that language can have. A semantic domain surely is a large set, but there are many things it does *not* contain, such as cars, animals, thoughts, movies, traffic laws, and so on. Therefore, this set still is useful in characterizing a language. It does that by describing what a user of the language can expect a sentence of that language to denote.

The collection of all individual sentences of a language and their associated meanings constitutes the semantics of a language. If a language is nonambiguous, each of its sentences has only one meaning,[1] and so picking out a sentence from the language will always lead to its meaning. In an ambiguous language, the fact that one sentence can have more than one meaning is reflected by its having multiple syntax trees, each of which can have a different meaning. The described view of meaning is referred to as *denotational semantics*, which is based on the idea of assigning meanings to sentences. There are several other approaches in computer science to defining the semantics of languages, but denotational semantics is probably the closest to our intuition and also easier to understand than some of the alternatives.

The major purpose of a language is the communication of meaning, but invented languages have no a priori obvious semantics. Therefore, for a language to be useful, it needs to be assigned a semantics. Since most languages consist of an infinite number of sentences, we cannot simply list all sentences and their meanings. There must be some other systematic way of defining the semantics of a language. This question ultimately boils down to finding an algorithm for defining the meaning of individual sentences. Such an algorithmic denotational semantics definition for a language consists of two parts. The first part is a mapping of terminal symbols to basic elements of the semantic domain. In this case this means mapping individual notes to sounds of a particular pitch and duration. The second part is given by rules that say for each nonterminal how to construct its meaning from the meanings of its children in the syntax tree. In this example, there are three nonterminals. The rule for *note* is trivial, since each note nonterminal has exactly one child, which means that its sound should be identical to that of its child. The meaning of *measure* is obtained by concatenating the sounds of its children in the order they appear. Finally, the meaning of *melody* is obtained in the same way as for *measure*, namely, through the concatenation of the sounds obtained as meaning for the melody's measures.

This example illustrates how the meaning of a sentence is systematically constructed via its abstract syntax tree by combining the meanings of leaves into meanings of their parents, followed by combining their meanings, and so on, until the meaning for the root of the tree is obtained. A semantics definition that has this form is said to be *compositional*. A compositional definition is appealing because it mirrors the way a grammar defines the syntax of an infinite language through a finite set of rules. A language whose semantics can be defined in a compositional way is also called compositional. The principle of compositionality was identified by the mathematician and philosopher Gottlob Frege during his investigation of languages and ways to formally define language semantics. Some degree of compositionality is principally required to obtain a finite description of the meaning for an infinite number of sentences given by a grammar. If a language lacks compositionality, then it is generally problematic to define its semantics, since the meaning of an arbitrary sentence cannot be obtained by composing the meanings of its parts but must be described separately. Such descriptions are exceptions that override the general rules for determining meaning.

The simplified music language described here is compositional, but many other languages are not, or only partly so. English is one such example (as are most other natural languages). For very simple examples of noncompositionality one has to look no further than compound words. While a firefighter is somebody who fights fires, a hot dog does not refer to a high-temperature canine, and a red herring does not refer to a fish of a specific color. Other examples are idiomatic expressions such as "kicking the bucket" or "spilling the beans," each of whose meanings is not obtained through the combination of the expression's words.

Staff notation also contains noncompositional elements. For example, a tie is a symbol that connects two consecutive notes of the same pitch, typ-

*why oh why can't I?*

ically the last note of a measure with the first note of the next measure. This occurs in "Over the Rainbow" at the very end of the song in the phrase "why oh why can't I?" where "I" is sung as one note that lasts for two whole measures. According to the rule for finding the meaning of a melody, one has to determine the meanings of the individual measures and then concatenate those. This would lead to two one-measure-long sounds instead of one sound that lasts two measures. Therefore, to properly get the meaning of notes tied across two (or more) measures, the rule for finding the meaning of a melody must be overridden by a rule that treats groups of measures whose notes are tied as one.

The rules for determining the meaning of a sentence are remarkably similar to the rules that musicians follow when interpreting music notation. This is not an accident because a denotational semantics for a language is an algorithm to compute the meaning for a given sentence from that language. A computer that understands the language in which the denotational semantics is given can execute the semantics and thus compute the meaning of sentences. A computer or algorithm that can execute semantics is called an *interpreter*. While it may seem strange to view Hansel and Gretel as interpreters of pebble-following instructions, calling Judy Garland an interpreter of Harold Arlen's music probably won't raise any objections. Just as an algorithm makes computation repeatable, a language definition can be used to create computers for executing sentences of the language and thus makes language execution repeatable. In the case of the music notation, anybody who understands the semantics for the music notation can learn how to interpret music notation. In other words, the semantics can be used to teach musicians without a music teacher; it allows people to teach themselves.

A question related to interpreters is what happens if we create a recording of the music performance. Do recordings somehow embody the meaning of a music piece? Not really. What happens is that the recording of music produces merely a different representation of the music. The first recordings of "Over the Rainbow" were produced on analog records, which contain grooves that are interpreted by the needle of a record player and transformed into sound waves. Later, sound waves were encoded digitally on a CD as a sequence of bits (zeros and ones) that are read by a laser and then interpreted by a digital-to-analog converter to reproduce the sound waves. Today, most music is represented using software formats, such as MP3, designed to support the streaming of music over the internet. Whatever the representation is, it is still a representation of the music in some specific format, or language, that requires a performer or computer for executing the language instructions to produce the intended sound effect. Thus, playing and recording a music piece is actually a form of translation from one language, say, staff notation, into another, say, bit representation of sound waves.

# Further Exploration

The song "Over the Rainbow" was used to illustrate that each sentence of a language has a structure that is important for understanding its meaning. Any other music piece could have been used as well to investigate the structure of songs and the potential ambiguity in notation, provided it could be described by some sufficiently expressive music notation. To understand the significance of notes, bars, and other structural elements of the notation, it is instructive to examine alternative notation systems for music and understand their limitations. In particular, the systematic restriction of existing notations results in new languages. For example, restricting the available pitches of notes leads to *percussion notation*, and ignoring pitches altogether leads to a language of rhythms. If we further reduce the available note lengths to only two ("short" and "long"), we obtain *Morse code*. *Chord symbols* ignore the melody and only show the harmonic progression of a music piece, while *Chord charts* combine chord symbols and rhythm notation to show the harmonic and rhythmic progression of a music piece.

Staff notation is more visual than a typical textual language, yet a sentence (that is, music piece) is still a linear sequence of note symbols that can be adapted by changing their position and appearance. This principle forms the basis for many notations that are not traditional textual languages. For example, in the universal graphical language *Bliss*, a sentence consists of sequences of words, which are symbols that can be composed out of simpler symbols. This is similar to part of *Egyptian hieroglyphs*, in which symbols can be combined in different ways, depending on their size and the intent of what is being expressed. Bliss and hieroglyphs are general languages, intended to express arbitrary thoughts. In contrast, the staff notation is targeted at a narrow domain and is thus much simpler. An example of a special-purpose notation is *chemical formulas* that describe the composition of molecules out of atoms (for example, the formula $H_2O$, for water, says that each water molecule consists of one oxygen and two hydrogen atoms).

The previous examples are still mostly linear notations, that is, a sentence in these languages is a sequence of symbols. Visual languages can be more expressive if they employ a two-dimensional layout. For example, chemical formulas only represent the proportions of atoms that constitute a molecule and ignore the spatial arrangement of the atoms. In contrast, *structural formulas* provide a description of the geometric arrangement of atoms. Similarly, *Feynman diagrams* are a two-dimensional language, used in physics to describe the behavior of subatomic particles.

All of these languages employ a static one- or two-dimensional representation, which means one can take a picture of a sentence and send it to somebody else, who can then interpret it. Other languages transcend this snapshot limitation and employ a temporal dimension as well. For example, *gestures* are a form of language. Movements of body parts cannot be captured well by a single picture. To define a language of body movements one typically needs videos or sequences of pictures. In user interfaces for computers, tablets, and cell phones, hand movements such as swiping or pinching are interpreted as actions to be performed. In addition to gestures, there are also notations for describing dance, for example, *Labanotation*. A sentence in that language is an algorithm to be executed by a dancer, which produces a dance as a computation. *Origami instructions* are a similar kind of language for describing algorithms to fold paper objects. Language is not even restricted to humans. For example, in the series of books about the adventures of *Doctor Dolittle*, animals communicate by movements of noses, ears, and tails. But even outside of fiction we find, for example, the *waggle dance* of bees to communicate the location of food sources.

The meaning of language is defined by rules that translate the abstract syntax of a sentence into values of a semantic domain. Communication can be successful only if the communicating partners agree on those rules. Lewis Carroll's books *Alice's Adventures in Wonderland* and *Through the Looking-Glass* illustrate what happens if the rules are violated or interpreted differently by the communicating partners.

# Control Structures and Loops

———◇———

*Groundhog Day*

# Force of Habit

Back at the office, your first task is to send out several letters. Without thinking about it, you fold each letter twice horizontally to reduce its height to about one-third and then put it into an envelope. This works perfectly every time, since the paper and the envelope you are using have a fixed size, and you figured out long ago that this particular folding scheme makes the letter fit into the envelope.

The folding process is a computation described by an algorithm—a basic example of origami. Despite its simplicity, the paper-folding algorithm illustrates a number of points about languages.

The first is that the algorithm can be described in two slightly different ways. If *fold* means to fold a piece of paper a specific distance from the top (for example, one-third of the total paper length), then we could say either "fold and fold" or "fold twice." It may not seem like a big difference, but these are two fundamentally different descriptions of a repeated action. The first lists an action to be repeated explicitly as many times as needed, whereas the second merely says how often an action is to be repeated. The difference becomes clearer when you have to send a larger sheet of paper that needs additional folding steps. For example, for folding three times, the two approaches would read "fold and fold and fold" and "fold three times," respectively. Next, envision the case for 500 or more repetitions, and you can see which approach remains practical.

The first description is a *sequential composition* of individual steps, whereas the second is a *loop*. Both are examples of *control structures*, which are components of an algorithm that don't do any actual algorithmic work but rather organize the work of other steps. This is similar to workers and managers in a factory. Managers don't manufacture anything directly but coordinate the actions of the workers who do. Control structures are essential components of any language for describing algorithms, and loops (or recursion) in particular are employed in most nontrivial algorithms.

There is actually a third algorithm for folding a piece of paper, which simply says "fold until paper fits." This algorithm also employs a loop control structure, but this loop is different from the previous one in an important way. It does not explicitly say how many times an action should be repeated, but instead defines a condition that must be fulfilled for the repetition to end. This algorithm is actually more general than the previous two, since it works for paper of arbitrary size, and thus it solves a more general problem. It would be impossible to express this algorithm without a loop (or recursion). In contrast, a loop with a fixed number of repetitions can always be rewritten as a sequence of that many steps.

Assume you have to send not only a single letter but a whole bunch of documents. Whenever you have more than five sheets of paper, instead of folding them all and stuffing them into a small envelope, you use a larger envelop into which you can place the stack of papers directly without folding. Making this decision, to fold or not to fold, is an example of another control structure, the *conditional*, which executes one of two possible actions depending on a *condition*. In this case the condition is that the number of pages is five or less, in which case you fold the paper and use the small envelope. Otherwise, you don't fold the paper and use the large envelope.

A condition is also needed for determining when to end the repetition of a loop. The condition to end the loop "fold three times" is expressed with a counter having reached a particular value, namely, 3. In contrast, the condition of the loop "fold until paper fits" tests a property of the paper that is transformed by the actions in the loop. The latter kind of condition is more powerful, as evidenced by the fact that it expresses a more general algorithm. But with this increased *expressiveness* also comes a cost. While the counter-based loop can easily be shown to terminate (since the counter does not depend on what the actions in the loop do), this is not so obvious for the more general kind of loop, and we cannot be certain whether an algorithm using this kind of loop will ever stop (see chapter 11).

Much of what we do is repetitive and can often be described by loops. Sometimes whole days seem repetitive. This view is taken to the extreme in the movie *Groundhog Day*, which guides the exploration of loops and other control structures in chapters 10 and 11.

# 10 Weather, Rinse, Repeat

Any algorithm is given in some language, whose semantics determine the computation represented by the algorithm. We have seen that different languages can have different semantics and can be targeted for different computers. For example, an algorithm expressed in a programming language is executed on an electronic computer and typically denotes the computation of data. On the other hand, an algorithm in the language of music notation is executed by a musician and denotes sounds. Despite these differences, most nontrivial languages share an intriguing property, namely, that they consist of two kinds of instructions: (1) *operations* that have a direct effect, and (2) *control structures* for organizing the order, application, and repetition of operations.

Control structures not only play a crucial role in formulating algorithms, but also determine the expressiveness of languages. This means that the definition of control structures and the decision as to which control structures to include in a language determine which algorithms can be expressed in a language and thus which problems can be solved using it.

One such control structure is the so-called loop, which allows the description of repetitions. We have seen many examples of loops already, as in Hansel and Gretel's way-finding algorithm that instructs them to repeatedly find the next unvisited pebble, or in selection sort, which works by repeatedly finding the smallest element in a list. Even music notation contains control structures for expressing loops. Though I have employed loops extensively already, I haven't discussed them in detail yet. This is done in this chapter. Following the weather reporter Phil Connors, who relives Groundhog

Day over and over again, I explain how loops and other control structures work. I show different ways of describing loops and the differences in the computations they can express.

## Forever and a Day

You may have heard about Groundhog Day, the tradition according to which a groundhog can foreshadow—literally—six more weeks of winter or an early spring. This works as follows. Each year, on the second day of February, a groundhog comes out of its burrow. If on a sunny day it sees its own shadow, it retreats into the burrow, indicating that winter will last for six more weeks. If on a cloudy day it can't see its own shadow, this means an early arrival of spring.

Growing up outside of the United States, I learned about this tradition through the 1993 movie *Groundhog Day*, in which Phil Connors, an initially arrogant and cynical weather reporter from Pittsburgh, reports about the Groundhog Day festivities in the small town of Punxsutawney. The intriguing feature about the movie is that Phil Connors has to relive the same day over and over again. Each morning he wakes up at 6:00 a.m. to the same song on the radio and has to experience the same series of situations. The plot of the story unfolds as he reacts differently to these situations over the course of the movie.

Repetition plays an important part in all of our lives. Learning a skill makes sense only if we can expect that it will be applicable in the future. More generally, any use of past experience works only in circumstances that are similar to the one in which the experience was gained. Every day we repeat many things: getting up, getting dressed, having breakfast, commuting to work, and so on. An action (or a group of actions) that is repeated immediately several times is called a *loop*. The action that is repeated is called the *body* of the loop, and each execution of a loop's body is called an *iteration* of the loop. Talking to someone at a bar, Phil Connors reflects on his situation:

> Phil: *What would you do if you were stuck in one place and every day was exactly the same and nothing that you did mattered?*
>
> Ralph: *That about sums it up for me.*

This exchange can be summarized in the following characterization of one's life by a loop:

**repeat** *daily routine* **until** *you die*

What makes Phil Connors's daily routine so maddening to him—and so funny to the viewer of the movie—is that everything happens in exactly the same way as the day before, that is, everything that is not a direct response to his actions during the day. Otherwise, the movie would quickly become boring, like a monotonously repeating refrain at the end of a song.

Our days are typically less frustrating than the ever-repeating Groundhog Day because our actions yesterday have an effect on today. Therefore, each day, no matter how repetitive it may seem, happens in a different context, and the knowledge that what we and others do makes a difference provides us with a sense of continuous change and progress. These observations suggest a distinction between two kinds of loops, namely, loops that produce on each iteration the same outcome and loops that yield different outcomes. An example of the first kind is a loop that prints the name of the city you were born in, say, New York. Barring any renaming of the city, this loop will produce a steady stream of the same outputs, such as "New York" "New York" "New York" . . . . In contrast, a loop to report whether it is raining will produce a stream that contains a mix of yes and no values—unless you live in Cherrapunji,[1] where it's likely to produce a constant stream of yes values.

Note that even in a loop that produces varying outcomes, the loop body is the same for each iteration. The variation is achieved by *variables*. A variable is a name that points to part of the world. Through the variable name the algorithm can observe and manipulate the world. For example, the variable *weather* points to the current weather condition, say, sunny, and an algorithm that checks the current weather by accessing this variable would obtain the corresponding value. The variable *weather* cannot be changed by an algorithm, but the variable *pebble* that refers to the next pebble Hansel and Gretel walk toward changes with each pebble visited. Similarly, in the instruction to find the smallest element in a list that is part of selection sort, the variable *smallest element* changes in each iteration unless the list contains duplicates.

Since the term loop is sometimes used for both the description of the loop (the algorithm) and the computation it generates, this is a good time to recall the difference between the description of a computation and its execution. A loop for the daily weather report looks as follows:

**repeat** *report weather* **until** *forever*

The result of executing this loop is a sequence of values, which is a very different thing from the loop description itself. For example, the execution of the algorithm could lead to the following sequence:

rainy cloudy sunny sunny thunderstorm sunny . . .

This weather-reporting loop describes the kind of loop that Phil Connors finds himself in: each morning he has to prepare a report on the forecast of his colleague, the groundhog Punxsutawney Phil. (Interestingly, despite all the dramatic variations he creates for the day—at one time he even tries to kill Punxsutawney Phil—he never seems to miss his report about the groundhog's forecast.) Of course, Phil Connors hopes that the loop he is in does not repeat forever. In fact, he assumes the loop is of the following form:

> **repeat** *report weather* **until** *'some hidden condition'*

His initial attempts to escape this loop are essentially efforts to discover the hidden condition, which is a critical component of any loop, called its *termination condition*. Toward the end of the story we learn that the termination condition is his becoming a good person, somebody who cares about and helps other people. His reincarnation every day provides an opportunity to perfect his karma, which is the key to his leaving the purgatory-like Groundhog Day.

The Groundhog Day loop is an instance of the following general loop schema:[2]

> **repeat** *step* **until** *condition*

The termination condition appears at the end and is evaluated after the body of the loop has been executed. If the condition is true, the loop stops. Otherwise, the body will be executed again, after which the condition is also checked again to determine whether to continue or end the loop, and so on.

It is clear that a termination condition that is false at one time can become true later only if it contains a variable that can be changed by the actions of the loop body. For example, efforts to start a car that has run out of gas will not succeed until gas is refilled. Thus, if the repeated actions include only turning the ignition key or maybe kicking the tires or the incantation of a magic spell, they won't help. The termination condition thus lets us distinguish between *terminating loops* whose termination condition eventually becomes true, and *nonterminating loops* whose termination condition always remains false.

It has been said that insanity is doing the same thing over and over again and expecting different results.[3] We might be tempted therefore to brand nonterminating loops as insane, but there are examples of perfectly valid loops that do not terminate. For example, a web service is a loop that takes a request, processes it, and then continues to take the next request, ad infinitum. However, when a loop is part of an algorithm—in particular, when it is followed by other steps—we expect it to end eventually because otherwise steps that follow the loop could never be executed, and the algorithm would not terminate either.

Termination is one of the most important properties of a loop. The termination condition determines whether a loop ends, but it is the effect the loop body has on the world that is critical for the loop's termination, specifically the effect on those parts of the world on which the termination condition depends. Reporting the weather does not change the world very much and seems unlikely to have an effect on the unknown termination condition in Phil Connors's Groundhog Day loop. In frustration, he tries out more and more extreme actions, including different forms of suicide and killing Punxsutawney Phil, desperately hoping to affect the world so that the termination condition finally becomes true.

## Everything under Control

When Groundhog Day starts to repeat itself, Phil Connors is everything but in control of his life. On the contrary, he is under the control of the Groundhog Day loop and is painfully aware of this fact. Here being under the control of a loop means that he lives inside the body of a loop that controls when the repetition ends and when he can escape.

A loop controls how often its body is executed, but the effect of the loop is obtained solely by the steps of its body. In other words, a loop itself does not have any effect directly but rather indirectly through the repetition of the steps of its body. Since it generally matters how often an algorithmic step is executed, a loop exerts its influence through the number of times it executes its body. Since a loop controls the effect of its body (through the termination condition), it is called a *control structure*. A loop is a control structure for repeatedly executing a group of algorithmic steps. The other two major control structures are sequential composition and the conditional.

*Sequential composition* connects two (groups of) steps into an ordered sequence of steps. I have previously used the word *and* for this purpose, but to indicate that both steps are to be executed in sequence, not in parallel, it might be better to use a keyword such as *andThen* or *followedBy*. However, for simplicity and succinctness I adopt the notation used in most programming languages, namely, connecting two steps by a semicolon. This notation is similar to how we write down lists of items. Moreover, it is short and doesn't distract from the actual steps of the algorithm. For example, *get up*; *have breakfast* means to first get up and then have breakfast. The order of the steps matters, of course, and for some people *have breakfast*; *get up* is a welcome change of routine on Sundays. The general form of sequential composition is as follows:

*step*; *step*

Here *step* is a nonterminal that can be substituted by any simple or compound step. In particular, *step* can be another sequential composition of other steps. Thus, if you want to squeeze in a shower between getting up and having breakfast, you can use sequential composition twice by expanding the first *step* to *get up; take a shower* and the second one to *have breakfast*, which altogether produces *get up; take a shower; have breakfast.*[4]

As with the example of folding a piece of paper twice, "fold and fold," which we now write as *fold; fold*, the steps connected by ; need not be different. Executing a loop **repeat** *fold* **until** *paper fits* (or **repeat** *fold three times*) yields the same computation as the sequence *fold; fold; fold*, which illustrates that loops are a tool to describe sequences of actions. The important contribution of a loop is that it produces arbitrarily long sequences of steps while having to mention the actions to be repeated only once.

The *conditional* selects one of two (groups of) steps for execution depending on a condition. Like a loop it uses a condition to make the decision. The general form of a conditional is as follows:

**if** *condition* **then** *step* **else** *step*

Whenever Punxsutawney Phil is asked to foretell the weather, he essentially executes the following weather-reporting algorithm:

**if** *sunny* **then** *announce six more weeks of winter* **else** *announce early spring*

The conditional is a control structure that allows algorithms to make choices and select between alternative steps. The preceding conditional is part of a yearly loop for Punxsutawney Phil and a daily loop for Phil Connors. This illustrates that control structures can be combined in arbitrary ways, that is, conditionals can be part of loops or sequential compositions, loops can occur in the alternatives of a conditional or as part of a sequence of steps, and so on.

The basic steps of an algorithm are like the moves in a game (for example, passing the ball or taking a shot on a goal in soccer, or attacking a piece or castling in chess). Then the control structures define strategies in those games, for example, **repeat** *pass* **until** *in front of goal* (or if you are Lionel Messi, **repeat** *dribble* **until** *in front of goal*), that is, control structures compose basic moves into bigger plays.

As shown in chapter 8, there are many different notations to describe music. Similarly, there are different notations for algorithms. Each programming language is an example of a specific notation for algorithms, and while languages can differ significantly in which specific control structures they offer, most provide some form of loop, conditional, and composition.[5] A notation that nicely illustrates the difference between control structures is a flowchart. A *flowchart* depicts an algorithm as boxes connected

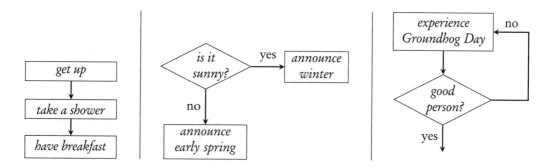

**Figure 10.1**  Flowchart notation for control structures. *Left:* A sequence of steps Phil Connors takes every morning. *Middle:* A conditional showing the decision that Punxsutawney Phil faces on each Groundhog Day. *Right:* A loop expressing the life of Phil Connors during the movie *Groundhog Day.* The "no" arrow and the arrow to the condition form a cycle through the two nodes.

by arrows. Basic actions are displayed inside the boxes, and decisions are enclosed in diamond shapes. The arrows indicate how the computation progresses. For sequential composition this means to follow single arrows from box to box, but for conditionals and loops, whose conditions have two outgoing arrows, which arrow to follow depends on the condition. Some examples of the flowchart notation are shown in figure 10.1.

It is striking how similar the notations for conditionals and loops are. Both consist of a condition with two possible continuations. The only crucial difference is that the "no" path from the condition in the loop leads to a step that continues back to the condition. The cycle thus formed provides a nice visual explanation of the name *loop* for this control structure.

Flowcharts are a *visual language.* In contrast to a textual language that presents an algorithm as a linear sequence of words and symbols, a visual language presents symbols in two- (or three-)dimensional space, connected by spatial relationships. Flowcharts use arrows to express the "execute next" relationship between actions, which are represented as boxes. A flowchart looks similar to a transportation network. The junctions are places where actions take place, and the connections lead from one action to another. Think of moving through an amusement park. The park can be regarded as an algorithm for having fun. Different people will visit individual attractions in a different order and a different number of times, depending on their predispositions and experiences with the attractions. Or envision the aisles of a supermarket that connect different sections and shelves. The supermarket can be viewed as an algorithm for different shopping experiences.

Flowcharts were quite popular in the 1970s, and they are sometimes still employed for the documentation of software, but they are rarely used these days as a programming notation. One reason is that the notation does not scale well. Even moderate-sized flowcharts are difficult to read—the profusion of arrows has been called spaghetti code. Moreover, the similarity between the notation for conditional and loop, while quite helpful to illustrate their relationship, makes it hard to identify and distinguish between control structures in flowcharts.

The control structures presented here are those used by algorithms for single computers. Modern microprocessors come with multiple cores that can execute operations in parallel. People, too, can compute in parallel, especially when they are in a team. To make use of parallelism, an algorithm needs control structures that are specifically dedicated for this purpose. For example, we could write *walk* || *chew gum* to instruct somebody to walk and chew gum at the same time. This is different from *walk*; *chew gum*, which means first walk and then chew gum.

Parallel composition is useful when two results that do not depend on each other are needed by another computation. For example, Sherlock Holmes and Watson often split their investigative work in solving a crime. On the other hand, one cannot get up and take a shower at the same time. Those two actions must be executed strictly in sequence (and the order matters).

Related to parallel computing is distributed computing, in which computation happens through communication among interacting agents. For example, when Phil Connors and his team create a report about the groundhog's prognostication, they need to synchronize the operation of the camera with Phil Connors's talking. An algorithm to describe this coordination requires its own control structures, in particular, for sending and receiving messages.

In general, any domain-specific language, that is, a language for a specialized application area, may have its own control structures. For example, music notation contains control structures for repetition and jumps, and languages for recipes contain constructs for choice that allow for the creation of variety in recipes. Control structures are the glue to connect primitive operations into larger algorithms for describing meaningful computations.

# A Loop Is a Loop Is a Loop

In his attempt to escape the Groundhog Day loop, Phil Connors is effectively trying to discover its termination condition. This is a rather unusual way to deal with algorithms in general, or loops in particular. Typically, we express an algorithm and execute it to achieve a desired computation. In contrast, Phil Connors is part of a computation whose describing algorithm he doesn't know. In his search for an action that will turn the termination condition true, he is trying to reverse-engineer the algorithm.

Loops and their termination play an important role in computation. Loops (and recursion) are arguably the most important control structures, since they get computation off the ground. Without loops we can only describe computations with a fixed number of steps, which is limiting and misses out on the most interesting computations.

Given the importance of loops, it comes as no surprise that there are different ways to describe loops. The loop schema we have used so far, **repeat** *step* **until** *condition*, is called a *repeat loop*. It has the property that the loop body will be executed at least once, no matter what the termination condition is. On the other hand, a *while loop* executes the body only if its condition is true, and thus it may not execute it at all. A while loop has the following form:

> **while** *condition* **do** *step*

Even though both loops are controlled by a condition, the role of the condition is different in each loop. Whereas the condition controls the exit of a repeat loop, it controls the (re-)entry of a while loop. In other words, if the condition is true, the repeat loop ends, whereas the while loop continues; if the condition is false, the repeat loop continues, whereas the while loop ends.[6] This difference is also highlighted by the flowchart notation for the two loops, shown in figure 10.2.

Despite their apparently different behaviors, one can express a repeat loop using a while loop, and vice versa. For this, one has to negate the condition, that is, transform the condition so that it is true in exactly those cases when the original condition is false. For example, the termination condition for the Groundhog Day repeat loop, "being a good person," becomes the entry condition "not being a good person" or "being a bad person" for the corresponding while loop. Moreover, one must be careful to ensure the same number of iterations. For example, the repeat loop lets Phil Connors experience Groundhog Day at least once, no matter what, whereas the while loop does that only if he is a bad person. Since this is the case in the story, both loops behave the same.

The language representation lets us express the equivalence between the loops more formally through a simple equation:

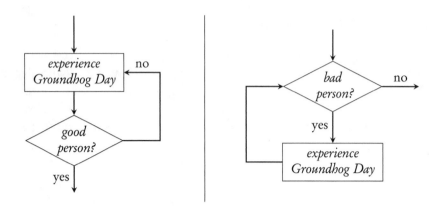

**Figure 10.2**  Flowchart notation illustrating the different behavior of repeat and while loops. *Left:* Flowchart of a repeat loop. *Right:* Flowchart of a while loop.

**repeat** *step* **until** *condition*  =  *step*; **while** *not condition* **do** *step*

Again, the initial *step* before the while loop is required because its body might not be executed at all, unlike the body of the repeat loop, which is executed at least once. The difference between the two loops sometimes really matters. Consider, for example, Hansel and Gretel's algorithm. Expressed as a repeat loop, it reads as follows:

**repeat** *find pebble* **until** *at home*

The problem with this algorithm is that if Hansel and Gretel executed this algorithm when they were already at home, the loop would never terminate, since they could not find a pebble. Humans would never do such a silly thing and instead abort the loop, but a strict adherence to the algorithm would lead to a nonterminating computation.

Yet another description of loops can be achieved using recursion. I explain recursion in detail in chapter 12, but the basic idea is easy to grasp. (In fact, recursion was described in connection with divide-and-conquer algorithms in chapter 6). For a recursive description of an algorithm, we first need to assign it a name, then use that name in its own definition. The Groundhog Day loop can thus be described as follows:

*GroundhogDay = experience the day*; **if** *good person?* **then** *do nothing* **else** *GroundhogDay*

This definition effectively emulates a repeat loop: after living through the day, the conditional checks the termination condition. If it is false, the computation simply terminates by doing nothing. Otherwise, the algorithm is executed again. The recursive execution of the algorithm is like a jump to the beginning of the sequence and triggers the reexecution of the loop.

All the different loop descriptions encountered so far (repeat, while, and recursion) have in common that their termination is controlled by a condition that is reevaluated before or after each execution of the body. The termination of the loop depends on the body to have an effect that ultimately makes the termination condition true (or the entry condition false, in the case of a while loop). This means that it is not known in advance how many iterations a loop will go through; it is not even clear that any such loop will terminate at all. This uncertainty is actually an important part of the Groundhog Day loop that Phil Connors experiences.

For some computations described by loops, however, it is clear how many times the loop should be executed. For example, if the task is to compute the square of the first ten natural numbers, it is clear that this computation can be achieved by a loop that repeats the squaring operation exactly ten times. Or, recall the algorithm to fold a piece of paper to fit into an envelope, which is described by a loop that is executed exactly twice. For cases like these, we employ *for loops*, which have the following general form:[7]

**for** *number* **times do** *step*

Using this schema, the paper-folding loop would be expressed as **for 2 times do** *fold*. The advantage of a for loop is that it is absolutely clear even before it is executed how many iterations will be performed. This is not the case for the other loops because one finds out only when executing the loop. This is an immensely important difference, since the for loop is guaranteed to terminate, while the other loops may run forever (see chapter 11).

Closely related is the question of the runtime of loops. It is clear that a loop that is executed, say, 100 times takes at least 100 steps. In other words, a loop is linear in the number of its iterations, and this is the case for every kind of loop. In addition to the number of iterations we also have to consider the runtime of the loop's body. The runtime of a loop is the number of its iterations times the runtime of the body. For example, selection sort is a loop whose body consists of finding a minimum in a list. The loop is linear in the size of the list, and the body takes, on average, time proportional to half of the list length. Therefore, the runtime of selection sort is quadratic in the size of the list.

Given that a for loop seems to behave so much more predictably than all the other kinds of loops, why not use for loops exclusively? The reason is that for loops are less expressive than while loops and repeat loops (and recursion), that is, there are problems that can be solved using a while loop or a repeat loop that can't be solved by a for loop.

The Groundhog Day loop is an example where it is not known at the beginning (at least, not to Phil Connors) how many iterations it will take. It is easy to see that any for loop can be represented by a while (or repeat) loop by explicitly maintaining the for loop counter, but the reverse is not true because one cannot immediately see how many iterations a while loop or a repeat loop needs before it terminates.

Predictability has its price. While uncertainty about the duration or outcome of adventures is welcome, we would rather know in advance how long a computation takes before we use it and rely on it—in particular, if it might run forever.

# Stop at Nothing

After you've folded your letters and put them into envelopes, it is time to welcome your new colleague who recently moved into an office one floor above you. Your walk to her office is the result of executing an algorithm that repeats taking steps until you have reached her office. But what if you don't know the exact location of her office? In that case, you have to walk around the floor and try to find her name on the office door. But what if her start date was pushed back and she hasn't even moved in yet? In that case, your simple algorithm that takes steps until the target office is reached won't terminate; rather, it will continue forever.

Of course, you wouldn't actually do that. You would execute a different algorithm, which, after searching the whole floor (maybe repeatedly, just to be sure), would abandon the search and lead back to your own office. This algorithm has a more sophisticated termination condition. It would not require only finding the office but would also allow for termination after a certain time.

Loops that do not terminate seem like a silly idea. Although some computations are the result of executing a loop without a termination condition (for instance, a web service or even a simple timer or counter), a computation to produce one fixed result would only use loops that are intended to terminate because a nonterminating loop would prevent the result from being constructed.

In general, algorithms are expected to terminate because otherwise they would not be an effective method for solving problems. It would therefore be helpful if we had a way of telling whether an algorithm terminates when executed. Since the only reason for an algorithm not to terminate is that one of its loops doesn't terminate,[1] judging the termination of an algorithm boils down to determining whether the loops employed by it actually terminate. The different algorithms for folding paper all do in fact terminate. This is clear for the for loop *fold three times*, since it explicitly mentions the number of iterations of the loop. The repeat loop *fold until paper fits* also terminates, but this may not immediately be obvious. Even if we know that each folding step reduces the size of the paper, we also have to assume that folding happens along different axes when needed. In that case, the size of the folded paper must eventually become smaller than that of the envelope, since it halves with every folding step. While it is not clear how many iterations the loop will go through and thus how long the algorithm will take, it is clear that the algorithm terminates eventually.

However, this is not the case for loops in general. The walking loop to find your colleague's office will not terminate if the termination condition is to find an office that doesn't exist. The reason you wouldn't search for a nonexisting office forever is that the office-finding problem is only a small part of a much larger set of goals for your workday, and if the algorithm is unable to solve the subproblem, it will be abandoned, and either a different method will be adopted or the goal will be replaced by another goal. If you consider programming a robot that simply executes the office-finding loop and that does not understand it as part of a bigger mission, the robot would go on forever (or until it runs out of energy or is stopped by a human).

So how can we distinguish between a terminating and a nonterminating loop? As we have seen, the answer is trivial in the case of for loops, which have a fixed number of iterations and thus always terminate. In the case of repeat loops (and while loops) we have to understand the relationship between the termination condition and the steps in the body of the loop. An interesting question to be investigated in chapter 11 is whether there is an algorithm that we can use to determine the termination behavior of loops. The answer may surprise you.

The runtimes of algorithms matter. A linear algorithm is preferable to a quadratic one, and an exponential algorithm is impractical for all but trivial input sizes. However, an exponential algorithm is still better than one that never terminates even for small inputs. The question of termination of an algorithm comes down to the question of termination of loops; it is one of utmost importance. This is also the question that haunts Phil Connors as he desperately tries to identify and satisfy the termination condition of the Groundhog Day loop.

# 11

# Happy Ending
# Not Guaranteed

Loops and recursion inject power into algorithms. Loops enable algorithms to process inputs of arbitrary size and complexity. Without loops, algorithms could deal only with small and simple cases of inputs. Loops get algorithms off the ground. They are to algorithms what wings are to airplanes: without wings, airplanes still can move, but their full transportation potential cannot be realized. Similarly, there are some computations that algorithms can describe without loops, but the full power of computation can be realized only with loops. Such power also needs to be controlled, however. As the *Groundhog Day* story illustrates vividly, a control structure over which one has no control is not a blessing but a curse. Goethe's poem "The Sorcerer's Apprentice" may also come to mind (which may be better known in the United States through the Mickey Mouse sequence in the film *Fantasia*). The key to controlling a loop is to understand the condition that decides when it ends. Phil Connors can eventually end the loop he is in, leading to a happy ending. But this happens more as a coincidence than by following a plan.

Since algorithms are generally expected to terminate, one would like to know before executing an algorithm whether all the loops in it will terminate. Trying to figure this out can be quite a tedious and complicated endeavor, and therefore we ideally would like to delegate this task to an algorithm itself. The quest for an algorithm that can decide whether another algorithm will terminate is a famous problem in computer science called the *halting problem*. This chapter explains and discusses this problem and shows that it is actually unsolvable, which means that no such algorithm can exist. This is a rather surprising fact that reveals a lot about the limitations of algorithms and computation in general.

Even though the events that are unfolding in the *Groundhog Day* story look like a loop, the script of the story does *not* contain a loop. Instead, all repetitions of actions are spelled out in detail. Thus, it is not hard to determine that the story does end. After all, a movie producer must know the length of a movie before starting the project. But we can imagine a version of the story as a play in which the acting is not prescribed but improvised. That description *could* include a loop with a termination condition, but for the improv performance of *Groundhog Day*, it is not clear how long it would take. And if it weren't for the ultimate exhaustion of the actors (and the audience), we wouldn't know in advance if it terminated at all.

## Out of Control

On his second day in Punxsutawney, Phil Connors starts to suspect that he might be reliving the previous day, after he wakes up to the same song on the radio and meets the same people in the same situations. Being deferred by someone on the phone to the next day, he replies:

> *Well, what if there is no tomorrow? There wasn't one today.*
> [Phone disconnects.]

During the many repetitions of Groundhog Day, most events and encounters are identical to the day before. However, some details vary because Phil Connors reacts differently each time. Initially, as he gets used to his new situation, he tries to take advantage of and manipulate people by accumulating information over successive iterations of the Groundhog Day. This is most prominent in his attempt to learn everything about his producer-turned-lover Rita.

His strategy works, in principle at least, because of the fundamentally different way in which he and other people experience the Groundhog Day loop. Most important, while he perceives the repetition of the day, all other people are not aware of it at all. In fact, when he tries to share his plight with others, for example, with Rita or later with a psychiatrist, they think he is crazy. This fact provides him with an important advantage, since, in contrast to other people, he has the ability to remember information that happened in previous iterations.

A similar situation exists in the loops of algorithms. Some things remain constant over different loop iterations while others change. For example, in the loop to find an element in a list (see chapter 5) the list of elements doesn't change, and neither does the element that we are looking for, but the current position in the list and thus the currently inspected element changes in every iteration until the element is found or the end of the list is reached.

A closer look reveals that the loop body and the termination condition have access to the state of the world, also just called *state*. As explained in chapter 10, this access happens through *variables*. The instructions of the loop body can both read the variables and change their values. In contrast, the termination condition can only read the variables to produce a true or false value to end or continue the loop, respectively.

In the element-finding algorithm the state consists of the list to be searched, the element to be found, and the position in the list that is currently being searched. To make the discussion more concrete, I use the following analogy.

Suppose you have taken a picture of a flower on one of your recent hikes and want to know what kind of flower it is. To this end, you want to look it up in a book of plants that contains on each page a description for a particular flower, including a picture. Assuming that the pictures in the book are not given in any particular order, you have to go through all the pages of the book to find the page that describes your flower. To make sure you find an entry for your flower, you have to look at each page until you have found it or exhausted all the pages. A simple method is to start with the first page, then look at the second, and so on.

The state for this search consists of three items: the picture of your flower, the book, and the current page in the book, given, for example, by a bookmark. This state is read by the termination condition, which checks whether the bookmark for the current page has reached the end of the book or whether the picture on the current page shows the same flower as your picture. In either of these two cases, the loop ends, but only in the latter case with a successful search. The loop must also contain an instruction to turn the page if the picture has not been found yet and when there are more pages with pictures to inspect. This step modifies the state of the loop because it changes the current page. This is also the only modification of the state that occurs in the loop.

It is clear that the state modification is critically important for the search algorithm because without turning pages you would not be able to find the picture (unless it happens to be on the first page).

This fact is clear to Phil Connors, and he therefore tries to change things around Punxsutawney to let the Groundhog Day termination condition become true so that he can exit the loop. But not only is the state of the Groundhog Day loop much larger—it includes all the people (and Punxsutawney Phil), their thoughts and attitudes, and so on—it is not even clear what the state consists of. And so it is rather by coincidence that he is able to finally escape the loop.

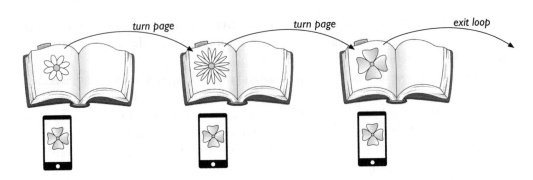

**Figure 11.1** Unfolding a loop means to create a sequence of copies of its body. For each iteration of the loop a separate copy of the loop body is created. The figure shows the state that is modified and how it changes (if at all). If the state never changes so that the termination condition is fulfilled, the sequence becomes infinite.

You may object that the Groundhog Day loop analogy to computing is invalid because the computer that executes it and the rules by which it operates are completely fictional—some kind of metaphysical purgatory engine to produce good people. While the Groundhog Day story is certainly fictional, its loop metaphor is apt. It also illustrates that computation can happen under very different circumstances, with computers that operate under a vast variety of rules. In fact, computation is often used to simulate hypothetical worlds and scenarios. As long as the rules for computation are logical and consistent, there is no limit to the computational scenarios that our imagination can create.

## Are We There Yet?

As mentioned in chapter 1, the description of an algorithm and its execution are two very different things. Loops and their termination behavior bring this issue to the fore, as one may wonder how a finite description of a loop can lead to an infinitely long computation. This phenomenon can be best understood through a method for tracing the execution of a loop called *loop unfolding* (see figure 11.1). In the example of finding a flower picture in a book, the loop body consists of the action to turn the page. Unfolding the loop body means to produce a sequence of "turn page" instructions.

In the case of the Groundhog Day, the unfolding is less obvious, but the idea still applies. Phil Connors lives each day acting according to his goals, guided by his character, and reacting to the encounters he makes. Since we don't have a precise description of this behavior, we can't call it an algorithm, but the execution of the Groundhog Day loop still unfolds the actions from each day into a long sequence that eventually leads to the satisfaction of the termination condition. We cannot pin down a specific action that changed the state so that the termination condition was fulfilled. This is different from the example of finding a picture in a book, where it is clear that turning the page is a necessary action to change the state so that the search algorithm can terminate.

For example, suppose that we alternate between flipping forward and backward a page. While this is changing the state by turning pages, it obviously will prevent the algorithm from terminating (unless the book has only two pages). Of course, few people would do such a thing, but this example illustrates that changes to the state are not enough to ensure the termination of an algorithm. Rather, an algorithm must make the right changes to achieve termination.

A related aspect is that we want the algorithm not only to terminate but also to produce a correct result. Correctness in this example means that we either stop on the page that contains the sought flower (if it is in the book), or we stop on the last page knowing that the flower is not contained in the book. But now consider the following variation of the algorithm, which turns not one single page but two or more pages at a time. In this case, we may miss the picture in the book. The algorithm will still terminate, but when we have reached the last page, we can't be sure that the flower is not contained in the book.

The termination condition of the Groundhog Day loop is Phil Connors's being a good person. Since he doesn't know this, he initially tries out all sorts of actions to change the state to achieve termination. This includes different forms of suicide and even the murder of Punxsutawney Phil—all to no avail. As he realizes that he has no control over the loop, he changes his attitude from cynical to making the best of the day by helping other people. Ultimately, as his transformation into a good person is complete, he can successfully exit the moral loop. And to make the happy ending perfect, Rita reciprocates his love for her.

The task that Phil Connors faces is especially hard, since he is flying blind. He has to satisfy the termination condition of the Groundhog Day loop without even knowing what it is. Moreover, he doesn't know what the underlying state is and how to change it. A truly daunting task. Surely, finding out the termination of an algorithm must be much easier because we can see the termination condition, know what the underlying state is, and can see how the actions in the loop body might change the state.

# No End in Sight

Suppose you are presented with an algorithm and have to decide whether the algorithm is worth running, that is, whether it produces a result in a finite amount of time. How would you go about it? Knowing that the only source of nonterminating behavior is loops, you would first identify all the loops in the algorithm. Then, for each loop you would try to understand the relationship between the termination condition and the instructions of the loop body, because the termination of a loop depends on the termination condition and how the values on which it depends are transformed by the loop body. This analysis will allow you to decide whether a particular loop terminates and whether the algorithm has a chance of terminating. To ensure the termination of the algorithm, you have to perform this analysis for each loop in the algorithm.

Since termination is such an important property of algorithms—it separates algorithms that actually solve a problem from those that don't—it would be nice to know the termination property for any algorithm that one may want to use. However, performing a termination analysis for an algorithm is not an easy task, and it might take a considerable amount of time to carry out. Thus, we are tempted to automate this task, that is, to create an algorithm, say, *Halts*, that does the termination analysis automatically. Since we have many other algorithms for analyzing algorithms (for example, for parsing, see chapter 8), this doesn't seem like such an outlandish idea.

Unfortunately, it is impossible to construct the algorithm *Halts*. It is not that this is too difficult at the moment or that computer scientists have not thought about the problem long and hard enough. No, we know that it is impossible *in principle* to craft an algorithm *Halts*. It is impossible now, and it will never be possible. This fact is often referred to as the *unsolvability of the halting problem*. The *halting problem* is a major problem in computer science. It was conceived by Alan Turing in 1936 as an example of an undecidable problem.

But why can't we create the algorithm *Halts*? Since any algorithm to be analyzed by *Halts* is itself given by a finite description, it seems we would have to inspect only a finite number of instructions and how they affect the state that determines the termination condition.

To understand why it is indeed impossible to define *Halts*, let us first construct an algorithm, *Loop*, whose termination behavior is clear (see figure 11.2). *Loop* takes a number as a parameter and assigns it to the variable $x$. Application of *Loop* to the number 1—written as *Loop*(1)—yields a computation that assigns 1 to the variable $x$ and stops, since the termination condition of the repeat loop is true (middle graphic in the figure). Otherwise, for any other number, it loops back to the assignment of the

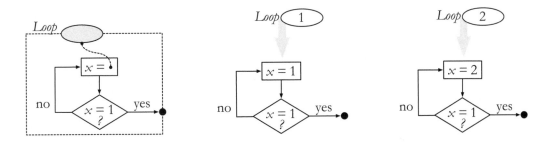

**Figure 11.2**  The algorithm *Loop* stops when called with the number 1 as an argument but loops forever when called with any other argument. *Left:* The definition of the algorithm *Loop*. *Middle:* Application of *Loop* to the number 1. *Right:* Application of *Loop* to the number 2.

parameter to $x$. For instance, application of *Loop* to the number 2, *Loop*(2), yields a computation that assigns 2 to the variable $x$ and loops forever, since the termination condition of the repeat loop is false (right-hand graphic in the figure).

The strategy to show that *Halts* cannot exist is to assume that it does and then demonstrate that this assumption leads to a contradiction. This strategy is called *proof by contradiction* and is widely used in mathematics.

Thus, what would the algorithm *Halts* look like? As illustrated by the algorithm *Loop*, the termination behavior generally depends on the input to an algorithm, which means that *Halts* should have two parameters: one parameter, say, *Alg*, for the algorithm to be examined, and another parameter, say, *Inp*, for the input that the algorithm should be tested with. Thus, the algorithm *Halts* has the structure illustrated in figure 11.3.[1]

Equipped with the algorithm *Halts*, we can define another algorithm, *Selfie*, which leads to a contradiction in the assumption that *Halts* can exist. *Selfie* employs *Halts* in a rather peculiar way: it tries to determine whether an algorithm terminates when executed given its own description as input. In that case, it enters a nonterminating loop. Otherwise, it stops. The definition of *Selfie* is shown in figure 11.4.

It might seem odd to give an algorithm its own description as input, but this is not really such a strange idea. For example, *Loop*(*Loop*), that is, *Loop* applied to itself, would not terminate because *Loop* only terminates for the input 1. What happens if we apply *Halts* to itself? Would *Halts*(*Halts*) terminate? Yes, since *Halts* by assumption says for any algorithm, whether or not it halts, it has to terminate to do this; so it should terminate specifically when applied to itself.

The rationale for the definition of *Selfie* becomes clear when we consider what happens when we execute the algorithm *Selfie* with itself given as input. This, in fact, leads to a paradoxical situation that calls into question the possibility of *Halts*'s existence. We

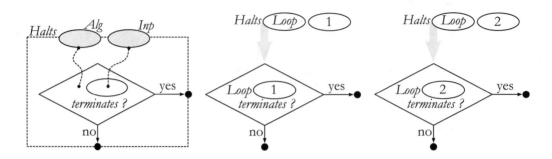

**Figure 11.3** *Left:* The structure of the algorithm *Halts*. It takes two parameters, an algorithm (*Alg*) and its input (*Inp*), and tests whether the algorithm applied to the input *Alg*(*Inp*) terminates. *Middle:* Application of *Halts* to the algorithm *Loop* and number 1, which results in "yes." *Right:* Application of *Halts* to *Loop* and the number 2, which results in "no."

can get a glimpse of what's going on by unfolding the definition of *Selfie* when applied to itself. To do so, we substitute *Selfie* for the parameter *Alg* in its definition. As shown in the middle graphic of figure 11.4, this leads to a loop that terminates when *Selfie* applied to its own definition does *not* halt, because if *Halts*(*Selfie*,*Selfie*) is true, the algorithm loops back to test the condition again, and otherwise stops.

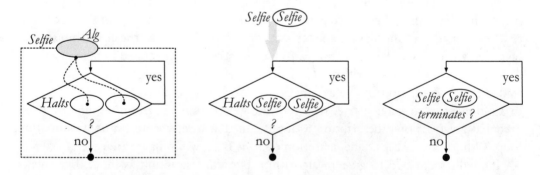

**Figure 11.4** *Left:* The definition of the algorithm *Selfie*. It takes an algorithm (*Alg*) as a parameter and tests whether the algorithm applied to itself terminates. In that case *Selfie* will enter a nonterminating loop. Otherwise, it will stop. *Middle:* Application of *Selfie* to itself leads to a contradiction: If *Selfie* applied to itself terminates, then it goes into a nonterminating loop, that is, it doesn't terminate; if it doesn't terminate, it stops, that is, it terminates. *Right:* Expanding the definition of *Halts* provides a slightly different view of the paradox.

The resulting flowchart describes a computation that seems to behave as follows. If *Selfie* applied to itself halts, it runs forever, whereas if it doesn't halt, it stops. The contradiction may become even more obvious if we replace the call of *Halts* by its definition, as shown in the right graphic in figure 11.4. So, does *Selfie(Selfie)* terminate or not?

Let's assume it does. In that case, the algorithm *Halts*—which we assume can correctly determine whether an algorithm halts on a specific input—will say that *Selfie(Selfie)* halts, but that will cause *Selfie(Selfie)* to select the "yes" branch of the conditional and enter the nonterminating loop. This means, if *Selfie(Selfie)* terminates, it doesn't terminate. So that assumption is clearly wrong. Let's then assume that *Selfie(Selfie)* doesn't terminate. In this case, *Halts* yields false, causing *Selfie(Selfie)* to select the "no" branch of the conditional and halt. This means if *Selfie(Selfie)* doesn't terminate, it terminates. This is wrong as well.

Thus if *Selfie(Selfie)* halts, it runs forever, and if it doesn't halt, it halts—a contradiction in either case. This can't be true. So what went wrong here? Except for standard control structures (loop and conditional), all we have used in constructing the algorithm *Selfie* is the assumption that the algorithm *Halts* can correctly determine the termination behavior of algorithms. Since this assumption has led to a contradiction, it must be wrong. In other words, the algorithm *Halts* cannot exist, because assuming its existence leads to a logical contradiction.

This way of reasoning is reminiscent of logical paradoxes. For example, let's consider the following variation of the well-known barber paradox.[2] Suppose Punxsutawney Phil can see the shadow of only those groundhogs that can't see their own shadow. The question is, Can Punxsutawney Phil see his own shadow? Let's assume that he can. In that case, he does not belong to the groundhogs that can't see their own shadow, but these are the only groundhogs whose shadow he can see. Since he is not one of them, he can't see his own shadow, which is a contradiction to our assumption. So let's assume he can't see his own shadow. But now he is one of those groundhogs whose shadow he can see, again a contradiction to the assumption. So, no matter what we assume, we obtain a contradiction, which means that a groundhog that fits the given description cannot exist. In the same way, there cannot be an algorithm that fits the description of *Halts*.

As with the example of searching for a picture in a book, we can judge the termination behavior of particular algorithms quite well. Doesn't this contradict the fact that the algorithm *Halts* cannot exist? No, it only shows that we can solve the halting problem for particular cases, which doesn't imply that there is a single method for doing so in all cases.

The nonexistence of an algorithm *Halts* is a surprising but also profound insight. It tells us that there are computational problems that *cannot* be solved algorithmically. In other words, there are computational problems that computers cannot solve—ever. Such problems for which no algorithms exist are called *uncomputable* or *undecidable*.[3]

Learning about the existence of undecidable/uncomputable problems might be disappointing if you thought that every mathematical or computational problem could be solved automatically. But maybe there are only a few such cases, and for the majority of problems algorithms do exist? Unfortunately, that is not the case. In fact, the overwhelming majority of problems are undecidable. It is not easy to fathom this point because it involves two different notions of infinity.[4] To visualize the difference, think of a two-dimensional grid that extends infinitely in all directions. Each decidable problem can be placed on one grid point. There are infinitely many grid points, so the number of decidable problems is really large. But the number of undecidable problems is even larger; it is so large that we couldn't place the problems on the grid points. There are so many of them that if we placed them on the plane together with the decidable problems, they would occupy all the space between the grid points. If you consider a small portion of the grid, say, a small square spanned by four grid points, for these four decidable problems, there are infinitely many undecidable problems that fill the space between them.

The fact that most problems cannot be algorithmically solved is certainly sobering news, but it also provides us with deep insight into the fundamental nature of computer science as a discipline. Physics reveals to us important limitations about space, time, and energy. For example, the first law of thermodynamics about the conservation of energy says that energy cannot be created or destroyed; it can only be transformed. Or, according to Einstein's special theory of relativity, information or matter cannot be transmitted faster than the speed of light. Similarly, knowledge about (un)decidable problems shows us the scope and limits of computation. And knowing one's limits is probably as important as knowing one's strengths; in words attributed to Blaise Pascal, "We must learn our limits."

# Further Exploration

The movie *Groundhog Day* has illustrated different aspects of a loop. A crucial feature in the movie is the question of whether the loop will ever end. In the movie, the protagonist Phil Connors tries to find a combination of actions that will end the loop. Similarly, in the movie *Edge of Tomorrow*, an Army public relations officer named Bill Cage, who dies while reporting about an alien invasion of earth, is repeatedly sent back in time to the previous day to relive the experience. In contrast to *Groundhog Day*, where every loop iteration takes exactly one day, later iterations in *Edge of Tomorrow* take Bill Cage further into the day and delay his death as he is trying out alternative actions in every iteration. (The movie is also known under the title *Live. Die. Repeat.*, making the loop algorithm obvious.) This is similar to replaying a video game over and over again, learning from past mistakes and trying to reach a higher level each time. *Dark Souls* is a video game that exploits this phenomenon and makes it a feature of its game play. The novel *Replay*, by Ken Grimwood, also contains characters who relive parts of their lives. However, the relived episodes get shorter and shorter, ending always at the same time and starting closer to the end point. Moreover, the people have no control over their replays. This is also the case for the protagonist in the movie *Source Code*, where a passenger on a commuter train into Chicago is in an eight-minute time loop, trying to prevent a bomb attack. In this story, the protagonist himself has no control over the loop, since it is a computer simulation managed from the outside.

A loop works by changing in each iteration parts of an underlying state until the termination condition for the loop is fulfilled. Relevant for the effect and termination of a loop are only those parts of the state that transcend each iteration. In the case of *Groundhog Day*, the state that can be changed is only the person Phil Connors. Everything else (the physical surroundings, the memories of other people, etc.) is reset on each iteration and cannot be affected by Phil Connors. Analyzing a story from this perspective helps uncover implicit assumptions about the effect of actions, memories of people, and so on, and thus supports the understanding of the story. It also helps with discovering inconsistencies and plot holes.

When the actions in a loop don't affect the parts of the state that can make the termination condition true, a loop will not terminate. The movie *Triangle* seems essentially to consist of one big nonterminating loop. However, since some of the actors have doppelgängers, the loop structure is actually more intricate and indicates the existence of several interleaved loops. A nonterminating loop is displayed most prominently in the story of Sisyphus. According to Greek mythology, Sisyphus was punished by Zeus by forcing him endlessly to push a boulder up a hill. When he reaches the top of the hill, the boulder rolls down again, and Sisyphus has to begin all over again. The story of Sisyphus is interpreted philosophically in Albert Camus's *The Myth of Sisyphus*, which contemplates how to live in a world that is ultimately devoid of meaning and where no action can have any lasting effects.

# Recursion

---

*Back to the Future*

# Read This Again

You are back in your office and have several phone calls to make. Calling someone is simply a matter of a few clicks on your smartphone, or you might ask an electronic assistant to initiate the call for you. But without a computer to help, you would have to find the number in a phone book. How do you do that? You probably won't start on the first page and search through all the names one by one, that is, you won't treat the phone book as a list. Instead you will probably open the phone book somewhere in the middle and compare the name you are looking for with the one you see. You may get lucky and immediately find the name on the current page. If so, you are done. Otherwise, you will continue your search either before or after the current position, again by opening a page somewhere in the middle of the identified unexplored page range. In other words, you will employ *binary search* to find the phone number. The same algorithm is used to find a word in a printed dictionary or a book among the shelves in a library.

This algorithm, discussed in some detail in chapter 5, is recursive, since it occurs as part of itself. This becomes clear when you try to explain the algorithm to somebody else. After describing the steps of the first round (opening the book, comparing the name, deciding whether to search forward or backward), you need to explain that the same steps have to be repeated again. You could say, for example, "Then repeat these actions." It is the compound noun "these actions" that refers to what needs to be repeated. If we decide to give a name to the whole algorithm, say BinarySearch, then we can actually use this name in the instruction: "Then repeat BinarySearch" to express the repetition in the algorithm. Employing the name BinarySearch in this way results in a definition of the algorithm that uses that name in its own definition, and this is what descriptive recursion is: it uses a name or symbol or some other mechanism to express self-reference, that is, to refer to itself in its definition.

When executed, the algorithm leads to the repetition of a few steps (for example, opening a book on a particular page or comparing names) potentially many times. In this respect, recursion is similar to a loop, which also causes the repetition of the steps of an algorithm. Does it matter whether we employ a loop or recursion in an algorithm? As far as the computation itself is concerned, it doesn't—any computation that is described using recursion can also be represented using loops, and vice versa. However, the understanding of an algorithm is affected by the way it is expressed. In particular, divide-and-conquer problems such as binary search or quicksort are often most easily expressed using recursion because the recursion is not linear, that is, the algorithm is referenced recursively more than once. In contrast, computations that repeat a fixed set of actions until a condition is fulfilled, which corresponds to linear recursion, are often most easily described by loops.

But recursion does not only appear in algorithms as a descriptive phenomenon; sequences of values can themselves be recursive. If you are singing "99 bottles of beer on the wall" while searching the dictionary, this would emphasize the recursive nature of the process. There are two versions of this song, one that stops once you've counted  down to zero, and one that recurses back to 99 and starts all over again. Unlike physical embodiments of recursion, such as the Matryoshka dolls, which always terminate at a certain point, linguistic recursion may go on forever. Binary search does terminate, since sooner or later either the name is found or you run out of pages to search, but never-ending songs, as their name suggests, do not—at least, if understood strictly algorithmically.

Here is an experiment to illustrate this point. See whether you can perform the simple task described in the following sentence:

> Read this sentence again.

If you are reading this sentence now, you didn't follow the instructions of the task; otherwise you wouldn't have come this far. Just as you aborted the fruitless search for your colleague's office, you have made a decision outside of the algorithm (the preceding sentence in this case) to stop executing the algorithm. Just as loops are prone to nontermination, so are recursive descriptions, and detecting nontermination is algorithmically impossible for recursion, as it is for loops.

Chapter 12 explains different forms of recursion using time travel as a metaphor. By taking a close look at paradoxes—in time travel and in recursion—we can better understand what the meaning of a recursive definition is.

# 12

# A Stitch in Time
# Computes Fine

The word *recursion* has two different meanings, which can be a source of confusion about the concept. Since recursion plays an important role in the description of computation, it should be understood well. While recursion in algorithms can be replaced by loops, recursion is actually more fundamental than loops because, in addition to defining computations, it is also used for defining data. The definitions of lists, trees, and grammars all require recursion; there is no alternative version that is based on loops. This means if one had to decide between the two concepts and pick only one, it would have to be recursion, because many data structures depend on it.

Deriving from the Latin verb *recurrere*, which roughly means "run back," the word *recursion* is used to indicate some form of self-similarity or self-reference. These two different meanings lead to different notions of recursion.

Self-similarity can be found in pictures that contain themselves in smaller form, such as the picture of a room that contains a TV that displays the same view of the room, including a smaller version of the TV that shows the room, and so on. In contrast, self-reference occurs when a definition of a concept contains a reference to itself, usually through the use of a name or symbol. As an example consider the definition of *descendant* (which was used as a basis for an algorithm for computing descendants in chapter 4). Your descendants are all your children and the descendants of your children. Here the definition of what your descendants are includes a reference to the word *descendant*.

In this chapter I present different forms of recursion and specifically explain the relationship between the self-similarity and self-reference forms of recursion. I use the movie trilogy *Back to the Future* and the idea of time travel to illustrate several aspects concerning recursion. Time travel can be viewed as a mechanism that works like recursion in describing sequences of events. Starting from the observation that recursive definitions can be understood as time travel instructions, I explain the problem of time paradoxes and how it is related to the question of making sense of recursive definitions through the concept of *fixed points*.

This chapter also points out several features of recursion. For example, the TV room recursion is direct in the sense that the picture of the room is immediately contained as part of itself. Moreover, the recursion is unbounded, that is, the containment goes on forever, so that if we could repeatedly zoom in and expand the TV screen to the size of the picture, we would never reach an end of the containment. This chapter examines examples of indirect and bounded recursions and explores their impact on the concept of recursion.

Finally, I explain the close relationship between loops and recursion by demonstrating how algorithms involving loops, such as Hansel and Gretel's pebble-tracing algorithm, can also be described using recursion. I show that loops and recursion are equivalent in the sense that any algorithm that uses a loop can always be transformed into an algorithm that computes the same result using recursion, and vice versa.

## It's about Time

Like many stories about time travel, the movie trilogy *Back to the Future* employs time travel as a means for solving problems. The general idea is to identify a past event as the cause of a problem in the present and go back in time to change the event, hoping that the ensuing events then unfold differently and avoid the problem. In the *Back to the Future* story, the scientist Doc Brown has invented a time machine in 1985, which lets him and his friend Marty McFly, a high school student, experience a number of adventures. In the first movie, Marty by accident goes back to the year 1955 and interferes with his parents' falling in love, which threatens his and his siblings' existence. He is ultimately able to restore (most of) the course of history and safely return to 1985. In the second movie, Marty, his girlfriend Jennifer, and Doc Brown return from a trip to 2015, in which they had to rectify a problem with Marty and Jennifer's children. They find a dark and violent 1985 in which Biff Tannen, Marty's antagonist from the first movie, has become a rich and powerful man. Biff has murdered Marty's father and married Marty's mother. Biff built his wealth with a sports almanac from 2015 that predicts the outcomes of sports events. He had stolen the almanac from Marty in 2015 and given it to his younger self by traveling to 1955 with the help of the time machine. To restore the reality of 1985 to what it was before they left for 2015, Marty and Doc Brown travel back to 1955 to take the sports almanac away from Biff.

> Doc Brown: *Obviously the time continuum has been disrupted, creating a new temporal event sequence resulting in this alternate reality.*
>
> Marty: *English, Doc!*

All this jumping back and forth in time sounds quite confusing, and Doc Brown has to explain some of the consequences of a planned trip with the time machine to Marty using a drawing on a blackboard, similar to the diagram shown on the right.

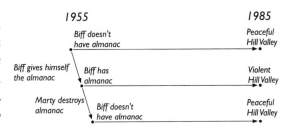

Some of the difficulties in making sense of these and other time travel stories are rooted in our experience of reality as a single stream of events with one past and one future. The possibility of time travel challenges this view and presents the potential for multiple alternative realities. Yet, time travel and alternative realities are not completely foreign to us. First, we all actually travel through time, albeit in a very limited fashion. As Carl Sagan put it, "We're all time travelers—at a rate of exactly one second per second."[1] We also contemplate alternative realities when we are planning ahead and when we reminisce about events in the past, although we never really experience alternative realities.

Time travel is a fascinating topic, but what does it have to do with computation and, in particular, with recursion? As illustrated by the stories and daily activities described so far, a computation corresponds to a sequence of actions taken by a computer (human, machine, or other actor). Therefore, traveling into the past to perform actions corresponds to inserting actions into the stream of actions that lead to the present state of the world. The purpose is to bring the state of the world into a desired shape that allows specific actions to be taken at present.

For example, when Marty, Jennifer, and Doc return from 2015 to 1985, Marty expects to go with Jennifer on a long-planned camping trip. However, the violent state in which they find the world doesn't allow that, and thus they travel into the past and change it by taking the sports almanac away from Biff so that the sequence of actions leading to the present will generate the state they expect. But time travel is not limited to a single step into the past. Right after Marty and Doc Brown have finished their mission of retrieving the sports almanac from Biff, the time machine is struck by lightning and transports Doc into 1885. Marty later finds out that Doc was killed a few days after he had arrived in 1885 by the outlaw Buford "Mad Dog" Tannen. He therefore follows Doc back to 1885, using the time machine that Doc had hidden in an old gold mine in 1885 for Marty to recover in 1955. In 1885 he helps Doc avoid being shot by Buford Tannen and ultimately manages to return to 1985.

Recursive algorithms do something very similar and can be understood as inserting instructions into a stream of instructions. Each step of an algorithm is either some basic instruction, or it can be an instruction to execute another algorithm, which effectively causes the instructions of that algorithm to be inserted into the current sequence of instructions. In the case of recursion, this means that the instructions of the current algorithm itself are inserted where the algorithm is called.

Since the execution of each algorithmic step produces some intermediate value or has some other effect, a recursive execution of an algorithm makes its value or effect available at the place where it is called. In other words, a recursive call of an algorithm can be viewed as an instruction to travel back in time to start the computation that makes the required result available now.

As a first example, let's describe Marty's actions by a recursive algorithm. Specifically, we can define an algorithm *ToDo* through several equations that tell Marty what to do at what time:[2]

> *ToDo*(1985) = *ToDo*(1955); *go camping*
> *ToDo*(1955) = *retrieve sports alamanac*; *ToDo*(1885); *return to 1985*
> *ToDo*(1885) = *help Doc avoid Buford Tannen*; *return to 1985*

We could extend this algorithm to include the time travel to 2015, but the three shown cases suffice to illustrate a number of points about recursion. First, the equation for *ToDo*(1985) reveals that the actions to be taken in 1985 require actions to be taken in 1955, since in order to be able to go camping with Jennifer the world needs to be in a different state. This requirement is expressed using recursion in the algorithm *ToDo*. One of the steps in the algorithm *ToDo* is an execution of *ToDo* itself. Second, the recursive execution *ToDo*(1955) uses a different argument than the equation for *ToDo*(1985), of which it is a part. This means that the recursion does not lead to an exact replication (unlike the picture of the room containing a TV). This is significant for the termination behavior of computations.

Let's consider how the computation unfolds when the algorithm is executed with the argument 1985. The first step of the computation *ToDo*(1985) is the execution of *ToDo*(1955), which means that before Marty can go camping, he has to travel back in time to 1955 to retrieve the sports almanac from Biff. But before he can return to 1985, he has to take the steps described by *ToDo*(1885), that is, he has to travel further back in time, to 1885, to save Doc Brown. After that he returns to 1985, when he finally can go on the long-planned camping trip with his girlfriend.

When we examine the third equation carefully, we observe something peculiar. Instead of returning to 1955, the time Marty came from when the computation $ToDo(1885)$ was started, the algorithm directly returns to 1985. This is what actually happens in the third *Back to the Future* movie. This makes a lot of sense, because jumping back to 1955, only to then directly jump back to 1985 would not be very useful. (Most people prefer direct flights over layovers.)

However, this behavior is not how recursion typically works. When a recursive computation is completed, it automatically returns to the point where it left off, and the computation then continues right after it. In this example, it would have meant the jump to 1885 returning to 1955. The reason for this behavior is that the recursive computation generally doesn't know how the computation is being continued, and thus the safe thing to do is to return to the point of departure in order to not miss anything important, even though in this particular case, since the next step is to return to 1985, the direct jump is fine. Whether there are two consecutive jumps or just a single one is a matter of efficiency. In *Back to the Future* this really matters because the flux capacitor that makes time travel possible in this story requires a lot of energy for each time jump. Doc Brown laments in 1955 about his car design from 1985:

> *How could I have been so careless! 1.21 gigawatts! Tom* [Thomas Edison], *how am I gonna generate that kind of power? It can't be done, it can't!*

## No Matter When

To use Doc Brown's time machine one needs to provide the exact target date and time of the time travel. However, since the purpose of time travel is to change the causal chain of events, the exact date/time doesn't really matter as long as one arrives before the event that is to be changed. Assuming that we have a table containing the dates/times for all the events we are interested in changing, we could express the *ToDo* algorithm differently, employing intended causal changes instead of explicit time jumps. In fact, the algorithmic style in *ToDo* of using direct jumps is quite old. It is how low-level languages for programming microprocessors operate, namely, by labeling pieces of code and then using jump instructions to move between pieces of code. All the control structures discussed in chapter 10 can be realized using such jumps. However, programs that employ jumps are difficult to understand and reason about, especially if the jumps are used in a haphazard way, in which case the resulting code is often called spaghetti code. Jumps have therefore been mostly retired as a way of expressing algorithms, even though they are still used in the low-level representation of code that runs on computer hardware. Instead, algorithms employ conditionals, loops, and recursion.

Since explicit jumps are a deprecated control structure, how can we express the *ToDo* algorithm without them? In this case, instead of using specific years for labeling sequences of actions, we can employ names for goals the algorithm is supposed to achieve. When an algorithm is called with a particular goal, we can find the equation for that goal among the equations. Moreover, once a recursive execution is finished, we automatically return to the point where it was started. While the exact years are very important for the movie to establish different cultural contexts, they do not matter for establishing the correct sequence of steps, which only depends on a relative ordering that respects the causal dependencies of the actions. We can therefore replace the algorithm *ToDo* with a new algorithm *Goal*, defined as follows:

*Goal(live now)*      = *Goal(restore world)*; go camping
*Goal(restore world)* = *retrieve sports alamanac*; *Goal(save Doc)*
*Goal(save Doc)*      = *help Doc avoid Buford Tannen*

The computation for this algorithm unfolds in the same way as for the algorithm *ToDo*, except that the times are not made explicit and that the return to 1985 happens in two steps.

## Just in Time

The computation that results from executing the recursive *ToDo* or *Goal* algorithm has an effect on the state of the world and is not directly visible by tracing the steps of the algorithms as they unfold. To illustrate the connection between recursive execution and computation more clearly, let us look at another example and consider a simple algorithm for counting the elements in a list. As a concrete analogy, think of counting the cards in a deck.

This algorithm has to distinguish two cases. First, if the deck is empty, it contains 0 cards. Second, if the deck is not empty, the number of cards can be determined by adding 1 to the number of cards in the deck without the card on top. If we represent the deck of cards as a list data structure, the algorithm has to correspondingly distinguish between an empty and a nonempty list. In the latter case, it adds 1 to the result of applying the algorithm to the list's tail (which is the list without its first element). Since any recursive call to a nonempty list will itself lead to the addition of 1, the algorithm will add as many 1s as there are elements in the list. The algorithm *Count* can be described by the following two equations that deal with the cases empty list and nonempty list:

$$Count(\ ) \qquad = 0$$
$$Count(x{\rightarrow}rest) = Count(rest) + 1$$

The two cases are distinguished by displaying different forms of arguments for *Count* on the left sides of the equation. In the first equation a blank space indicates that this equation applies to empty lists that don't contain any elements. In the second equation the pattern $x{\rightarrow}rest$ represents a nonempty list, where $x$ stands for the first element and *rest* stands for the tail of the list. The definition in this case counts the elements in the list's tail by *Count(rest)* and then adds 1 to the result. This way of selecting between different cases for an algorithm is called *pattern matching*. Pattern matching can often replace the use of conditionals and leads to a clear separation of the different cases to be considered by the algorithm. Pattern matching also provides direct access to parts of the data structure that the algorithm is working on, which sometimes can make definitions shorter. In this case $x$ refers to the first element of the list, but it is not used in the definition on the right side of the equation. But since *rest* names the tail of the list, it can be employed as the argument for the recursive call to *Count*. Another nice benefit of pattern matching is that it clearly separates the recursive from the nonrecursive part in the definition.

The recursive equation for *Count* can be understood as the following hypothetical statement: If we knew the number of elements in the list's tail, the total number of elements could be obtained by simply adding 1 to that number. Imagine somebody had already counted the number of cards in the deck without the top card and had left a sticky note with the number on it. In that case, the total number of cards could be determined by simply adding 1 to the number on the sticky note.

However, since this information is not available, we have to compute it—recursively—by applying *Count* to the tail of the list, *rest*. And here is the connection to time travel. Consider the times when the different computation steps occur. If we want to add 1 now, the computation of *Count(rest)* must already be completed and therefore must have been started sometime in the past. Similarly, if we want to compute the total number of cards immediately, we could have asked somebody else to count the number of cards in the deck without the top card a few minutes ago to have the result available now. Thus we can regard a recursive call of an algorithm as a trip into the past to create computational steps that will be completed in the present so that the remaining operations can be carried out immediately.

To see an example computation of a recursive algorithm, let's count the different things Marty takes with him to 1885, which are cowboy boots (B), a pair of walkie talkies (W), and the hoverboard (H). When we apply *Count* to the list B→W→H, we have to use the second equation, since the list is not empty. To perform this application, we have to match the pattern $x$→*rest* against the list, which causes $x$ to refer to B, and *rest* to refer to W→H. The defining equation for *Count* then instructs to add 1 to the recursive call of *Count* to *rest*:

$$Count(B→W→H) = Count(W→H) + 1$$

In order to carry out this addition, we need the result of *Count*(W→H), which we know to be 2, but the corresponding computation with *Count* must have started earlier if we want to be able to use the result now.

In order to get a more precise understanding of the timing, we assume that a basic computation step, such as adding two numbers, takes one time unit. We can then talk about the duration of a computation in terms of such time units. The start and completion of a computation relative to the present can be expressed as a distance of time units. If we designate the present as time 0, a basic step taken now will be completed at time +1. Similarly, a computation that takes two steps and completes now must have been started at time −2.

It is not obvious how long a recursive computation will take because it very much depends on how often a recursive step occurs, and this depends in general on the input. In the example *Count*, the number of recursions, and thus the runtime, depends on the length of the list. As with algorithms that use loops, the runtime for recursive algorithms can be described only as a function of the size of the input. This observation raises a question for the travel-into-the past view of recursion: How far back in time does the recursive call of *Count* have to travel to complete its work just in time and deliver its result for the addition? It seems that we have to travel far enough back into the past to have enough time for all the required expansions and additions, but since we don't know the length of the list, we don't know how far back we should go.

Fortunately, we don't have to know the size of the input to employ time travel effectively. The key observation is that it is sufficient to start a recursive computation only one time unit into the past, because no matter how long a recursive computation takes, any additional time that would be required to execute further recursive computations is gained by sending the corresponding recursive calls even further into the past. How this works is illustrated in figure 12.1.

As shown, the execution of *Count*(B→W→H) generates the computation of *Count*(W→H) + 1. Once the recursive computation is completed, *Count* takes exactly one step to add 1 to result of the recursive call, and we have the final result 3 available at time +1. To have the result of a recursive call available at some specific time, it is sufficient to start the computation one time unit earlier. For example, to obtain the value

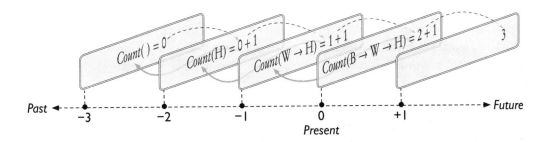

**Figure 12.1** Recursively counting the number of elements in a list by traveling into the past. The execution of the algorithm *Count* on a nonempty list triggers a computation that adds 1 to the result of the computation of *Count* for the list's tail. Executing the computation of the tail one step in the past makes its result available in the present, and the result of the addition will be available one step in the future. Executing *Count* on a nonempty list in the past leads to a further execution of *Count* even further back in the past.

of *Count*(W→H) in the present, that is, at time 0, we need to send the computation only one time unit into the past. As shown in the figure, this computation results in the expression $1 + 1$ at time −1, which evaluates then in one step to 2 at time 0, exactly when it's needed. And how is it possible for *Count*(W→H) to produce $1 + 1$ instantaneously? This is achieved, again, by sending the involved recursive call *Count*(H) one step into the past, that is, to time −2, where it produces the expression $0 + 1$, which also evaluates in one step and makes its result 1 available one time unit later at time −1. The 0 in the expression is the result of the call *Count*( ) that was sent back to time −3. Altogether we can see that by repeatedly starting recursive computations in the past, we can finish the original computation only 1 time unit into the future. This is true regardless of how long the list is; a longer list would simply generate more time travel further back in time.

Note that the time travel analogy might make recursion look more complicated than it really is. When a recursive algorithm is executed by a computer, no timing tricks and fancy scheduling are required. This was evident with binary search in chapter 4 and the quicksort and mergesort algorithms in chapter 6.

The time travel analogy illustrates two forms of recursion and how they are related. On the one hand, algorithms such as *Goal* or *Count* employ recursion in their definitions through self-reference. I call this form of recursion *descriptive*, since the recursion occurs in the description of the algorithm. On the other hand, when a recursive algorithm is executed, the resulting sequence of similar events or computations comprises instantiations of the recursive description with different values used for the parameters. I call this form of recursion *unfolded*. As figure 12.1 illustrates, the repeated expansion of recursive algorithm applications transforms a descriptive recursion into an unfolded recursion. In other words, executing a descriptive recursion (that is, a recursive algorithm) yields a corresponding unfolded recursive computation, a view that can be summarized in the following equation:

Execution(Descriptive Recursion) = Unfolded Recursion

The recursive picture of the room with a TV showing this room is an example of an unfolded recursion. Given the above relationship, is there a descriptive recursion of it that, when executed, produces it? Yes. One could consider the instructions to take a still image with a video camera of the room and feed the picture into the TV that is located in the room. Carrying out the instructions would produce the unfolded recursive picture.

In *Back to the Future* the descriptive recursion is captured in the algorithms *ToDo* and *Goal*. In particular, the goals and plans for changing the past are a form of descriptive recursion. And when the plans are executed, the story unfolds into events that are often quite similar to one another, such as the déjà vu cafe/saloon and skateboard/hoverboard scenes.

It is not only fictional characters in time-traveling movies who formulate goals and plans that contemplate changes in the past. In fact, we all sometimes engage in descriptive recursion by asking, What would have happened if I had done that differently? However, unlike characters in a movie, we cannot execute such plans.

## Fighting Paradoxes with Fixed Points

Time travel is such an intriguing and entertaining subject in part because it can create paradoxes, impossible situations characterized by logical contradictions that something is and at the same time is not. A well-known example is the *grandfather paradox*, referring to a time traveler who goes back in time to kill his own grandfather (before the grandfather has conceived the time traveler's father or mother). This makes the time traveler's own existence impossible, including his time traveling and the killing of the grandfather. The grandfather paradox has been used to argue that time travel into the past is not possible, since it can lead to such logically impossible situations that contradict our understanding of causality. In *Back to the Future II*, Doc Brown warns about the possible consequences should Jennifer encounter her future self:

> *The encounter could create a time paradox, the results of which could cause a chain reaction that would unravel the very fabric of the space-time continuum,*

*and destroy the entire universe! Granted, that's a worst-case scenario. The destruction might in fact be very localized, limited to merely our own galaxy.*

One response to the problem of paradoxes is to assume that it's actually not possible to take actions that will cause a paradox. For example, even if you could travel into the past, it would be impossible for you to kill your grandfather. Concretely, suppose you try to kill your grandfather with a gun. Then maybe you would fail to get hold of a gun, or if you tried to use the gun, it would jam, or your grandfather would dodge the bullet, or even if it hit him, he would only be injured and recover. Maybe the nature of the space-time continuum is such that it permits only actions in the past that are consistent with what is certain to happen in the future.

Does the equivalent of the grandfather paradox exist in the realm of computation? Yes. For example, any nonterminating execution of a recursive algorithm can be considered such a paradox. In the following I explain this view in more detail, using the concept of a *fixed point.*

To produce a paradox, it seems that we need to identify a recursive computation that triggers a trip into the past and changes it so that the triggering computation disappears or becomes impossible. Stopping short of actually going back in time, the closest we can probably get is an algorithm that deletes itself or destroys the computer on which it is running. In such a situation, the execution of the algorithm would simply stop, so there is no real paradox to be resolved in that case. But this example only looks at unfolded recursion. There are many cases of descriptive recursion that are paradoxes. Recall the recursive definition of *Count*, which was given by an equation that said that the number of elements in a list is obtained by adding 1 to the number of elements in the list's tail. There is no paradox here, but suppose we changed the definition slightly by applying *Count* recursively to the whole list and not the list's tail:

$$Count(\underline{list}) = Count(\underline{list}) + 1$$

This seems to be defining the number of elements as one more than the number of elements, a clear contradiction. A similar example is the following equation, which tries to define a number *n* that is 1 larger than itself:

$$n = n + 1$$

Again, this is a contradiction, or paradox, and the equation has no solution. In terms of the time-traveling analogy, the attempt to go back in time to compute a value for *n* or *Count*(<u>list</u>) will not terminate and thus can never reach the point where we could add 1. In other words, there is no way that the desired actions in the past can be carried out to be consistent with the action in the present, which amounts to the paradox that the number of elements in a list should be two different values at the same time.

In reality, apparent paradoxes are often resolved by the constraints of physics. For example, the seemingly infinite recursion in the picture of the room with the TV stops with the resolution of the camera. Once a deeply nested TV picture gets as small as one pixel, the recursion stops and will not present a picture of the room as part of that pixel. Similarly, in the case of audio feedback when the output of an amplifier is input (fed back) to a microphone connected to it, the amplification does not proceed infinitely. The paradox in this case is resolved by the physical limitations of the microphone and amplifier, which are both limited with respect to the amplitude of signals they can handle.

Chapter 9 discussed the fact that languages have semantics and that the semantics of an algorithm expressed in some programming language is a computation that is carried out when the algorithm is executed. From this perspective, the meaning of algorithms that are contradictory and lead to paradoxes is undefined, that is, there is no computation that would do what the algorithm demands. How can we tell whether a recursive algorithm is contradictory and entails a paradox?

The example of a recursive number definition can help illuminate the problem. Consider the following equation, which says the number being defined is equal to its own square:

$$n = n \times n$$

This is actually not a contradiction. There are two natural numbers for which the equation is true, namely, 1 and 0. And this is the key to understanding recursive definitions. The defined number is a solution to the equation, that is, it is a number that when substituted for the variable $n$ will yield a true statement and not a contradiction. In the case of this number equation, we obtain, for example, $1 = 1 \times 1$, which is true, so 1 is a solution for that equation. In contrast, the equation $n = n + 1$ does not have a solution. Similarly, the equation $Count(\underline{list}) = Count(\underline{list}) + 1$ does not have a solution either, but the original equation does. In that case, it is a computation that computes the number of elements contained in a list.

An equation that contains the same variable on both sides can be viewed as being defined by a transformation. For example, the equation $n = n + 1$ says that $n$ is defined by adding 1 to itself, or $n = n \times n$ says that $n$ is defined by multiplying it by itself. Any number $n$ that is unaffected by a transformation is called a *fixed point* of that transformation. As the name suggests, the value does not change and remains fixed.

Examples of fixed points that make the term *point* more fitting arise for geometric transformations. Consider, for example, the rotation of a picture around its center. All points change their position except for the center, which stays at its place. The center is a fixed point of the rotation transformation. In fact, the center is the only fixed point of the rotation. Or consider reflecting a picture along one of its diagonals. In this case all of the points on the diagonal are fixed points of the reflection transformation. Finally, shifting a picture to the left does not have any fixed point, since all points are affected. For the number examples, the "adding 1" transformation has no fixed points, whereas the "multiply by itself" transformation has the two fixed points: 1 and 0.

What is the transformation that corresponds to the equation defining *Count*? First, we observe that the changed definition *Count*(*list*) = *Count*(*list*) + 1 is very similar to the definition $n = n+1$ except that it has a parameter. This definition corresponds to the transformation that says *Count* applied to *list* is defined by adding 1 to this application. This transformation, like the one for the equation for $n$, does not have a fixed point. In contrast, the transformation for the original definition *Count*(*x*→*rest*) = *Count*(*rest*)+1 says that *Count* applied to *list* is defined by removing the first element of *list* in that application and then adding 1. This transformation (together with the equation defining the case for the empty list) does have a fixed point, which turns out to be the function that counts the elements in a list.

The meaning of a recursive equation is the fixed point of its underlying transformation—that is, if such a fixed point exists.[3] When the recursive equation describes an algorithm, the fixed point describes a computation that is stable under a transformation that makes it applicable to a large number of cases. The transformation typically adapts the argument of the algorithm, and it might also modify the result of the recursive call. In the case of *Count*, the argument list has its first element removed, and the result is increased by 1. In the case of *Goal*, the recursive equations execute *Goal* with different goals and add other activities that are pertinent to each case.

Viewed from the time-traveling perspective, the fixed point of a recursive algorithm describes a computation whose effects in the past are consistent with those in the present. This is why fixed points are relevant for recursion. Recursive algorithms, like time travelers, must behave properly and avoid paradoxes to be successful. If a recursive algorithm has a fixed point, it denotes a meaningful computation. Otherwise, it amounts to a paradox. However, unlike time travel paradoxes, it doesn't destroy the universe; it simply doesn't compute what you want. Understanding the meaning of a recursive algorithm as a fixed point is not easy. Chapter 13 demonstrates another way of making sense of recursive algorithm descriptions.

# To Loop or Not to Loop

Recursion is a control structure that is equivalent to loops, that is, any loop in an algorithm can be replaced by recursion, and vice versa. In some examples one or the other feels more natural, but this impression is often due to a bias from prior exposure to either control structure. For example, how could one not view Hansel and Gretel's pebble-tracing algorithm as a loop?

Find a pebble not visited before, and go toward it until you are home.

It clearly is an example of a repeat loop. While this is indeed a clear and simple description of the algorithm, the following equivalent recursive version, *FindHomeFrom*, is only slightly longer:[4]

*FindHomeFrom(home) = do nothing*
*FindHomeFrom(forest) = FindHomeFrom(next unvisited pebble)*

Like the other recursive algorithms presented here, *FindHomeFrom* is given by multiple equations that distinguish the different cases to consider by a parameter. In this case, the parameter represents a position from which the algorithm finds the way home, and the two cases are whether the current position of Hansel and Gretel is already home or still in the forest.

The recursive algorithm is arguably a bit more precise than the loop version, since it terminates in case Hansel and Gretel's father leads them into their backyard. In that case Hansel would not drop any pebble, since they never left home. However, the loop algorithm instructs them to find a pebble, which would lead to a nonterminating computation. This is not a problem with loops per se, but rather a consequence of using a repeat loop to describe the algorithm where a while loop, "While you are not home, find a pebble not visited before, and go toward it," would have been more appropriate because it tests the termination condition before executing the body of the loop.

The recursive formulation illustrates how a loop can be expressed using recursion. First, the two outcomes of the termination condition (having reached home or still being in the forest) are represented explicitly as parameters of equations. Second, the loop's body becomes part of the equation whose parameter represents the nonterminating case (here, the position being in the forest). Third, the continuation of the loop is expressed as a recursive execution of the algorithm with an appropriately changed argument (here the position of the next unvisited pebble).

I have shown a recursive version of the Groundhog Day loop in chapter 10 using a conditional. Using equations and pattern matching we can also express the Groundhog Day loop in the following way:

*GroundhogDay(true) = do nothing*
*GroundhogDay(false) = experience the day; GroundhogDay(good person?)*

Compared with the loop **repeat** *experience the day* **until** *good person*, this seems to be more complicated. But it would be incorrect to conclude that loops are always easier to program with than recursion. Recursion is particularly well suited for problems that can be decomposed into subproblems (see divide-and-conquer algorithms in chapter 6). Recursive algorithms for those problems are often simpler and clearer than their loop-based counterparts. It is an instructive exercise to try to implement an algorithm such as quicksort *without* recursion to appreciate this point.

## The Many Faces of Recursion

Recursion is often portrayed as being mysterious and difficult to use, which is regrettable, since such a reputation is undeserved. Much of the confusion about recursion can be resolved by contemplating the different aspects of recursion and how they are related. We can distinguish different forms of recursion according to a number of categories, such as the following:[5]

- Execution: unfolded vs. descriptive
- Termination: bounded vs. unbounded
- Reach: direct vs. indirect

I have already discussed the difference between unfolded and descriptive recursion and the way they are related through computation. Recall that the execution of a descriptive recursion produces an unfolded recursion, which can be helpful in making sense of a recursive situation. On the one hand, when confronted with an unfolded recursion, one can try to think of the descriptive recursion which, when executed, would result in the unfolded recursion. The descriptive recursion can often provide a compact characterization of the situation, particularly when the recursion is also unbounded. On the other hand, given a descriptive recursion, it can often be helpful to execute the definition to see the unfolded version, especially in cases when the recursion has a more complicated form, such as when it involves multiple recursive occurrences. For the picture containing the TV example, what would the result be if one added a second camera and a second TV so that the cameras could record each other's projected picture plus both TV pictures? Seeing how the descriptive recursion produces the unfolded recursion helps with making sense of recursion.

A bounded recursion is one that terminates. Only for unfolded recursion does it make sense to distinguish between bounded and unbounded recursion. However, we can ask what the requirements for descriptive recursion are to produce bounded recursion. One condition is that the description of the recursion must contain some part that does not itself invoke recursion, such as the definitions for *Goal*(*save Doc*) or *Count*( ). Such equations are called *base cases*. While a base case is always required to end the recursion, it is not a guarantee for termination because the recursive case(s) could be such that the base case is never reached. Recall the definition *Count*(*list*) = *Count*(*list*) + 1, which will never terminate when applied to a nonempty list, even if it has a base case for the empty list.

Is unbounded recursion useful at all? It would seem that recursive computations that do not terminate could not produce any result and would therefore be meaning-less. This may be so if such computations are considered in isolation, but as components of other computations unbounded recursions can be quite useful. Suppose a computa-tion produces an infinite stream of random numbers. Such a stream can be useful for implementing simulations. As long as only a finite portion of the infinite stream is consumed, the computation can behave well and simply ignore the infinite parts. As another example, consider the following definition of an infinite list of 1s, which says that the list has 1 as its first element and is followed by a list of 1s:

$$Ones = 1 \rightarrow Ones$$

Executing this definition will lead to an infinite sequence of 1s:

$$1 \rightarrow 1 \rightarrow 1 \rightarrow 1 \rightarrow 1 \rightarrow 1 \rightarrow \cdots$$

Like the picture of the room with the TV, this list contains itself as a part. The equation shows this, as does the unfolded list. The infinite list of 1s starts with a 1 and is followed by a list of 1s, which is also infinite.

This view of self-containment also helps to explain self-similarity as a result of re-cursion. If we write the list computed by *Ones* on one line, and the list computed by $1 \rightarrow Ones$ on the line beneath it, we will see two lists that are absolutely identical. Since both lists are infinite, the one on the second line does not contain an additional element.

Unbounded recursion can also be found in music, as in never-ending songs ("99 bottles of beer on the wall" and the like) or the drawings of M. C. Escher, such as "Drawing Hands" and "Print Gallery."[6] The work "Drawing Hands" shows one hand drawing a second hand, which in turn draws the first hand. There is no base case, and the recursion does not end. Similarly, "Print Gallery" displays a nonterminating recursion. It is the picture of a town with a gallery in which a man looks at a picture of that same town that includes him in the gallery looking at the picture.

The two Escher drawings illustrate the difference between direct and indirect re-cursion. In "Drawing Hands" the recursion is indirect, since instead of drawing itself, each hand draws a different hand—the one by which it is drawn. In contrast, the "Print Gallery" picture contains itself directly, since it immediately shows the town with the print gallery in which that man looks at the picture. "Drawing Hands" also demonstrates that indirect recursion does not guarantee termination. This situation is similar to that for base cases: they are required for termination but are no guarantee for it.

A popular example of indirect recursion is the definition of the algorithms *Even* and *Odd* to determine whether a number is divisible by 2. The definition of *Even* says that 0 is an even number and any other number is even if its predecessor is odd. In the second equation the definition of *Even* refers to the algorithm *Odd*. The definition of *Odd* says that 0 is not an odd number and any other number is odd if its predecessor is even. In the second equation the definition of *Odd* refers to the algorithm *Even*.

$$Even(0) = true \qquad\qquad Odd(0) = false$$
$$Even(n) = Odd(n-1) \qquad\qquad Odd(n) = Even(n-1)$$

Thus, *Even* refers recursively to itself indirectly through the reference to *Odd* (and vice versa). This can be seen when evaluating a simple example:

$$Even(2) = Odd(2-1) = Odd(1) = Even(1-1) = Even(0) = true$$

We see that the call *Even*(2) is reduced to the call *Even*(0), but only indirectly via *Odd*. The definitions of *Even* and *Odd* are similar to "Drawing Hands" in that each one defines the other. An important difference, however, is that the recursion in the algorithms is bounded (any computation will terminate with one of the base cases),[7] whereas the recursion in the painting is unbounded.

Another example of direct recursion is the following dictionary-style definition of recursion:[8]

Recursion [n], see *Recursion*.

This tongue-in-cheek definition incorporates several essential components of recursive definitions, in particular, the use of what is being defined in its own definition and the fact that this is accomplished with the help of a name. The nontermination and empty meaning of this "definition" also captures the uncanny sensation that recursive definitions sometimes evoke. Chapter 13 presents two methods for unraveling recursive definitions and making sense of them.

# State of the Art

You are done with your work for the day and get back home. Before dinner you have some time to work on your latest sewing project. The quilting pattern you have chosen details the different fabrics and how much of them you need. Since you started the project a few weeks ago, you have bought the fabrics, cut and ironed most of the pieces, and have already begun to sew together some of the quilt blocks.

The quilting pattern with its associated instructions is an algorithm. Since making a quilt is a lot of work and typically can't be finished in one session, the execution of the algorithm must be repeatedly interrupted and continued at a later time. Despite the care and attention it takes to make a quilt, it is surprisingly easy to interrupt quilting and pick it up again at a later time, because the state of the quilting process is perfectly represented at each stage by its current results. If you don't have the fabrics, the next thing to do is buy the fabrics; if you have all the fabrics but don't have the pieces yet, you have to cut the fabrics next; and so on. The situation is similar for other crafting projects, such as building a birdhouse or folding an origami figure, but there are some tasks that require extra effort to represent the state of computation. Suppose, for example, that you are counting the number of baseball cards in a box of collectibles, and you are interrupted by a phone call. In order to continue the counting, you have to make sure to separate the counted items from the yet-to-be-counted ones and to remember the number of items counted so far.

In addition to supporting the interruption of work, intermediate results can serve as an explanation of the computation produced by an algorithm, since they keep track of computational steps and provide a trace of what has been done so far. A trace is given by a sequence of computation states that starts with a simple item (for example, a collection of fabrics in quilting, or a plain sheet of paper in origami) and then contains increasingly more accurate approximations of the final result. Each of the approximations is obtained from a preceding one by performing changes to it as described by the algorithm that defines the computation. The sequence of the initial item, all intermediate steps, and the final result is the trace of the computation. And just as a trace of footsteps in the sand explains the movement of a person and how they got from one place to another, the trace of a computation explains the process of how the initial item was transformed into the final result.

Building a trace is also an effective approach to understanding a recursive description. Even though most quilting patterns are not recursive, we can find some fascinating recursive designs, for example, those that employ Sierpinski triangles. The quilt illustrates nicely the recursion on which it is based. An upright triangle is built of three mostly light-colored upright triangles that enclose one upside-down dark-colored triangle; and an upside-down triangle consists of three upside-down triangles enclosing one upright triangle. Each of the smaller upright triangles is again composed out of three  smaller upright triangles enclosing an upside-down triangle, and so on. Note the similarity to the indirect recursion in Escher's "Drawing Hands" and the *Even* and *Odd* algorithms (see chapter 12).

There are different kinds of traces. In some cases, the algorithm is completely separated from the trace. For example, many assembly descriptions contain numbered steps that describe what to do and then have a separate, correspondingly numbered sequence of pictures that show what the results of the steps are. But there are also traces that consist of pictures containing instructions directly. Both kinds of traces have their strengths and shortcomings, especially when it comes to traces for recursive algorithms. One challenge with executing recursive algorithms is to keep track of all the different executions and their different parameters. For example, the execution of *Count*(B→W→H) leads to three more executions of *Count*, all with different lists as parameters. The approach that keeps instructions as part of traces does this very well and without any additional help. The individual steps of the trace are the only representations of the computation and contain all relevant information to continue the computation. However, instructions within a trace can be confusing, and this method can also lead to huge traces, full of redundancy and containing too many snapshots. In contrast, the approach that keeps instructions separate from traces has to manage the correspondence between algorithm and trace but can produce more succinct traces.

The meaning of an algorithm is given by the set of all computations it can produce.[1] Traces make computations concrete and therefore contribute to the understanding of algorithms. Methods for producing traces are thus important tools for elucidating the relationship between algorithms and their computations.

# 13

# A Matter of
# Interpretation

The focus of chapter 12 was on explaining what recursion is, the different forms of recursion, and how recursion is related to loops. The executions of the algorithms *ToDo* and *Count* demonstrated that the execution of descriptive recursion yields unfolded recursion, revealing that the connection between self-reference and self-similarity is computation. However, we have not yet looked in detail at how recursive computation works.

This chapter illustrates how recursive algorithms can be executed. One intriguing aspect is that the execution of an algorithm leads, through recursion, to many executions of the same algorithm. The dynamic behavior of recursive algorithms can be illustrated in two ways.

First, the use of *substitution* allows the construction of computation traces out of recursive definitions. The substitution of an argument for a parameter is a fundamental activity that is invoked whenever we execute an algorithm. For executing a recursive algorithm, substitution additionally is employed to replace the call of an algorithm by its definition. In this way, substitution can eliminate descriptive recursion and transform it into a trace that can serve as an explanation of a recursive algorithm.

Second, the notion of an *interpreter* provides an alternative approach to explaining recursive algorithms. An interpreter is a specific kind of computer that executes algorithms using a stack data type (see chapter 4) to keep track of recursive (and nonrecursive) calls and multiple copies of arguments that arise as a consequence of recursive algorithm executions. The operation of an interpreter is more complicated than substitution, but it provides an alternative perspective on the execution of recursive algorithms. Moreover, an interpreter can produce traces of computations that are simpler than the substitution-generated ones because they contain only data and no instructions. In addition to explaining how recursion works, these two models help explain one further aspect of recursion, the difference between linear and nonlinear recursion.

## Rewriting History

An algorithm as a tool for solving problems is of interest only if it can solve a number of related problems (see chapter 2). If a specific algorithm could solve only one problem, such as finding the shortest route from your home to work, you could execute the algorithm once and then remember the route and forget the algorithm. If, on the other hand, the algorithm is parameterized and can find shortest routes between different places of interest, it becomes very useful, since it is applicable in many situations.

When an algorithm is executed, the resulting computation works on input values that are *substituted* for the parameters. The getting-up algorithm in chapter 2 consists of the instruction "Wake up at *wake-up-time*." To execute that algorithm, a concrete time value such as 6:30 a.m. must be supplied (for example, by setting the alarm), and so the instruction becomes "Wake up at 6:30 a.m.," obtained by substituting the value 6:30 a.m. for the parameter *wake-up-time* in the algorithm.

The substitution mechanism applies to all algorithms and their parameters: cups of water for making coffee, pebbles for finding a path, weather conditions for weather reports, and so on. Of course, parameter substitution also applies to recursive algorithms. For example, quicksort and mergesort require the list that is to be sorted as input; binary search has two parameters, the item to be found and the data structure (tree or array) to perform the search in; and the algorithm *Count* (see chapter 12) takes the list to be counted as input for its parameter.

In addition, another kind of substitution is at play in the execution of recursive algorithms, namely, the substitution of the definition of an algorithm for its name, for instance, in the demonstration of how *Count* computes the number of items Marty took with him on his trip to 1885. Let's take another look at the equation that defines what the *Count* algorithm does for nonempty lists:

$$Count(x \rightarrow \underline{rest}) = Count(\underline{rest}) + 1$$

First, there is the substitution of the argument list for the parameter. Executing *Count* on the list B→W→H means to substitute the list for the parameter of *Count*. Since the parameter of *Count* is represented in the equation as a pattern that consists of two parts, the process of matching the list against this pattern produces two substitutions, B for $x$ and W→H for *rest*. The substitution affects the right-hand side of the equation, which defines the steps of the algorithm—in this case the execution of the algorithm *Count* on *rest* and the addition of 1 to the resulting number. This leads to the following equation:

$$Count(B{\rightarrow}W{\rightarrow}H) \;=\; Count(W{\rightarrow}H) + 1$$

This equation can be understood as the definition of the algorithm instantiated for a particular example case, but it can also be viewed as a substitution of the call of the algorithm by its definition.

This becomes clearer if we employ the notation for derivations first mentioned in chapter 8. As you may recall, an arrow was used to indicate how a nonterminal grammar symbol is expanded by its defining right-hand side. A sequence of such expansions can be used to derive a string or syntax tree using the grammar rules for a language. We can view the defining equations of a recursive algorithm in the same way as rules for deriving a computation. Using the arrow notation we can rewrite the preceding equation as follows:

$$Count(B{\rightarrow}W{\rightarrow}H) \;\xrightarrow{\;Count_2\;}\; Count(W{\rightarrow}H) + 1$$

The arrow notation emphasizes that *Count*(W→H) + 1 is the result of replacing, or *substituting*, the call of the algorithm *Count* by its definition. The label $Count_2$ above the arrow indicates that we have used the second equation for *Count* to do that. Since the result contains a call of *Count*, we can apply this strategy again and substitute its definition for it, making sure to also substitute the new argument list W→H for the parameter. Again, we have to use the second equation, since the argument list is not empty:

$$Count(B{\rightarrow}W{\rightarrow}H) \;\xrightarrow{\;Count_2\;}\; Count(W{\rightarrow}H)+1 \;\xrightarrow{\;Count_2\;}\; Count(H)+1+1$$

This last step shows that substitutions generally happen within a context that is unaffected by the substitution. In other words, the substitution replaces a part of a bigger expression and makes a change only locally. This is very much like replacing a light bulb. The old light bulb is removed, and in its place a new one is inserted, leaving the lamp and other parts of the environment unchanged. In the example, the substitution of *Count*(H) + 1 for *Count*(W→H) occurs in the context of " + 1." We need two more substitution steps to complete the expansion and remove all recursive occurrences of *Count*:

$$Picture =$$

**Figure 13.1**  Recursive picture definition. A name is given to a picture, which contains the name and thus a reference to itself. The meaning of such a self-referential definition can be obtained by repeatedly substituting a scaled-down copy of the picture for its name, thus producing step-by-step an unfolded recursion.

$$Count(B{\to}W{\to}H) \xrightarrow{\ Count_2\ } Count(W{\to}H) + 1$$
$$\xrightarrow{\ Count_2\ } Count(H) + 1 + 1$$
$$\xrightarrow{\ Count_2\ } Count(\ ) + 1 + 1 + 1$$
$$\xrightarrow{\ Count_1\ } 0 + 1 + 1 + 1$$

Note that the last substitution step employs the first rule for *Count*, which applies to the empty list. Now that we have eliminated all recursion and obtained an arithmetic expression, we can evaluate it and obtain the result.

We can apply the same strategy to the algorithms *ToDo* and *Goal* and use substitution to trace the execution of a recursive time-traveling algorithm, producing a sequence of actions:

$$Goal(\textit{live now})$$
$$\xrightarrow{\ Goal_1\ } Goal(\textit{restore world}); \textit{Go camping}$$
$$\xrightarrow{\ Goal_2\ } \textit{retrieve sports almanac}; Goal(\textit{save Doc}); \textit{go camping}$$
$$\xrightarrow{\ Goal_3\ } \textit{retrieve sports almanac}; \textit{help Doc avoid Buford Tannen}; \textit{go camping}$$

These examples show how the potentially mystifying self-reference in descriptive recursion can be resolved by the repeated substitution of a name by its definition. The repeated substitution of definitions works even for the recursive picture that shows a room containing a TV showing a picture of that room (see figure 13.1).

Here are the first few steps that show how repeated substitution transforms the descriptive recursion into an unfolded one:

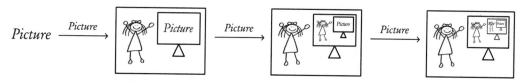

Of course, this substitution process doesn't end, since the recursion is unbounded and has no base case. This situation is similar to the definition of the infinite list of 1s:

$$Ones = 1 \rightarrow Ones$$

When executing this definition, substitution will produce an ever-growing list. In each step, another 1 is added to the list:

$$Ones \xrightarrow{\;Ones\;} 1 \rightarrow Ones \xrightarrow{\;Ones\;} 1 \rightarrow 1 \rightarrow Ones \xrightarrow{\;Ones\;} 1 \rightarrow 1 \rightarrow 1 \rightarrow Ones \cdots$$

The process of repeatedly substituting names by definitions is also called *rewriting*, so when we view Marty's time travels as computations, he is indeed rewriting history.

## A Smaller Footprint

Substitution is a simple mechanism for producing a trace of a computation, which is basically a sequence of snapshots of intermediate results or states. It works for nonrecursive and recursive algorithms alike, but it is particularly useful for recursive algorithms because it eliminates self-reference and systematically turns a descriptive recursion into a corresponding unfolded one. When we are only interested in the result of a computation and not in the intermediate steps, substitution is doing more than is needed, but the value of a substitution trace lies in its ability to provide an explanation of the computation that has taken place. The *Count* trace provides such an example.

However, while a substitution trace can be illuminating, it can also be distracting when it gets too large. Consider again the insertion sort algorithm (see chapter 6). Here is a recursive definition of the algorithm *Isort*, which uses two lists, the list of elements still to be sorted and the list of elements already in sorted order:

$$Isort(\,, list) = list$$
$$Isort(x \rightarrow rest, list) = Isort(rest, Insert(x, list))$$

$$Insert(w,\,) = w$$
$$Insert(w, x \rightarrow rest) = \textbf{if } w \leq x \textbf{ then } w \rightarrow x \rightarrow rest \textbf{ else } x \rightarrow Insert(w, rest)$$

$$Isort(B{\to}W{\to}H,\ ) \xrightarrow{\ Isort_2\ } Isort(W{\to}H, Insert(B, ))$$

$$\xrightarrow{\ Insert_1\ } Isort(W{\to}H, B)$$

$$\xrightarrow{\ Isort_2\ } Isort(H, Insert(W, B))$$

$$\xrightarrow{\ Insert_2\ } Isort(H, \textbf{if } W \le B \textbf{ then } W{\to}B \textbf{ else } B{\to}Insert(W, ))$$

$$\xrightarrow{\ \textbf{else}\ } Isort(H, B{\to}Insert(W, ))$$

$$\xrightarrow{\ Insert_1\ } Isort(H, B{\to}W)$$

$$\xrightarrow{\ Isort_2\ } Isort(\ , Insert(H, B{\to}W))$$

$$\xrightarrow{\ Isort_1\ } Insert(H, B{\to}W)$$

$$\xrightarrow{\ Insert_2\ } \textbf{if } H \le B \textbf{ then } H{\to}B{\to}W \textbf{ else } B{\to}Insert(H, W)$$

$$\xrightarrow{\ \textbf{else}\ } B{\to}Insert(H,W)$$

$$\xrightarrow{\ Insert_2\ } B{\to}(\textbf{if } H \le W \textbf{ then } H{\to}W \textbf{ else } W{\to}Insert(H, rest))$$

$$\xrightarrow{\ \textbf{then}\ } B{\to}H{\to}W$$

**Figure 13.2**    Substitution trace for the execution of insertion sort.

The algorithm *Isort* has two arguments. It traverses its first list and executes the auxiliary algorithm *Insert* for each element of the list. If the list of elements to be sorted is empty, no more sorting is needed, and the second parameter, *list*, contains the final result. Otherwise, the algorithm *Insert* moves an element $w$ from the unsorted list to the correct position in the sorted list. If that list is empty, $w$ alone constitutes the resulting sorted list. Otherwise, *Insert* compares $w$ with the first element ($x$) of the list into which it is to be inserted. If $w$ is smaller than or equal to $x$, the correct position has been found, and $w$ is placed at the beginning of the list. Otherwise, *Insert* keeps $x$ in place and tries to insert $w$ into the remaining list *rest*. Of course, this works only if the list into which it is to be inserted is itself already sorted, which is indeed the case because that list is built exclusively using the *Insert* algorithm.

As figure 13.2 demonstrates, the actual construction of the sorted list takes many steps, and the effect of the different executions of the *Insert* algorithm is partly obscured by the presence of the conditional and the fact that intermediate lists are temporarily represented *twice* in the alternatives of the conditional. While the trace produced by substitution is precise and shows exactly what the algorithm does, it also requires a lot of attention and focus to slog through all the details and to distinguish the data from the instructions.

Another aspect of the substitution approach that can be confusing is that in many cases different substitutions are possible, and while the choice does not generally affect the result, it can affect the size of the trace and its understandability. For example, figure 13.2 shows that the first substitution yields *Isort*(W→H, *Insert*(B, )), to which two substitutions are applicable: we can either use the first equation for *Insert* or the second equation for *Isort*.

Chapter 6 showed a data-only trace to illustrate different sorting algorithms: for each element that was moved, only the unsorted and sorted lists were shown (see illustration of insertion sort in figure 6.2). If we apply the same visualization to the example here, we obtain a trace that is much shorter and more concise than the one in figure 13.2:

| Unsorted List | | Sorted List |
|---|---|---|
| B→W→H | | |
| W→H | | B |
| H | | B→W |
| | | B→H→W |

The data-only trace looks so much simpler because it does not contain any instructions from the algorithm. (This reveals how an interpreter typically works: it keeps the algorithm or program description and the data to be manipulated separate.) Also, the data-only trace shows only the effects of *Isort* on the two lists, leaving out the details of how *Insert* moves elements within the second list. Moreover, the program is represented only once and is not changed at all. When an algorithm is interpreted, a data-only trace presents only the data as it evolves.

Whereas the trace in the substitution approach serves the double duty of tracking the evolution of the data and the progress of the computation, an interpreter uses a stack data type for each of these two tasks. In particular, for a recursive algorithm, an interpreter must keep track for each recursive call where it left off to be able to go back and continue the computation after the recursive call is finished. Since each recursive execution of an algorithm has its own argument, the interpreter also has to be able to maintain multiple versions of parameters.

Both these needs can be fulfilled by storing program addresses and parameter values on a stack. Let's see how this works by executing the algorithm *ToDo*. To facilitate jumps back from recursive calls, we have to mark positions in the algorithm, for which we use numbers. Since the parameter of the algorithm *ToDo* is not used in any of the definitions, we can ignore it and only store positions on the stack. The algorithm

| Current Instruction | Stack | State of the World |
|---|---|---|
| ① *ToDo*(1955) | - | Year: 1985, *Biff has almanac, Mayhem in 1985* |
| ④ *destroy almanac* | ② | Year: 1955, *Biff has almanac, Mayhem in 1985* |
| ⑤ *ToDo*(1885) | ② | Year: 1955, *Doc in danger in 1885* |
| ⑦ *save Doc* | ⑥② | Year: 1885, *Doc in danger in 1885* |
| ⑧ *return* | ⑥② | Year: 1885 |
| ⑥ *return* | ② | Year: 1955 |
| ② *go camping* | - | Year: 1985 |

**Figure 13.3** Interpretation of *ToDo*(1985). If the current instruction is a recursive call, the address following it is remembered on the stack to allow the continuation of the computation after it is completed. This happens whenever a *return* instruction is encountered. After the jump back, the address is removed from the stack.

is reproduced in a slightly modified way, where numbers mark the positions between instructions:

$$ToDo(1985) = {}_①\ ToDo(1955)\ {}_② \text{ go camping } {}_③ \text{ return}$$
$$ToDo(1955) = {}_④ \text{ destroy almanac } {}_⑤\ ToDo(1885)\ {}_⑥ \text{ return}$$
$$ToDo(1885) = {}_⑦ \text{ save Doc } {}_⑧ \text{ return}$$

An interpreter executes an algorithm applied to an argument such as *ToDo*(1985) by performing the instructions one by one and by keeping addresses to jump back to on a stack. Whenever an instruction is a recursive execution of the algorithm, the address following that instruction is pushed onto the top of the stack before the interpreter jumps to the instruction indicated by the recursive call. In the example, the first instruction is such a jump that causes the following address ② to be pushed onto the stack and makes ④ the next instruction.

This is illustrated in the first two lines of figure 13.3, which shows how the current instruction and the stack evolve during the execution of the algorithm. The second column displays the stack with its top on the left and bottom on the right. The figure also shows part of the world as it is changed through the execution of the instructions, for example, the current year or the possession of the sports almanac. This particular fact about the world changes after Marty has destroyed the sports almanac in 1955. Note, however, that the fact that Doc Brown is in danger is not a consequence of the current algorithm execution. However, changing it is part of the next steps of the algorithm. After traveling to 1885, which causes another return address, ⑥, to be pushed onto the stack, the action to save Doc Brown changes the fact about his being in danger. The next instruction in the algorithm is to return to where the algorithm left off when the recursive jump was made. The target for the return jump is the last address pushed onto the stack and can thus be found on top of the stack. Therefore, the execution of the *return* instruction causes the next instruction to be the instruction at the address ⑥, which is another *return* that also pops the return address off the stack. This reveals the target address for the next *return* instruction, which is ②, the point where Marty and Jennifer can finally go camping.

The *ToDo* example demonstrates how nested calls of an algorithm lead to return addresses being stored on the stack, but it did not require storing parameter values on the stack. To illustrate this aspect of an interpreter, we consider again the algorithm *Isort*, which does require this. However, we don't need to store return addresses because each algorithmic step is given by just one expression, not a sequence of several, as in the case of *ToDo*.

To sort the list of Marty's items, an interpreter starts evaluating the call *Isort*(B→W→H, ) with an empty stack. Matching the arguments against the parameter patterns of *Isort* leads to *bindings*, which are associations of parameter names used in the patterns and values. These bindings are pushed onto the stack, resulting in the stack shown in figure 13.4A. It may seem strange that while the *Isort* algorithm takes two inputs, the application to a nonempty first input produces bindings for three parameters on the stack. This is because the first argument is matched against a pattern, *x*→*rest*, which contains two parameters that have the purpose of splitting the argument list into two parts, the first element and the tail of the list. The first equation only produces a binding for one parameter, because the first input is known to be the empty list and need not be referred to by a name.

After the pattern matching, which produces parameter bindings on the stack, the algorithm instructs to compute *Isort*(*rest*, *Insert*(*x*, *list*)). As in the substitution method, the interpreter now has two possible routes to proceed: either continue with the outer *Isort* call, or first deal with the nested *Insert* call. Most programming languages evaluate arguments before executing an algorithm.[1] Following this strategy, the interpreter evaluates *Insert*(*x*, *list*) before further evaluating the *Isort* call. The values for *x* and *list* can be retrieved from the stack and lead to the evaluation of *Insert*(B, ). This evaluation can be carried out with a separate stack and produces the resulting list B, which means that the evaluation of the *Isort* call becomes *Isort*(*rest*, B).

The interpreter evaluates *Isort*(*rest*, B) with the stack shown in figure 13.4A. First, the value of *rest* is retrieved from the stack, which means that the interpreter actually evaluates the call *Isort*(W→H, B). Then pattern matching produces new bindings for the parameters of *Isort* to be pushed onto the stack, as shown in figure 13.4B.

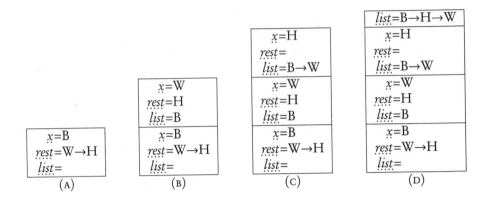

**Figure 13.4** *Snapshots of stack values during the interpretation of Isort(B→W→H, ).*

It is striking that the parameters *x*, *rest*, and *list* appear twice on the stack. This is because the recursive call of *Isort* operates with different arguments for its parameters and thus requires separate storage for them. Once the nested call of *Isort* has been processed by the interpreter, the bindings for the parameters are removed from ("popped off") the stack, and the computation of the previous call of *Isort* can continue, having access to its own arguments.[2]

However, before it can be completed, the call of *Isort* leads again to an execution of the second equation for *Isort*, which prompts the evaluation of *Isort*(*rest*, *Insert*(*x*, *list*)). The bindings are again found on the stack. But since there are multiple bindings available for each parameter name, the question is which of these should be used, and how to find them. It is here where the stack data type comes into play again. Since the parameter values for the latest *Isort* call have been pushed onto the stack most recently, they are found on top of the stack. The resulting call is thus *Isort*(H, *Insert*(W, B)). Since *Insert*(W, B) results in B→W, the next call of *Isort* to be evaluated is *Isort*(H, B→W), which triggers again the second equation for *Isort* and leads to another call *Isort*(*rest*, *Insert*(*x*, *list*)) with the stack shown in figure 13.4C.

Finding the arguments for the parameters on top of the stack, this call leads to evaluating *Isort*( , *Insert*(H,B→W)), which in turn results in *Isort*( , B→H→W) after the evaluation of *Insert*(H, B→W). Since now *Isort*'s first argument is the empty list, the interpreter is given *list* to evaluate by the first equation for *Isort*. The evaluation happens in the context of the stack shown in Figure 13.4D.

At this point, the value for *list* is found on the stack and returned as the final result. Finally, the end of each *Isort* call is accompanied by removing its parameter bindings from the stack, leaving the stack empty. We can observe how a stack grows with each (recursive) call and shrinks after a call is completed.

The two-list trace for insertion sort shown earlier can be systematically reconstructed from the stacks in figure 13.4. In fact, the stack that represents the complete nesting of all *Isort* calls (figure 13.4D) is sufficient for that purpose. Specifically, each group of bindings in the stack produces one step of the trace. Recall that each nonempty input list to *Isort* is split when *Isort* is called to produce the bindings for the two parameters *x* and *rest*. This means that the input list for the first three *Isort* calls is given by the list *x*→*rest*, and the output is given by *list*. For the final call of *Isort*, when the input list is empty, the input list is the empty list, which is not represented by a parameter, and the output list is given by *list*. Thus the bottom entry of the stack yields the pairs of lists B→W→H and the empty list, the second entry yields W→H and B, the third yields H and B→W, and the top entry gives us the empty list (the input list, not bound to a parameter) and B→H→W.

Substitution and interpretation are two methods to understand the execution of algorithms, in particular, of recursive algorithms. Substitution is simpler, since it only works with a trace that is rewritten step-by-step, whereas interpretation employs an auxiliary stack. Substitution mixes code and data, whereas interpretation keeps them cleanly separated, which simplifies the extraction of simple traces. In the case of unbounded recursion, substitution produces something useful, whereas interpretation does not terminate.

## Doppelgängers Get More Done

When Marty goes back to 1955 a second time (after returning with Doc from 2015 to the violent 1985), he exists in 1955 *twice*, because the past he is traveling back to is the past to which he has traveled before (by accident in the first movie). The two Martys don't interact, and they do different things. The first Marty is trying to get his parents to fall in love, whereas the second Marty tries to take the sports almanac away from Biff. Similarly, when old Biff travels from 2015 to 1955 to give his younger self the sports almanac, he exists twice in 1955. In contrast to the two Martys, the two Biffs do interact. The old Biff gives the young Biff the sports almanac. Fortunately, the space-time paradox that could bring about the destruction of the universe doesn't occur.[3] Moreover, the time machine that Marty uses to go back from 1985 to 1955 is the same that old Biff has used to go from 2015 to 1955. Therefore, at the time when Marty observes that old Biff gives young Biff the sports almanac, two copies of the time machine must exist in 1955. In fact, *three* time machines must exist at the same time in 1955 because the first Marty has also come to 1955 with the time machine.

This demonstrates that an inevitable consequence of time travel into the past is the duplication of the time-traveling objects and people—at least, when multiple travels happen to that same time in the past. The situation with recursion is very similar. Since the second equation for *Count* contains only one recursive occurrence of *Count*, it will create when executed only one instance at any time in the past, because each recursive call will travel one time unit into the past from when it occurred. This form of recursion, in which the defined is referred to only once in its definition, is called *linear recursion*. Linear recursion in algorithms leads to isolated occurrences of algorithm calls in the past. Linear recursion can be easily transformed into loops, and it generally does not lead to opportunities for concurrent execution.

In contrast, the case when a definition refers to the defined more than once is called *nonlinear recursion*. Since all the calls happen at the same time, the corresponding executions are also started at the same time in the past and thus occur concurrently. This does not mean that a computer (electronic or human) actually *has* to execute the calls in parallel. It only means that they *could be* executed in parallel. And this is a stunning aspect of well-designed divide-and-conquer algorithms. Not only do they divide the problem quickly so that a problem can be solved with few steps, they also support the parallel execution by many computers.

Quicksort and mergesort are two examples of such algorithms (see chapter 6). The definition of quicksort is as follows. The first equation says that an empty list is already sorted, and the second equation says that to sort a nonempty list one should take all elements from the tail of the list (*rest*) that are smaller than $x$, sort them and put them in front of $x$ and similarly place the result of sorting all larger or equal elements after $x$:

$$Qsort(\,) = $$
$$Qsort(x \rightarrow rest) = Qsort(Smaller(rest, x)) \rightarrow x \rightarrow Qsort(Larger(rest, x))$$

Notice that the second equation reveals the nonlinear recursion of *Qsort*. Quicksort performs best when $x$ repeatedly allows the tail to be split into two sublists of roughly equal size. This may not happen in the worst case, when the list is already (almost) sorted, but quicksort performs very well on average.

It's actually fun to execute quicksort or mergesort with the help of a group of people. To execute quicksort, all people line up in a queue, and the first person starts sorting by applying the second equation and splitting the list of all elements into two sublists depending on whether they are smaller than the first element. She keeps the first element and hands each sublist to a new person from the queue who performs quicksort on the list handed to him and possibly also recruits new people from the queue for the sorting of sublists. A person who is handed an empty list is immediately done and can return that empty list, following the definition of the first equation.[4] Once a person has finished sorting her list, she hands the sorted list back to the person who gave her the list. And everyone who receives a sorted sublist as a result creates his own sorted list by placing the list with the smaller elements before $x$ and the list with the larger elements after $x$. If we stop the recursion when lists have only one element, then we need as many people to sort the list as the list contains elements, because each person hangs on to only one element. This strategy may seem a waste of resources for simply sorting a list, but with ever-decreasing computing costs and increasing computing power, it illustrates the power of divide-and-conquer and shows that many hands make light work.

# Further Exploration

A recursive algorithm for solving a problem tries to first solve the same problem for smaller input. The time travel in *Back to the Future* illustrates how solving a problem in the past is a prerequisite for proceeding in the present. The same situation can be found in the movies *Twelve Monkeys* and *Déjà Vu*, where time travel is employed to solve a problem in the present by first solving a related problem in the past. With a similar premise but a changed perspective, in the *Terminator* movies robots are sent to the present to change reality now to create a different future. The future-to-present time travel also is the basis of the movie *Looper*.

The problem of time paradoxes is often skirted in time travel stories because reading an inconsistent story is not very satisfying. Attempts to deal with paradoxes, and thus with undefined recursions, can be found in Stephen King's *11/22/63*, in which a teacher travels through a time portal back in time to prevent JFK's assassination, which causes reality in the present to break down. A similar story line can also be found in Gregory Benford's *Timescape*.

The idea of making sense of recursive definitions through fixed points is dramatically illustrated in Robert Heinlein's *All You Zombies*, which tells the story of a woman who falls in love with the turned-male version of herself traveling back in time from the future. She gets pregnant, and her baby girl is abducted and brought back in time, where she grows up to be the woman the story starts out with. The interesting aspect is that all the strange events can be reconciled, since the woman is her own mother and father, a fact that amounts to the fixed point of the story's causal constraints. This story has been made into the movie *Predestination*. In the movie *Los Cronoscrímenes* (Timecrimes), the fixed point is obtained by creating doppelgängers of the protagonist.

When recursive definitions are executed, they unfold into nested structures. This is clear for Sierpinski triangle quilts, Matryoshka dolls, or nested TV pictures. But it also happens in stories. Perhaps one of the oldest examples is the collection of stories *One Thousand and One Nights*, also known as *Arabian Nights*. A narrator tells the story of Queen Scheherazade, who tells stories in which people tell stories about people who tell stories, and so on. Douglas Hofstadter's *Gödel, Escher, Bach* contains a dialogue that tells a nested story, which, among other things, illustrates the stack model of recursion. The book contains a lot of material on recursion, including several drawings by M. C. Escher.

David Mitchell's book *Cloud Atlas* consists of several stories that are nested within one another. Nested stories play a central role in the movie *Inception*, where a group of people steal ideas from other people's minds by infiltrating and manipulating their dreams. For a difficult mission, they have to perform their dream manipulation recursively, that is, once being within the dream of their victim, they have to perform the manipulation to the person in the dream.

Mutual recursion occurs in Richard Cowper's *Worlds Apart*, which tells two stories, one of a married school teacher on earth who invents a world with a married couple, and the other of a married man on another planet who invents a story about a married school teacher on earth. A similar story unfolds in the movie *The Frame*, which is about a paramedic who watches a TV show about a thief who himself watches a TV show about the life of the paramedic. Mutual recursion also appears in Lewis Carroll's *Through the Looking-Glass* when Alice encounters a Unicorn and both consider each other fictional creatures.

# Types and Abstraction

---◦○◦---

*Harry Potter*

# Time for Dinner

After finishing the work on your quilt, it is time to prepare dinner. Which silverware you need to set the dinner table depends on what will be served. If you prepare soup, you will use spoons, for spaghetti you will need (also) forks, and for meat you will need both knives and forks. The properties of different dishes call for different features of eating utensils. The shape of the spoon supports carrying liquids, the tines of the fork help with catching and holding on to the spaghetti strands, and the blade of the knife makes it easy to cut the meat into pieces. The rules about when to use spoons, forks, and knives illustrate several important aspects about language.

First, the rules talk about *types* of eating utensils, that is, they do not distinguish between different individual spoons, forks, or knives. All those are grouped together into categories, and the rules talk about arbitrary members of those categories. This is important, since it allows for an economical description that employs as few rules as possible. Suppose the word *fork* were not available to collectively describe all the forks in your kitchen drawer, and instead you had names for each fork, say, Pointy, Spiky, Sharpy, and so on. To express a rule about needing a fork for eating spaghetti, you would need to mention each individual fork. If you had to talk in the same way about spoons, knives, plates, and so on, you would have a hard time coming up with names and remembering them all, and the rules would become quite complicated. If this sounds ridiculous, that's because it is—and it illustrates how important types are in making language effective. The words *soup*, *spaghetti*, and *meat* are also used as types in the rules, since they refer to general food categories, not to a particular dish made at a particular time and place. You may notice that the word *food* is also a type, which encompasses *soup*, *spaghetti*, and *meat*; it is a type at a higher level. This shows that types and individual objects can organize concepts into hierarchies, which make languages more efficient through generalizations. Types are a powerful linguistic tool for organizing knowledge in support of effective reasoning.

Second, the rules express relationships between different types, such as food and eating utensils. Rules put to work the knowledge about objects represented in types.

In particular, they facilitate reasoning about objects and allow us to draw conclusions about objects' behavior. The rule about using a fork to eat spaghetti indicates that using a fork for that purpose will be successful but using a spoon probably won't be. The rule encodes prior experiences about the interaction of objects, and by using types it can represent these experiences in a succinct form.

Third, the rules are predictive, which means that you can pick the silverware and set the table even before the meal is ready and still be certain that the chosen eating utensil will be appropriate for the dish. (It also means that by violating the rules, you may go hungry.) This matters, since it makes the dinner algorithm more efficient: it allows you to set the table while the meal is still cooking. Since the rule is a reflection of previous eating experiences, it saves you from having to find out every time you have soup that a fork or knife won't do the job.

Using a fork or knife to eat soup would be a mistake. This insight can be derived from the rules about proper eating utensils. Since the rules talk about the types of objects, irrespective of which individual spoon or fork or soup is used, any action that violates such a rule is called a *type error*. There are two kinds of type errors. First, there are errors that have failure as an immediate consequence. For example, using a fork to eat soup is such a failure. These errors are real in the sense that they make an intended action, such as eating, impossible. The algorithm gets stuck, and since no progress is possible, it has to be aborted. Second, there are errors that do not lead to failure but describe situations that are nevertheless considered wrong or ill advised. For example, it is possible to use a spoon to drink water, but few people would normally do that, probably because it's inefficient and doesn't provide a satisfying drinking experience. Similarly, while it is not unusual to use a straw for drinking water, this would be rather weird for wine. Again, this is not a mistake that makes the action impossible, but it is nevertheless considered foolish.

In computation, operations are applied to values. With their ability to impose structure, type-based rules about the composition of computation can help make sense of algorithms, predict their behavior, and identify errors in their execution. Just as phone jacks and electrical outlets have different shapes to protect appliances from damage and people from injuries, rules about types in algorithms can prevent computations from causing bad consequences. Chapter 14 examines the magical power of types through some of the adventures of Harry Potter and his friends.

# 14 The Magical Type

Of all the stories in this book, the tale of Harry Potter may be the one most widely known. Among the many factors that contribute to its popularity is that the story revolves around magic, which obeys different laws than the rest of the physical universe. Therefore, these stories must develop rules about what is and what is not possible in the realm of magic and indicate how these rules interact with the ordinary laws of nature. This last aspect is particularly important for the Harry Potter adventures because they, unlike many other stories involving wizards and magicians, take place in present-day England, not in some distant place or time.

If the magic in the *Harry Potter* books were arbitrary and not governed by laws, the stories would quickly become pointless. When readers cannot form reasonable expectations of what happens next or what the unknown cause for a particular event could be, they are less motivated to read on. Rules that capture the laws of nature, the "laws" of magic, and other regularities in our lives are important for understanding events and their causes. They are also essential for planning ahead. These laws are necessarily general and refer to types of things, not individuals, because a law's power lies in its ability to represent a large number of individual cases. Types not only characterize objects but also categorize actions. For example, teleportation, a train ride, or Hansel and Gretel's walk through the forest are all examples of movements. A simple law for movements is that moving something changes its position. Since this is true for any movement and any object, this law is about types, not individuals.

In the realm of computing, laws that describe regularities of computations are called *typing rules*. These constrain the admissible inputs and outputs of algorithms and thereby can find mistakes when executing algorithms. Moreover, since types operate on a fine-grained level, that is, for operations and their arguments in each step of an algorithm, typing rules can be employed to find *type errors* in algorithms. This is such an important task that it is done itself by algorithms that are called *type checkers*. If an algorithm doesn't violate any of the typing rules, it is said to be *type correct*, and its execution is guaranteed to be free of certain errors. Types and typing rules go a long way toward ensuring that algorithms behave as intended, and they can serve as guidelines for building reliable algorithms.

## The Types of Magic and the Magic of Types

The most fascinating aspect of magic is probably that it makes the impossible possible. The transformation of objects or people beyond what is reasonable under natural laws is captivating and stimulates the imagination. The *Harry Potter* books are, of course, full of such examples. However, the employed magic is subject to many restrictions and obeys a number of laws. One reason for limiting the power of the magic is that this makes the stories more mysterious and intriguing. Since not everything logically conceivable is actually possible in the world of Harry Potter, the reader has to wonder how Harry Potter and his friends will be able to master particular challenges in the different adventures. If they could always use some kind of superspell to solve any particular problem, the story would become boring. Since the magic is not all-powerful, a significant part of the *Harry Potter* books is devoted to explaining its rules, including its possibilities and limitations.

To help make sense of the magical world, it is categorized into a number of related concepts. For example, a person who can perform magic is called a wizard (or a witch), whereas an ordinary person who cannot perform magic is called a muggle. Wizards are further distinguished into different professions such as aurors, arithmancers, curse breakers, herbologists, and many others. Magical actions are called spells and are further classified into charms, curses, transfigurations, and other categories. The name assigned to a category is rather arbitrary and doesn't really matter; what is important are the properties and behaviors that all objects in one category have in common. And just as important as the meaning of individual magic categories are the relationships between them. For example, spells can be cast only by wizards, but a spell can affect wizards and muggles alike. The magic in *Harry Potter* can be quite complicated. To effectively cast a spell, a wizard typically needs to employ a wand and has to make an incantation.

However, experienced wizards can also cast nonverbal spells without wands. The effect of a spell is usually temporally bound, and it can also sometimes be protected against through a counterspell. Magic can also be conserved in potions, and this enables even muggles to perform magic if they have access to potions. That magic is not a trivial matter is also reflected in the fact that young wizards and witches have to attend wizarding school for seven years to master the subject.

The classification of people or objects into different categories according to particular properties or abilities applies, of course, not only to magic; it happens in virtually all domains of life. Classification is ubiquitous in science, and it is a basic component of our everyday understanding of the world; we employ it unconsciously in our reasoning all the time. Examples range from rather mundane tasks, such as selecting silverware for dinner or clothes according to the weather, to more abstract realms, such as classifying and reasoning about philosophical and political ideas. The process of classification itself is studied systematically in computer science because it can greatly enhance our understanding of computation and help us create more reliable software in practice.

In computer science, a class of objects that behave in a certain way is called a *type*. We have encountered types already in several different ways. In chapter 4 we saw different *data types* (set, stack, and queue) for storing and maintaining collections of objects. Each such data type has a distinctive way of inserting, retrieving, and removing elements from a collection. For example, a stack retrieves objects in the reverse order in which they were put into the stack (last in, first out), and a queue retrieves them in the order they were entered (first in, first out). Thus, a particular data type encapsulates a specific behavior for manipulating collections of elements. The behavior of a data type makes it suitable to support specific computation tasks. For example, in chapter 13, I used a stack data type to explain how an interpreter works and keeps track of different arguments when algorithms are invoked recursively.

Another use of types is in describing the required or expected input and output for algorithms. For example, the type of an algorithm for adding two numbers can be described as follows:

(*Number, Number*) → *Number*

The type of the algorithm's argument(s) is shown to the left of the arrow and the result type to its right. Thus the type says that the algorithm takes a pair of numbers and produces a number as a result. Note that the type of algorithms for subtracting, multiplying, or any other binary operation on numbers would be the same as that for addition. This shows that a type is not tied to a particular algorithm or computation, which is consistent with types being descriptions of classes of things. In this case, the type describes a wide range of computations.

As another example, consider the getting-up algorithm in chapter 2, which has the parameter _wake-up-time_ to tell the algorithm when to sound the alarm. This parameter needs as input a time value, that is, a pair of numbers indicating the hour and minute of the wake-up time. Moreover, the two numbers cannot be arbitrary: the hour value must be a number between 0 and 23,[1] and the minute value must be a number between 0 and 59. Numbers outside these ranges are meaningless and would cause the algorithm to behave in unexpected ways. We could therefore describe the type of the getting-up algorithm as follows:

> (_Hour, Minute_) → _Alarm_

Here _Hour_ and _Minute_ are types for subsets of numbers as described, and _Alarm_ is a type for alarm behaviors. An alarm behavior is making a particular sound at a specific time, and just as the type _Minute_ contains the numbers 0 through 59, the type _Alarm_ contains $24 \times 60 = 1{,}440$ different alarm behaviors, one for each minute of a day. If the alarm sound is configurable, then the algorithm needs another parameter, which must be reflected in the type as well, and the result type _Alarm_ has to be more general as well and incorporate different sounds.

We can see that the type of an algorithm tells us something about the algorithm. It doesn't tell us precisely what the algorithm does, but it narrows down its functionality. This is often enough to choose between algorithms. One would obviously not use an algorithm for addition for the problem of sounding an alarm at a specific time. Without even looking at the details of the addition and getting-up algorithms, one can tell this already from their different types. The type of an algorithm contains an arrow to separate the type of its arguments (to the left) from the type of its result (to the right). It says that the corresponding computation transforms input of one type into results of the other. The result type can be a value, as in the case of addition, or an effect, as in the case of the getting-up algorithm.

Since spells are transformations too, we can apply types to characterize their effects as well. For example, in the _Harry Potter_ books, objects can be levitated using the Wingardium Leviosa spell, in which the wizard has to move the wand, point it toward the object, and use the incantation "Wingardium Leviosa." Assuming that the types _Object_ and _Levitating_ denote arbitrary and levitating objects, respectively, the type of the spell can be described as follows:

> (_Wand, Incantation, Object_) → _Levitating_

Types are a useful notation to talk and reason about properties of algorithms and computations. The arrow to separate arguments from result types is one critical part of that notation. The use of *type parameters* is another. As an example, consider the sorting algorithms discussed in chapter 6. A sorting algorithm needs as input a list of items, and it produces a list of the same items as a result. Moreover, the items must be comparable in some way, that is, we must be able to determine for two items whether they are equal or whether one is larger than the other. Since numbers are comparable, the following type is a valid type for any sorting algorithm that sorts lists of numbers:

$$List(Number) \rightarrow List(Number)$$

Writing the type for lists of numbers as *List(Number)* indicates that different list types can be obtained by replacing *Number*. For example, since we can also sort textual information, a sorting algorithm can also have the type *List(Text)* → *List(Text)*. To express that sorting algorithms can have a number of different though related types, we can replace any specific item type such as *Number* or *Text* by a type parameter, which can be substituted by a specific type. We can thus express the type of sorting algorithms by the following template, where *comparable* stands for any type whose elements can be compared:[2]

$$List(comparable) \rightarrow List(comparable)$$

Any specific type, such as *List(Number)* → *List(Number)*, can be obtained from this type template by substituting an item type for the type parameter *comparable*.

By attaching a type to the name of an algorithm with a colon, one can assert that the algorithm has that particular type. For example, to assert that the sorting algorithm *Qsort* has this type, we would write the following:

$$Qsort : List(comparable) \rightarrow List(comparable)$$

The *Count* algorithm in chapter 12 also takes a list of items as inputs, but it doesn't require the items to be comparable, and it returns a number as a result. Thus the type of *Count* can be described as follows, where *any* is a type parameter that stands for an arbitrary type:

$$Count : List(any) \rightarrow Number$$

To know the type of something tells us what it can do and what can be done with it. Knowing the types of algorithms helps us select and apply them appropriately. The type information can help with that in several different ways.

First, if we want to execute a particular algorithm, its input type tells us what kind of arguments we need to supply. For example, a spell needs an incantation and a wand to be applied, whereas a potion has to be drunk. It makes no sense to drink a spell or to use an incantation and wand movement on a potion. Similarly, a sorting algorithm such as *Qsort* can be applied to a list, but it makes no sense to apply it to a time value. Without arguments of the required types, an algorithm cannot be executed.

Second, the type of an object tells us what algorithms we can use to transform it. For example, if we are given a list, we know that we can count the items in the list. If the items in the list can be compared, we know that we can also sort the list. An object can be levitated with the Wingardium Leviosa spell. Objects of a specific type can be transformed by any algorithm that has this type as an argument type.

Third, if we have to compute something of a particular type, the result types of algorithms tell us which computations can in principle be used for this task. Together with the types of available arguments, the set of applicable algorithms can be narrowed down further. For example, to levitate an object, the Wingardium Leviosa spell seems to be the right choice. Objects of a desired type can be built only by an algorithm that has the same result type.

The pervasive nature and use of types is due to their power to organize knowledge effectively. Types allow us to abstract from individual examples and reason about situations on a general level. For example, knowing that only a witch or a wizard can fly on a broomstick, we can infer that Harry Potter might be able to fly on a broomstick but his muggle aunt Petunia cannot. Or when Harry uses his invisibility cloak, he relies on its property that everything it covers is invisible. Numerous examples can be found in everyday, nonmagical life, as when we select a specific tool because of the general properties associated with it (screwdrivers, umbrellas, watches, blenders, etc.), or when we predict the outcomes of specific interactions (think of colliding objects, plugging-in an electrical gadget, or how people behave in different roles, such as, customer, patient, parent, and so on).

## Rules Rule

In addition to supporting the efficient derivation of information about particular objects, types enable reasoning about the interaction of objects and thus provide a way to make predictions about the world. This can be achieved through a set of rules, called *typing rules*, that describe whether and how objects of different types can interact. For example, if something fragile drops onto a hard floor, it will likely break. In this case, the prediction can be derived from a rule that invokes several types: the types of fragile and of broken things, the type of accelerated movements, and the type of hard surfaces. The rule says that something belonging to the type of fragile things will likely belong to the type of broken things after it has experienced an accelerated movement against a hard surface. This general rule can be employed to make predictions in many different scenarios involving all kinds of fragile things (eggs, glasses, ice cream cones), hard surfaces (paved roads, brick walls, driveways), and accelerated movements (dropping, throwing). The rule compresses a large set of facts into one compact description. The compression is achieved by using types instead of individual names to represent the pertinent properties.

A typing rule describes the type of an object under certain conditions. The conditions that must be fulfilled for a rule to be applicable are called its *premises*, and the statement about the type of an object that the rule derives from the premises is called its *conclusion*. The rule about the breaking of fragile objects has three premises, namely, that the object is fragile, that it is dropped, and that the surface it lands on is hard. The rule's conclusion is that the object is broken. A typing rule that has only a conclusion but no premises is called an *axiom* to indicate that it is unconditionally true. Examples are "Harry Potter is a wizard," "3 is a number," or "thin glass is fragile."

The identification of types and the assignment of types to objects is a matter of design and is guided by particular situations and purposes. For example, the distinction between muggles and wizards is important in the context of the *Harry Potter* story but is not useful in contexts where magic does not exist. Most rules about objects in everyday life originally evolved to help us with survival in the natural world. They help us to avoid lethal mistakes. With new technology and culture, new rules are required to effectively navigate all areas of modern life like how to operate an elevator or a cell phone or how to sign up for and use health insurance. These examples demonstrate that the design of types and typing rules is an ongoing process driven by specific goals.

The most important and fundamental typing rule for computation is the *application rule*. It relates the type of an algorithm to the type of the argument it is applied to and the type of the result it produces. The rule requires that an algorithm can be applied only to arguments whose type is identical to the algorithm's input type. In that case, the type of the result delivered by the algorithm is the same as the algorithm's output type. Typing rules are often shown by displaying the premises above a horizontal line and the conclusion beneath it. In this style, the rule for applying an algorithm to its arguments is as follows:

$$\frac{Alg : Input \rightarrow Output \qquad Arg : Input}{Alg(Arg) : Output}$$

The first premise of the rule requires an algorithm to have an input and output type. This requirement is closely related to Gamp's Law of Elemental Transfiguration, presented in *Harry Potter and the Deathly Hallows*, which says that food cannot be created out of thin air; it can only be summoned from a different place or enlarged in size. The application rule reflects a fundamental property of algorithms, namely, that they depend on input to produce variable output.

Only if all the premises of a rule are fulfilled can the conclusion of the rule be drawn. For example, an egg dropped onto a driveway will satisfy the rule about the breaking of fragile things, and thus the conclusion that the egg will be broken is warranted. Moreover, since 6 is a valid hour and 30 is a valid minute, and since the argument type of a wake-up algorithm is (*Hour, Minute*), we can apply this algorithm to the two arguments and conclude that the result is a valid behavior of type *Alarm*. An application of a typing rule is obtained by substituting a specific algorithm for *Alg* and argument(s) for *Arg* together with the corresponding types for *Input* and *Output*. The application of the algorithm typing rule to a wake-up algorithm looks as follows:

$$\frac{WakeUp : (Hour, Minute) \rightarrow Alarm \qquad (6, 30) : (Hour, Minute)}{WakeUp(6, 30) : Alarm}$$

Similarly, if *L* is a list of numbers, we can use the rule with the type *List(Number)* → *List(Number)* for *Qsort* to conclude that applying *Qsort* to *L* will produce a list of numbers:

$$\frac{Qsort : List(Number) \rightarrow List(Number) \qquad L : List(Number)}{Qsort(L) : List(Number)}$$

The ability to predict the outcome of situations from just the types of the involved objects is a powerful reasoning mechanism that causes rational people to use a spoon for eating soup or to undress before taking a shower. Types and typing rules provide us with a compact representation of similar objects and events that makes this process efficient. And this does not work just for reasoning about everyday situations but also in domains such as the magic world of Harry Potter or the world of computing.

In the realm of Harry Potter the power of magic overrides many of the laws of the natural world. Therefore, wizards sometimes reason differently about everyday objects and act accordingly. For example, wizards can avoid much of the tedious work that muggles are forced to do, as when Ron Weasley's mother uses magic to aid her with cooking and sweeping. For wizards it simply doesn't make sense to do this by hand. Another example is driving in a regular car, which is shunned by the wizarding community because it isn't economical compared to magical forms of transportation, such as teleportation, floo powder, portkeys, and, of course, flying.

Types of algorithms predict outcomes of computations and can be used to reason about those as well. Suppose you are tasked with sorting a list and you don't know how to do it. You are given three sealed envelopes A, B, and C that each contain a different algorithm. You don't know which algorithm is contained in which envelope, but you know that one of them contains the sorting algorithm. As a hint, the type of each algorithm is written on the outside of each envelope. The envelopes show the following types:

Envelope A: *(Hour, Minute)* → *Alarm*
Envelope B: *List(any)* → *Number*
Envelope C: *List(comparable)* → *List(comparable)*

Which envelope should you pick?

## When Rules Do Not Apply

Types and typing rules provide a framework for reasoning that is very effective when applicable. But there are often situations when the rules don't apply. Whenever one or more of the premises are not satisfied, a rule is not applicable, which means that its conclusion is not valid. For example, a hammer being dropped onto a driveway doesn't satisfy the premise regarding the fragile object, and a scenario in which an egg is dropped into a box of sawdust doesn't satisfy the premise regarding the hard surface. Therefore, in either case the conclusion about the breaking of the object cannot be drawn. Similarly, when Ron Weasley tries to perform the Wingardium Leviosa spell to levitate a feather, the feather doesn't move because his spell incantation is incorrect:

> *"Wingardium Leviosa!" he* [Ron] *shouted, waving his long arms like a windmill. "You're saying it wrong," Harry heard Hermione snap. "It's Wing-gardium Levi-o-sa, make the 'gar' nice and long."*

Since one of the premises of the levitation spell is not fulfilled, the rule doesn't apply, and its conclusion, the levitation of the feather, does not follow.

Encountering a situation in which a typing rule is not applicable does not mean that the rule is wrong; it only means that it is limited in its scope and cannot be used to predict the behavior in the current situation. Moreover, when a rule is not applicable, it does not follow that the conclusion of that rule is definitely false. It could still be true because of other factors that are not covered by the rule. For example, the rule "If it's raining, the driveway is wet" is not applicable when it's sunny. However, the driveway could still be wet if the sprinklers were running. Or, to take an example from *Harry Potter*, even if Ron doesn't perform the Wingardium Leviosa spell correctly, the feather could still start to levitate because somebody else could apply a spell to it simultaneously. Or the dropped hammer might still break when it hits the floor because its handle was already fractured to begin with. Therefore, when a rule is not applicable, no conclusion can be drawn either way.

Thus it may not seem like such a big deal when typing rules don't apply. However, that really depends on how important it is to ensure that a particular conclusion is true. While levitating feathers or the breaking of a dropped object are mere curiosities, there are many situations where the conclusion really matters. Think of all the "famous last word" jokes that play on incorrect conclusions, such as "The red wire is safe to cut," "Nice doggy," "These are the good kind of mushrooms," and so on. For a computation, getting the types correct is similarly important. While seldom lethal, operating on a value of the wrong type will in most cases cause a computation to fail. Here is why. Each step of an algorithm transforms one or more values, and each operation that is applied in this process relies on its arguments to be of a particular type because it is only defined to do something meaningful for such values. Remember, we can't sort a wake-up time, and we can't compute the square root of a list. If any step of an algorithm encounters a value of a type that is not expected, it doesn't know what to do with it and gets stuck. As a consequence, the computation cannot be completed successfully and cannot deliver a meaningful result. In short, the success of a computation depends on submitting only values of correct types to operations.

Therefore, typing rules are a crucial component of computation because they can ensure that operations don't get stuck on wrong values and that the computation as a whole can be completed successfully.[3] Just as typing rules can be used to identify meaningless sentences, such as "Harry Potter drank a spell," they can spot nonsensical applications of algorithms, such as *Qsort*(6:30am). And since an algorithm consists of many steps that involve the application of operations and other algorithms to values, typing rules can be used to identify mistakes within the definition of an algorithm, and they can actively support the construction of type-correct algorithms, a process sometimes called *type-directed programming*.

Typing rules prevent not only impossible applications of operations to values that get stuck but also ones that don't make sense in a certain context. For example, your height and age can be both expressed as numbers, but it doesn't make sense to add these two numbers. The addition makes no sense in this case because the two numbers are representations of different things (see chapter 3), and thus the sum of the two numbers is not a representation of anything and therefore meaningless.[4] We find examples in *Harry Potter* as well. For example, in the game of Quidditch two teams try to score goals by tossing a ball, the quaffle, into one of the opponent team's goal posts. Now this would be rather easy using a teleportation spell, but that would make the game rather boring, and it would undermine the goal of the game, which is to determine the better Quidditch team. Therefore, employing magic other than flying a broomstick is not allowed for the players of the game. Such restrictions are ubiquitous in games. The requirement to follow suit in a card game or move a bishop in chess only diagonally does not reflect the impossibility of playing a different card or moving the bishop in a straight line; it is a restriction in a particular context in support of the goals of the game. Types can be used to track these representations alongside computations to ensure that operations respect the rules of combination for the represented values.

A violation of a typing rule in an algorithm is called a *type error*. It indicates an inconsistency in the combination of operations and values. An algorithm that does not contain any type errors is said to be *type correct*. A type error in an algorithm can have different kinds of effects. First, it can cause the computation to get stuck, which in turn may lead to aborting the computation, potentially followed by reporting an error. The attempt to divide a number by zero typically has such an effect. In *Harry Potter and the Chamber of Secrets*, Ron's wand breaks and causes all his spells to malfunction. For example, the Eat Slugs spell that he casts on Malfoy backfires, and his attempt to transform a rat into a goblet results in a furry cup with a tail. While the exact outcome might be a surprise, the lack of success in Ron's magic was predictable, since his broken wand violates one of the premises of the typing rule for magic. In these cases, the effects of the nonworking magic are immediately visible. Second, a type error might not lead to any immediately noticeable effect, which means the computation continues and eventually finishes. But it does so with a meaningless value and thus ultimately produces an incorrect result. Adding the age and height of a person is such an example.

While an abrupt interruption of a computation without a final result seems bad, a computation that continues but leads to a meaningless result can be much worse. The problem in that case is that one might not recognize that the result is incorrect and base an important decision on that wrong result. An example of this is when Harry Potter mispronounces "Diagon Alley" as "Diagonally" when attempting to travel by floo powder, which causes him to end up incorrectly in Knockturn Alley instead. The travel was not aborted, and the floo powder still worked, but it produced a wrong result. It would have been better for Harry if the trip had simply aborted, because he nearly gets kidnapped and has a run-in with some dark artifacts in the store he ends up in.

## Law Enforcement

Since type correctness is an important prerequisite for the correct functioning of any algorithm, it is a good idea to check for type correctness automatically using an algorithm. Such an algorithm is called a *type checker*. A type checker determines whether the steps in an algorithm conform to the typing rules about control structures, variables, and values. A type checker can spot type errors in an algorithm and thus prevent erroneous computations.

The types in an algorithm can be checked in two different ways. One possibility is to check the types during the execution of the algorithm. This approach is called *dynamic type checking*, since it happens while the dynamic behavior of an algorithm comes into effect. Right before an operation is performed, it is determined whether the types of the arguments match the typing requirements of the operation to be applied. A problem with this approach is that it is not really of any help in case a type error is detected. In most cases, the only possibility is to abort the computation, which can be quite frustrating, in particular, in cases when much of the intended computation has already happened and the algorithm aborts right before the final result is obtained. It would be much better to know ahead of time whether the computation can be successfully completed without encountering a type error and not spend resources on a computation that is doomed to fail.

The alternative approach inspects the algorithm without executing it and checks whether all steps respect the typing rules. The algorithm is then executed only if no type errors are found. In this case, one can be sure that the algorithm will not abort with a type error. This approach is called *static type checking*, since it happens without considering the dynamic behavior of executing an algorithm, and it requires only the static description of the algorithm. Static type checking would have told Ron not to try any magic with his broken wand.

A further advantage of static type checking is that an algorithm needs to be checked only once. After that it can be executed repeatedly for different arguments without any more type checking. Moreover, while dynamic type checking has to check the operations in a loop repeatedly—in fact, as often as the loop is repeated—static type checking has to check any operation only once, which leads to faster execution of the algorithm. In contrast, dynamic type checking must be performed every time an algorithm is executed.

However, dynamic type checking has the advantage that it is generally more precise, because it takes into account the values processed by the algorithm. Whereas static type checking only knows the types of parameters, dynamic type checking knows the concrete values. Static type checking would have prevented Ron from using his broken wand at all, and thus would have prevented any failures, while dynamic type checking lets him try out spells, and succeed and fail in different situations. For example, when Ron tries to transfigure a rat into a cup, he only partly succeeds: the cup still has a tail.

Determining the precise typing behavior of an algorithm is, like determining its termination behavior, an undecidable problem (see chapter 11). Consider, for example, an algorithm in which only the "then" branch of a conditional contains a type error. This algorithm contains a type error only when the condition of the conditional evaluates to *true* and selects that branch. The problem is that figuring out the value of the condition might require an arbitrarily complicated computation (for example, the condition could be a variable whose value is computed in some loop). Since we cannot be sure whether such a computation terminates (since we cannot solve the halting problem), we cannot know in advance whether the condition will be true, and thus we cannot know whether the program will exhibit a type error.

To deal with this inherent inability to predict the behavior of an algorithm, static type checking approximates the types within an algorithm. To avoid computations that could lead to nontermination, static type checking is overcautious and reports a type error whenever there could be one. In the case of the conditional this means that a static type checker would require both alternatives to not contain a type error, since it can't compute the value of the condition. It would thus report a type error even if only one branch of the conditional contained one. Even though the algorithm might not exhibit any type error when executed, a static type checker would flag the algorithm as type-incorrect and not execute it. This is the price to be paid for the safety of static type checking: Some algorithms will be rejected even though they might not actually produce an error when executed.

Static type checking trades immediacy for accuracy. While an error might not necessarily happen later, it could. If the computation is important enough to not risk failure, it is better to fix the potential error in the algorithm before executing it. The cautious approach of static type checking is not unique to computing. There are many other domains in which checks are performed in advance. If you are boarding a plane, you rely on the pilots making sure there is enough fuel on board and that all important systems function. You are expecting static type checking of the rules for a successful flight. Consider the alternative of checking the systems after take-off. Detecting a problem at that time could be too late. Or, if you are to receive a medical procedure or prescription, the doctor should make sure that any contraindication is determined before the treatment to prevent any harm. Static type checking follows the maxim "Better safe than sorry." Following static typing, Ron should not have used the Eat Slugs spell;

because of his broken wand the rule for applying magic is not applicable and foreshadows a mistake during the execution of the spell. In contrast, dynamic typing is a less aggressive approach for enforcing typing rules that doesn't let any opportunity for computation pass, thereby running the risk of encountering errors during the execution of an algorithm. This is what Ron did. He took a chance, and it didn't work.

## Building Code

The violation of a typing rule is a sign that something is wrong. A type error in an algorithm indicates that it probably won't work correctly. Viewed positively, when all parts of an algorithm satisfy the typing rules, then some kinds of mistakes cannot happen, and the algorithm is correct to a certain extent. Of course, the algorithm can still produce incorrect results. For example, if we need an algorithm for adding two numbers, which has the type (*Number, Number*) → *Number*, but we accidentally create an algorithm for subtracting numbers, then this algorithm still has the correct type, but it doesn't compute the right values. Nevertheless, in a type-correct program a large number of errors have been ruled out, and one can be sure that the steps of the algorithm conform to an important level of consistency.

Shielding against incorrect or meaningless computation is an important role of types and typing rules, but it is not the only benefit they offer. Types also act as explanations of the steps of an algorithm. Without understanding the details of every step in an algorithm, we can get a high-level picture of what is being computed when we just look at the types. The ability to differentiate between computations by their types was illustrated by the task of picking the envelope with the right algorithm. The ability of types to summarize a large number of computations provides insights that cannot be gleaned by just looking at a few examples. Thus, types and typing rules also have explanatory value.

To illustrate, let's take another look at the game of Quidditch. The game can be explained without showing an actual game by describing the general rules and the roles of different players. This is, in fact, how Harry learns it from Oliver Wood in *Harry Potter and the Sorcerer's Stone*.[5] The rules of the game constrain the valid actions in the game and define how the score is kept. The important aspect is that the rules of the game are typing rules that use types for the roles of players (such as "seeker") and kinds of objects (such as "quaffle"). While seeing an example game would be helpful, it is not enough to understand the game. In particular, even after having watched many games, someone who doesn't know the rules can be easily surprised. For example, a Quidditch game ends immediately when a seeker catches the Golden Snitch. This may not have occurred in the examples that have been watched, so it would surprise an observer the first time it happened. Other games have special rules that can be surprising, for example, the offside rule in soccer or the en passant move in chess. It is difficult to learn a game by just watching examples, and it can take a very long time for all the rules to be acted out.

Similarly, it can be quite hard to understand what an algorithm does just by watching its inputs being transformed into corresponding outputs. While types are generally not sufficient to precisely describe the effect of an algorithm, they explain some of its behavior on a high level, and they support the understanding of how its parts (the individual steps and control structures) fit and work together.

Types structure the objects of a domain, and typing rules explain how they can be combined in meaningful ways. In computer science, types and typing rules ensure the meaningful interaction of different parts of an algorithm. They are thus important tools for building larger systems out of smaller ones. This is explored in chapter 15.

# At the End of the Day

As a long day of computing comes to an end, you reflect on all that has happened, and you note some of the events in your diary. Getting up in the morning wasn't really different from other days in any way. Nothing extraordinary happened that would warrant mention in the diary. Brushing your teeth a little longer than normal or even running out of toothpaste—these are not events that you would like to be reminded of years from now. The same is true for most of what happened during the day. Since you have breakfast every day and commute to work every workday, starting the diary entry with something like "This was mostly another ordinary workday" implies a standard getting-up and breakfast routine. Specifically, the name *workday* refers to a whole detailed description of getting up, having breakfast, commuting to work, and all the other routines that occur during an ordinary workday.

Assigning a (short) name to a (long) description and then using the name to refer to the description is a form of abstraction. Like representing different cities by the same kind of point on a map, the name *workday* ignores differences between weekdays and regards them as all the same. However, since the points on the map appear at different locations, they are not identical. Similarly, different mentions of *workday* occur at different times, so they are not identical either. The different positions in space and time provide context and additional meaning to references. For example, one city is located by the sea or can be reached by a particular highway, and one workday falls on election day or follows a holiday.

While effective in many situations, a plain name or symbol can sometimes be too abstract a representation. To supply different references with additional information, names and symbols can be extended by parameters. For example, points for representing cities are sometimes parameterized by size or color to distinguish larger from smaller cities. Or the shape of the symbol is varied to distinguish the capitals of states, and so on. Similarly, the name referring to a day can be parameterized. In fact, the name *workday* already distinguishes that day from, say, a holiday, on which you would not commute to work.

The full potential of parameters unfolds when they are referenced in the abbreviated descriptions. For example, suppose you want to add to your diary an entry about an important meeting or your visit to the doctor's office. Like *workday*, the terms *meeting* and *doctor's appointment* are abstractions that stand for a number of things that typically happen during such events. Most likely, in addition to writing that you had an important meeting, you would add whom you met with and what the purpose of the meeting was, and for the doctor's appointment you would probably mention what kind of doctor you had to consult and for what reason. This information would be represented by a parameter for the abstraction and used in its description. Just as when a bakery offers to customize birthday cakes with decorations for name and age, the abstraction *meeting* is extended by the parameters *who* and *purpose*, which then are referred to in the description of the abstraction. When you use an abstraction as in "meeting with Jill about hiring," the parameters are replaced by "Jill" and "hiring," and the description reads as if it were written just for this particular meeting.

Abstractions identify patterns and make them reusable. Through parameters, abstractions can be flexibly adapted to specific situations and still convey a lot of information in a concise form. Assigning a name to an abstraction and identifying its parameters defines its interface, which determines the proper use of the abstraction. Much of what computer scientists do on a daily basis is identifying, creating, and using abstractions to describe and reason about computation. Computer science studies the nature of abstractions and formalizes their definitions and uses to empower programmers and software engineers to develop better software.

In the final chapter of this book I explain what abstractions are and the role they play in computing. Since abstractions play an important role in natural languages and computer science, it is not surprising that stories can explain a lot about computing.

# 15

# A Bird's Eye View: Abstracting from Details

The examples of computation in this book were all rather small, which is good for illustrating concepts and principles, but do they scale up? The question of scalability arises in different places.

First, there is the question of whether algorithms work for large inputs. This problem is addressed by analyzing the runtime and space complexity of algorithms, discussed in the first part of this book, in particular, in chapters 2, 4, 5, 6, and 7. While some algorithms scale quite well (following a path, making coffee, searching, and sorting), others don't (optimizing a lunch selection with a limited budget). As explained in chapter 7, the runtime of exponential algorithms effectively prohibits the solution of some problems.

Second, there is the question of how to create, understand, and maintain large software systems. Designing and writing a small program is relatively easy, but producing large software systems still poses a major challenge for software engineers.

To see what the problem is, imagine a map of the city or country you live in. What would be a good scale? As explained by Lewis Carroll in his last novel *Sylvie and Bruno Concluded*, a scale of one to one is useless since, if the map were spread out, "it would cover the whole country and shut out the sunlight!" Thus any useful map has to be much smaller than what it represents, and it therefore has to omit many details. An important question in creating a map is, What scale is small enough to be manageable yet large enough to represent sufficient detail? Moreover, which details should be ignored and which should be kept? The answer to the latter question often depends on the context in which the map is used. Sometimes we need to see the roads and parking garages; in other situations we're interested in the bike paths and coffee shops. This means that the map should be configurable to individual needs.

Any description that is shorter than what it talks about faces these challenges of finding the right level of generalization and providing means for configuration. Such descriptions are called *abstractions*. Much of computer science is concerned with the question of how to define and effectively use abstractions. Most prominently, an algorithm is an abstraction of many different computations, and its parameters determine what particular computation will unfold when the algorithm is executed. An algorithm manipulates representations, which are also abstractions that preserve details to be exploited by the algorithm and ignore others. The level of abstraction in an algorithm and its arguments are related. Finding the right level of generality for an algorithm often involves a trade-off between generality and efficiency. To handle a wider range of inputs often requires a higher level of abstraction for the inputs, which means the algorithm has fewer details to exploit.

An algorithm is expressed in a language and is executed by a computer. All these concepts make use of abstractions too. And finally, the abstraction from individual computations achieved by algorithms requires abstraction also for the concepts of runtime and space efficiency because an effective characterization of an algorithm's efficiency needs to be independent of the size of the different inputs.

This chapter illustrates that abstraction permeates all major concepts of computer science. I first discuss the issues that arise in defining and using abstractions by contemplating an abstraction for the stories used in this book. Then I explain how abstraction applies to algorithms, representations, runtime, computers, and languages.

## To Make a Long Story Short

A variety of stories were mentioned in this book: a fairy tale, a detective story, an adventure story, a musical fantasy, a romantic comedy, a science fiction comedy, and a fantasy novel. While these stories are all quite different, they do have several things in common. For example, they all center on one or more protagonists who must face and overcome a challenge, and they all have a happy ending. All but one of the stories exist in book form, and all but one involve some form of magic or supernatural force. Even though these brief descriptions omit details from each individual story, they still deliver some information that helps to distinguish stories from, say, sports reports. However, there is a clear trade-off between the level of detail a description reveals and how many examples it applies to. There seems to also be a trade-off between the amount of detail provided and the time required to understand the description because more details lead to longer descriptions. This problem can be addressed by introducing names for specific descriptions, such as *detective story*, in which the protagonist is a detective who investigates a crime. Tag lines, movie previews, and other short summaries are important because they are an effective way to deliver relevant information about what to expect of a particular story, and they help us make faster decisions. For example, if you don't like detective stories, you can anticipate that you probably won't enjoy reading *The Hound of the Baskervilles*.

How would you go about generating a summary statement for a collection of stories? You could start by comparing two of the stories and remember all the aspects they have in common. Then you could compare the result with what is contained in the third story and keep those things all three stories have in common, and so on. This process filters out, step by step, aspects that do not apply to a particular story and keeps those that are common to all of them. This elimination of distinguishing details is called *abstraction*, and one also sometimes talks about the "abstraction from details."[1]

In computer science, the description that is the result of an abstraction is itself also called an *abstraction*, and the examples are called *instances* of the abstraction. Using the same name, *abstraction*, for the process and the result might be confusing. Why don't we just use a similar term, such as *generalization*? This seems to be fitting, since a generalization is also a summary that matches a number of specific instances. However, the term *abstraction* in computer science means more than generalization. In addition to the summarizing description, it typically has a name and contains one or more parameters that can be identified with concrete values in the instances. The name and the parameters are called the abstraction's *interface*. The interface provides a mechanism for using an abstraction, and the parameters link key elements of the instances to the abstraction. While generalization is solely driven by the instances, the need for defining an interface makes abstraction a more deliberate process that involves decisions about what details to omit. For example, we can elevate a story generalization "How protagonists overcome a challenge" to a story abstraction by giving it the name Story and identifying the parameters *protagonist* and *challenge*:

Story(*protagonist*, *challenge*) = How *protagonist*(s) solve(s) the problem of *challenge*

Like the parameters of an algorithm, the parameters of the Story abstraction are used in the description as placeholders to be substituted by whatever arguments Story will be applied to. (The potential singular/plural in *protagonist*(s) and *solve*(s) is used to have the description match both single and multiple protagonists, and replacing "overcome a" with "solve(s) the problem of" makes the following examples easier to read.)

In the story of Hansel and Gretel the protagonists are Hansel and Gretel, and the challenge is to find their way home. We can express this fact through an application of the Story abstraction to the corresponding values for the parameters:

Story(Hansel and Gretel, finding their way home)

This application denotes a story of two protagonists, Hansel and Gretel, who solve the problem of finding their way home.

It's worthwhile reflecting on what has been accomplished here. Suppose you want to quickly explain to somebody the gist of the story of Hansel and Gretel. You can do this by first saying that it is a story, that is, by referring to the Story abstraction. This works, of course, only if the other person knows what a story is, that is, if they understand the Story abstraction. In that case, a reference to the abstraction invokes in the other person the description of what a story is. Then you provide details to fill in the roles represented by the parameters *protagonist* and *challenge*, which turns the generic description of a story into a more specific one.

Technically, the application of the Story abstraction leads to replacement of the abstraction name by its definition and the substitution of the values "Hansel and Gretel" and "finding their way home" for the two parameters in the definition (see chapter 2). This substitution leads to the following instance:

How Hansel and Gretel solve(s) the problem of finding their way home

The relationship between instance and abstraction is illustrated in figure 15.1.

Once we have given a summary for the story of Hansel and Gretel in terms of the Story abstraction, we may want to refer to it even more succinctly by assigning it a name. In this case, the name of the story happens to be the same as that of the protagonists:

Hansel and Gretel = Story(Hansel and Gretel, finding their way home)

This equation says that Hansel and Gretel is the story of Hansel and Gretel solving the problem of finding their way home. That the story name and the names of the protagonists agree is purely coincidental, even though this actually happens fairly often. Here is an example where it doesn't occur:

Groundhog Day = Story(Phil Connors, escaping an endlessly repeating day)

Again, the instance represented by the application of the abstraction can be obtained by replacing the abstraction name with its definition and by substituting values for the parameters:

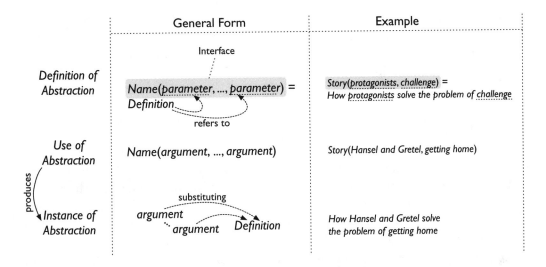

**Figure 15.1**   Definition and use of abstractions. The definition of an abstraction assigns it a name and identifies parameters that are referred to by its definition. The name and parameters are the abstraction's interface, which prescribes how the abstraction is to be used: through its name and by supplying arguments for its parameters. Such a use generates an instance of the abstraction, which is obtained by substituting the arguments for the parameters in the definition of the abstraction.

>  Groundhog Day = How Phil Connors solve(s) the problem of escaping an endlessly repeating day

In the story of Hansel and Gretel, finding their way home is not the only challenge they face. Another salient part of the story is that they have to escape the witch who tries to eat them. Thus the story could be described in the following way:

>  Story(Hansel and Gretel, escaping the witch)

This description uses the same Story abstraction. Only the argument for the second parameter is changed. This fact raises several questions about abstractions. First, what do we make of ambiguity in abstractions? Since the story of Hansel and Gretel can be regarded as an instance of the Story abstraction in different ways, and since both of the shown instances provide accurate information about the story, neither one of the two could be said to be more correct than the other. Does this mean that the definition of the abstraction is flawed? Second, the Story abstraction does not just *abstract* from the details of one particular challenge; it also *focuses* on one particular challenge (at least, for stories that contain several). For example, describing Hansel and Gretel with the Story abstraction leaves at least one challenge unmentioned, which raises the question of whether we could define the Story abstraction so that it accounts for multiple challenges in a story. This is not difficult, but what is the right level of detail for such an abstraction?

## Say When

When is an abstraction general enough to cover enough instances? When does it leave out too many details and lack precision? Whenever we are forming an abstraction, we have to decide how general it should be and how much detail it should provide. For example, we could use the description "sequence of events" instead of the Story abstraction to characterize the stories in this book. This would be accurate, but it would leave out some important aspects and be less precise. On the other hand, we could use more specific abstractions, such as "fairy tale" or "comedy." However, while these provide more details than the Story abstraction, they are not general enough to apply to all stories. In fact, even the fairly general Story abstraction is not general enough to cover stories in which the protagonists fail to solve the problem. We could address this shortcoming by adding another parameter that can be substituted by either "solve" or "don't solve," depending on the situation. Whether generalizing Story in this way is a good idea depends on the usage of the abstraction. If the "don't solve" case never comes up, the extra generality is not needed, and the current simpler definition is preferable. However, the usage context for abstractions may change, and thus one can never be absolutely sure about the chosen level of generality.

In addition to finding the right level of generality, another problem in defining an abstraction is deciding how many details to provide in the description and how many parameters to use. For example, we could add a parameter to the Story abstraction that reflects how the challenge was overcome by the protagonists. On the one hand, adding parameters to an abstraction makes it more expressive, since it provides a mechanism to expose more subtle differences between different instances. On the other hand, it makes the interface of the abstraction more complicated and requires more arguments when the abstraction is used. A more complex interface not only makes an abstraction more difficult to use but also makes applications of the abstraction more difficult to understand, because more arguments have to be substituted for parameters in more places. This counteracts one of the major reasons for using abstractions, which is to provide concise and easy-to-grasp summaries.

Balancing the complexity of interfaces and the precision of abstractions is one of the core problems in software engineering. We could actually characterize the plight of programmers through an instance of the Story abstraction:

Software Engineering = Story(Programmers, finding the right level of abstraction)

Of course, there are many other challenges for programmers, and some can be neatly summarized using the Story abstraction as well. Here is one more struggle that every programmer can empathize with:

Correct Software = Story(Programmers, finding and eliminating bugs)

Finding the right level of abstraction is also an issue for the Story abstraction. There are two different ways to define Hansel and Gretel as an instance of the Story abstraction. Picking one instance that focuses on one challenge means abstracting from (ignoring) the other. But what if we want to use both instances to provide a more comprehensive account of the Hansel and Gretel story? This can be done in different ways. First, we can simply mention both instances side by side:

Story(Hansel and Gretel, finding their way home) and
Story(Hansel and Gretel, escaping the witch)

This looks a bit clunky. In particular, the repeated mention of the protagonists and the Story abstraction seems redundant. This is apparent when we perform the substitution and generate the following instance:

How Hansel and Gretel solve(s) the problem of finding their way home,
and how Hansel and Gretel solve(s) the problem of escaping the witch

Alternatively, we could simply combine both challenges into one argument for the *challenge* parameter:

Story(Hansel and Gretel, finding their way home and escaping the witch)

This works reasonably well. You may have noticed that the same thing was done with the protagonists: Hansel and Gretel were grouped together and substituted as one text unit for the *protagonist* parameter. But we can also see that the flexibility of using single or multiple protagonists does not come for free. In the definition of the Story abstraction the use of *protagonist*(s) and *solve*(s) had to work grammatically with both singular and plural subjects. (To allow for multiple challenges this also had to be done with *problem(s)*.) It would be nice if the Story abstraction could generate separate, grammatically correct instances for each case.

This can be achieved by defining the Story abstraction so that its first parameter is a list of protagonists. Then two slightly different definitions are given, depending on whether the parameter is a single protagonist or a list of two:[2]

Story(*protagonist*, *challenge*) = How *protagonist* solves the problem of *challenge*

Story(*protagonist*$_1$→*protagonist*$_2$, *challenge*) = How *protagonist*$_1$ and *protagonist*$_2$ solve the problem of *challenge*

Now if Story is applied to a single protagonist, such as Phil Connors, the first definition using the singular verb is chosen, whereas when Story is applied to a list of two protagonists, such as Hansel→Gretel, the second definition with a plural verb is selected. In that case the second definition decomposes the list into its two elements and inserts *and* between them.

It seems that the Story abstraction provides a means to create English sentences. In chapter 8, I demonstrated grammars as a mechanism to do just that. So couldn't we alternatively define a grammar for story summaries? Yes. Here is one possible grammar that corresponds to the latest definition of Story.[3] Apart from minor notational differences, such as using an arrow instead of an equal sign or using dotted boxes to mark nonterminals rather than dotted lines to mark parameters, the two mechanisms basically operate in the same way by substituting values (or terminals) for parameters (or nonterminals).

*story* → How *protagonist* solves the problem of *challenge*

*story* → How *protagonists* solve the problem of *challenge*

*protagonists* → *protagonist* and *protagonist*

Table 8.1 in chapter 8 compares grammars, equations, and algorithms. It shows the common roles of the constituting parts of the different formalisms and thus emphasizes that grammars, equations, and algorithms are different but similar mechanisms for describing abstractions.

The preceding discussion shows that the design of an abstraction is not a straightforward task. By encountering new use cases one may recognize changing requirements that force changes in the definition of the abstraction. Such changes can lead to a more general abstraction or to one that exposes different details. In some cases, this might cause a change to the interface, for example, when a new parameter is added or when its type is changed. An example is the change of the *protagonist* parameter from a single value to a list. When the interface of an abstraction changes, all existing uses of the abstraction have to be changed as well to conform to the new interface. This can be a lot of work and might have a ripple effect of causing changes to other interfaces as well. Therefore, software engineers try to avoid changing interfaces whenever possible and consider it often only as a last resort.

# A Run of Abstractions

Consider the last definition of Story that uses a list of protagonists. While the equations work only for lists that contain either one or two elements, the definition can be easily extended to work for lists with an arbitrary number of elements using loops or recursion, as demonstrated in chapters 10 and 12. Using separate equations to distinguish between different cases and the idea of processing lists indicate that the Story abstraction might actually be an algorithm for producing short story descriptions. As it turns out, there is more to this than meets the eye, and I next discuss the relationship between algorithms and abstractions in more detail.

Given the importance of abstraction in computer science, it isn't surprising that one of its central concepts, the algorithm, is itself an example of an abstraction. An algorithm describes the commonality of a number of similar computations, whether following pebbles or sorting lists; see figure 15.2.[4] Different individual computations result when the algorithm is executed with different arguments substituted for its parameters.

The Story abstraction seems to be a post hoc generalization, that is, the summarizing description is created after having seen many existing stories. This may happen occasionally for algorithms as well. For example, after you have repeatedly prepared a certain meal, changing the ingredients and modifying the method to improve the outcome, you may finally decide to write down the recipe to ensure that the culinary experience can be repeated in the future. However, in many other cases an algorithm is a solution to an unsolved problem and is created before any computation is ever run. And this is what makes the algorithm abstraction so powerful. In addition to describing computations that have already happened, an algorithm can generate completely new computations as needed. An algorithm has the power to solve new problems not encountered before. In the context of the Story abstraction, think of some arbitrary protagonists and a specific problem, and you have the beginning of a new story.

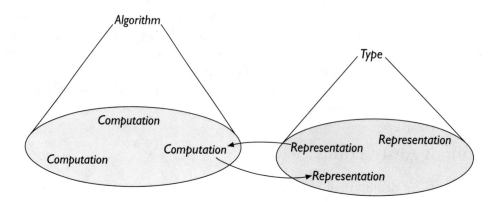

**Figure 15.2** An algorithm is an abstraction from individual computations. Each algorithm transforms representations. A type abstracts from individual representations. If *Input* is the type of representations accepted by an algorithm, and *Output* is the type of representations produced by it, then the algorithm has the type *Input* → *Output*.

The following analogy illustrates this point further. Consider a simple network of roads, and assume that two roads were built to connect the cities $A$ and $B$ and $C$ and $D$, respectively. It so happened that the two roads cross each other and that an intersection was built as well.  Suddenly, new connections become possible, and we can travel from $A$ to $C$, from $B$ to $D$, and so on. The road network facilitates not only the trips it was built for, but also potentially many others that were not anticipated.

The observation that algorithms are abstractions can be understood in two ways. First, the design and use of algorithms enjoys all the benefits of abstractions but also bears all the costs. In particular, the problem of finding the right level of abstraction is relevant to the design of algorithms because the efficiency of an algorithm is often affected by its generality. For example, mergesort takes linearithmic time. Mergesort works on any list of elements and only requires that elements can be compared to one another. It is thus the most general sorting method imaginable and is widely applicable. However, if the elements of the list to be sorted are drawn from a small domain, then bucket sort can be used (see chapter 6), which runs faster in linear time. Therefore, in addition to the potential trade-off between generality and precision, algorithms also have the trade-off between generality and efficiency.

Second, we can exploit algorithmic elements in the design of abstractions. The Story abstraction provides a good example of this. Its sole purpose is to produce descriptions of stories; no computation is intended. However, since a well-designed abstraction identifies key aspects of individual stories through the use of parameters, we notice the need for dealing with lists of protagonists and challenges in a more flexible way. In particular, the distinction between lists having different numbers of elements proves useful in producing specialized story descriptions.

Since the execution of algorithms is tantamount to functional behavior, algorithms are also called *functional abstractions*. But algorithms are not the only example of functional abstractions. Spells in *Harry Potter* are functional abstractions of magic. When executed by a wizard, a spell brings about magic. Each time it is executed, it brings about a different effect, depending on whom or what it is directed at and how well the spell was performed. Similar to an algorithm, which is expressed in some language and can be executed only by a computer that understands that language, a spell is expressed in the language of magic, which includes incantations, wand movements, and so on, and it can be executed only by a skilled wizard who knows how to perform that spell. Potions are another abstraction of magic. They are different from spells in that their execution is much easier. It doesn't take a wizard to unleash the effect of a potion. Anybody, even muggles, can do it.

Many machines are functional abstractions too. For example, a pocket calculator is an abstraction of arithmetic operations. As a potion expands access to magic beyond wizards, a calculator expands access to arithmetic to people who do not have the necessary skills to perform calculations. It can also expand access by accelerating the process even for people who do have those skills. Other examples are coffee makers and alarm clocks, which are machines that can be customized to reliably perform specific functions. The history of transportation vehicles illustrates how machines enhance the efficiency of the abstracted method (in this case traveling) and sometimes also simplify the interface to expand the access to more people. Carriages needed a horse and were relatively slow. Cars have been a big improvement but still require driving skills. Automatic transmissions, safety belts, navigation systems—all make the use of cars as a transportation method more accessible and safer. We can expect even more expanded access in the coming years with the advent of self-driving cars.

## One Type Fits All

Algorithms and machines (and spells and potions) are examples of functional abstractions, since they encapsulate some form of functionality. The passive representations that are being transformed in computations are also subject to abstraction, called *data abstraction*. In fact, the concept of a representation is inherently an abstraction, since it identifies some features of signs to stand for something (see chapter 3) and by doing so actively ignores other features, that is, it abstracts from those features.

When Hansel and Gretel find their way home by tracing pebbles, the size and color of the pebbles don't matter. The use of the pebbles as a representation for locations creates an abstraction that ignores the differences in size and color and focuses instead on their feature of reflecting the moonlight. When we say that Harry Potter is a wizard, we emphasize the fact that he can perform magic. In contrast, we do not care about his age or that he wears glasses or any other interesting piece of information about him. By calling Harry Potter a wizard we abstract from all those details. The same applies when we point out that Sherlock Holmes is a detective or that Doc Brown is a scientist. We highlight features commonly associated with those terms and temporarily ignore everything else about the person.

Terms such as *wizard*, *detective*, and *scientist* are, of course, types. They carry with them connotations of properties that are generally thought to be true of any one individual member of such a type. The notions of protagonist and challenge in the Story abstraction are also types, since they evoke a particular imagery that is required for the Story abstraction to convey its meaning. It seems that *protagonist* is a more general type than, say, *wizard* or *detective* because it provides fewer details. The fact that the latter two can be substituted for the former also supports this view. However, this is only part of the story. Take Lord Voldemort, for example. He is a wizard, but he is not a protagonist. Instead, he is a major antagonist in the *Harry Potter* stories. Since both Harry Potter, a protagonist, and Voldemort, an antagonist, are wizards, it now seems that the type *wizard* is more general because it ignores details on which the distinction between a protagonist and an antagonist relies. Therefore, neither *protagonist* nor *wizard* can be considered more abstract in general, which is not too surprising, since these types come from different domains, namely, stories and magic.

Within one domain, types are often arranged more clearly by placing them in hierarchies. For example, Harry Potter, Draco Malfoy, and Severus Snape are all members of Hogwarts, but only Harry and Draco are students at Hogwarts. If you are a student at Hogwarts, you are clearly also a member of Hogwarts, which means that the type *member of Hogwarts* is a more general abstraction than *student at Hogwarts*. Moreover, since Harry, but not Draco, is a member of the house of Gryffindor, the type *student at Hogwarts* is a more general abstraction than *student in the house of Gryffindor*. Similarly, magic is more abstract than a spell, which in turn is more abstract than a teleportation spell or a patronus charm.

Types found in programming languages are probably the most obvious form of data abstraction. The numbers 2 and 6 are different, but they have many things in common. We can divide them by 2, we can add them to other numbers, and so on. We can therefore ignore their differences and group them together with other numbers in the type *Number*. This type abstracts from the properties of individual numbers and exposes the commonalities between all its members. In particular, the type can be used to characterize parameters in algorithms, which can then be exploited to check the consistency of the algorithm with a type checker (see chapter 14). Thus data abstraction goes hand-in-hand with functional abstraction: an algorithm abstracts from individual values by using parameters. However, in many cases the parameters cannot be substituted by anything imaginable but require as arguments representations that can be manipulated by the algorithm. For example, a parameter that is multiplied by 2 must be a number, which is where types as data abstraction come into play. The type *Number* can also be regarded as more abstract than many more specialized number types, such as the type of all even numbers.

Finally, in addition to (plain) types such as *Number*, data abstraction applies specifically to data types (see chapter 4). A data type is defined solely by the operations it offers and their properties. The details of the representation are ignored, that is, abstracted from, which means that a data type is more abstract than a data structure that implements it. For example, a stack can be implemented by a list or an array, but the details of those structures and thus the differences between them are not visible when they are used to implement stacks.

Any well-chosen data abstraction highlights the features of the representation that support computations with them. Moreover, such an abstraction ignores and hides features that could interfere with the computation.

## Time to Abstract

As explained in chapter 2, the runtime of an algorithm is not reported in the same way as a fitness tracker reports the time of your most recent six-mile run. Reporting runtimes in seconds (or minutes or hours) would not be a very helpful piece of information, since it depends on a particular computer. When the same algorithm is run on a faster or slower computer, the runtime of the same algorithm would be different. Comparing your time for running six miles with that of your friend makes sense, since it provides information about the relative efficiency of two computers, that is, runners. However, the time doesn't say anything meaningful about the efficiency of the running algorithm itself, because both you and your friend are executing the same algorithm.

It is therefore a good idea to abstract from concrete times and to measure the complexity of algorithms in number of steps taken. Such a measure is independent of the speed of a computer and is thus not affected by technological development. Suppose your stride while running is relatively constant. Then you will always take about the same number of steps for your six-mile run regardless of the particular circumstances. Using the number of steps of a fixed stride abstracts from particular characteristics of the runner and thus provides a more stable characterization of the run. In fact, giving the number of steps is just a different way of saying that the run is six miles long. The length of a run is a better measure for its complexity than its duration, since it abstracts from the different speeds of different runners or even the same runner at different times.

However, the number of steps or operations, while more abstract than time, is still too concrete a measure for the complexity of an algorithm because this number varies with the input of the algorithm. For example, the longer a list, the longer it takes to find its minimum or sort it. Similarly, a six-mile run takes more steps to complete than a five-mile run. Remember that the goal is to characterize the complexity of the algorithm in general, not its performance for particular inputs. Thus it is not clear for which input we should report the number of steps. One could imagine creating a table showing the number of steps for several example cases, but it is not clear which examples to pick.

Therefore, time abstraction for algorithms goes further and ignores the actual number of steps taken. Instead it reports how the number of steps grows with larger input. For example, if the algorithm needs twice as many steps if the size of the input doubles, it grows at the same rate. As explained in chapter 2, such a runtime behavior is called *linear*. This is what happens with finding the minimum of a list or with running.[5] Even if the runtime grows by a factor higher than 2, the complexity of the algorithm is still considered linear because the relationship between the size of the input and the number of steps taken is expressed by multiplication with a constant factor. This is the case for the number of steps it takes Hansel and Gretel to find their way home. The runtime grows at a rate greater than 2, since pebbles are spread out by several steps. The runtime category of linear algorithms abstracts from this factor as well, and thus Hansel and Gretel's algorithm is still considered to be linear.

The two most important benefits of the runtime abstraction are its ability to tell us which problems are tractable and which algorithm to select for a particular problem. For example, algorithms with exponential runtime work only for very small inputs, and problems for which only algorithms with exponential runtime are known are therefore deemed intractable (see chapter 7). On the other hand, if we have several algorithms available to solve the same problem, we should pick the one with the better runtime complexity. For example, we would generally prefer the linearithmic mergesort over the quadratic insertion sort (see chapter 6). Figure 15.3 summarizes time abstraction.

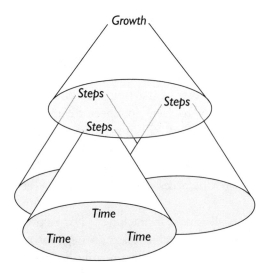

**Figure 15.3**   Time abstraction. To abstract from the different speeds of computers, we use the number of steps an algorithm needs during execution as a measure for its runtime. To abstract from the different number of steps needed for different inputs, we measure the runtime of an algorithm in terms of how fast it grows for larger input.

## The Language in the Machine

An algorithm cannot produce a computation by itself. As explained in chapter 2, an algorithm must be executed by a computer that understands the language in which the algorithm is written. Any instruction used in the algorithm must be in the repertoire of instructions the computer can process.

Tying an algorithm to a specific computer through a language is problematic for several reasons. First, independently designed computers will likely understand different languages, which means that an algorithm written in a language that can be understood and executed by one computer might not be understood and executed by another one. For example, if Hansel or Gretel used German to write down the algorithm for finding the way home using pebbles, a child growing up in France or England could not execute it without having been taught German. Second, over time the languages used by computers change. This may not be a problem for people, who can still reliably understand old, outdated language forms, but it is certainly a problem for machines, which may fail to execute an algorithm altogether if even one of its instructions has been slightly changed. The brittle language tie between algorithm and computer seems to make it difficult to share algorithms. Fortunately, software does not have to be rewritten every time a new computer enters the market. Two forms of abstraction can be credited for this: *language translation* and *abstract machines*.

To illustrate the idea of an abstract machine, let's consider the algorithm for driving a car. You probably learned how to drive one specific car, but still you are able to drive a variety of different cars. The driving skills you acquired are not tied to a specific model and make but are more abstract and can be described using concepts such as steering wheel, gas pedal, and brakes. The abstract car model is realized by various actual cars that differ in details but provide access to its functionality using the common general language of driving.

Abstraction applies to all kinds of machines. For example, we can abstract from the details of a coffee maker, a French press, or an espresso machine by saying that a machine for making coffee needs the ability to mix hot water with ground coffee for some time and then to separate the particles from the fluid. The algorithm for making coffee can be described in terms of this coffee-making abstraction, which is still concrete enough to be instantiated with different coffee-making machines. Of course, machine abstraction has its limits. We cannot use a coffee maker to execute a driving algorithm, and we cannot make coffee using a car. Yet abstract machines are an important way to decouple languages from specific computer architectures (see figure 15.4).

The most famous machine abstraction for computing is the *Turing machine*, named after the famous British mathematician and pioneer of computer science Alan Turing, who invented it in 1936 and used it to formalize the concepts of computation and algorithm. A Turing machine consists of a tape that is divided into cells, each containing a symbol. The tape is accessed through a read/write head that can also move the tape forward and backward. The machine is always in some particular state and is controlled by a program, given by a set of rules that say which symbol to write on the current cell of the tape, in which direction to move the tape, and which new state to go into, depending on what symbol is currently visible and what the current state is. The Turing machine has been used to prove the unsolvability of the halting problem (see chapter 11). Any program can be translated into a Turing machine program, which means that the Turing machine is an abstraction of all currently existing (electronic) computers. The importance of this insight is that whatever general property we can prove for the Turing machine also holds for any other existing computer.

The other strategy for abstracting from particular computers is to use language translation. For example, we can translate the pebble-tracing algorithm from German

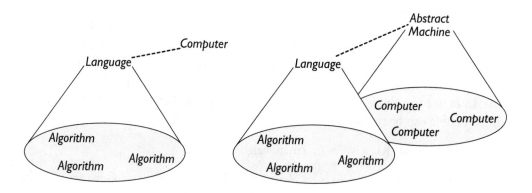

**Figure 15.4**   An abstract machine is an abstraction from concrete computers. By providing a simpler and more general interface, an abstract machine makes algorithmic languages independent of specific computer architectures and extends the range of computers that can execute them.

to French or English, which eliminates the language barrier and makes the algorithm accessible to a wider range of people. The same works, of course, for computer languages. In fact, almost all programs written today are translated in some way before they are executed by a machine, which means that almost none of the programming languages in use today are directly understood by a computer and that every algorithm has to be translated. A programming language abstracts from the details of a particular computer and provides a uniform access for programming a wide range of computers in one language. A programming language is therefore an abstraction of computers and makes the design of algorithms independent of specific computers. If a new computer is produced, all it takes to run existing algorithms on this new computer is to adapt a translator to produce changed code for that computer. The translation abstraction has made the design of programming languages to a large degree independent of the computers on which they will be executed.

There are different ways to define a Translate abstraction. As with any abstraction, the question is which details to abstract from and which to expose as parameters in the interface. The following definition abstracts from the program to be translated, the language it is given in, and the language it should be translated into:

Translate(*program*, *source*, *target*) = "Translate *program* from *source* into *target*"

Note that I use quotes around *"Translate . . ."* because translation is a sophisticated algorithm, much too long and complicated to be presented here. For example, the automatic translation of natural languages is still an open problem. In contrast, the translation of computer languages is a well understood and solved problem. Still, translators are long and complicated algorithms, which is why no details are shown here.

As an example of how to use the Translate abstraction, here is how the instruction to find a pebble can be translated from German into English:

Translate(Finde Kieselstein, German, English)

The instruction *Finde Kieselstein* is an element of the source language German, and the result of the translation is the instruction *Find pebble*, which is an element of the target language English.

In *Harry Potter* the language of spells and charms needs a wizard for execution. Some spells can be translated into a corresponding potion, which can then be executed by muggles as well. For example, the effect of some transforming spells can be captured in the Polyjuice Potion, which allows the drinker to change his or her appearance. While the Polyjuice Potion is apparently very difficult to produce, even for experienced wizards, some other spells have a straightforward translation. For example, the killing curse Avada Kedavra translates into any ordinary lethal poison.

Since every Translate abstraction is itself an algorithm, we can abstract from all translations through a language in which they can be expressed, just as we abstracted from all algorithms using a language. The top left part of figure 15.5 illustrates this case. Since every language corresponds to a computer or abstract machine that can execute its programs, this means that language can abstract from computers, as shown at the top right of figure 15.5.

Just as the Turing machine is the ultimate abstraction of any computing machine, *lambda calculus* is the ultimate abstraction of any programming language. Lambda calculus was invented around the same time as the Turing machine by the American mathematician Alonzo Church. It consists only of three constructs for defining abstractions, referencing parameters in definitions, and creating instances of abstractions by supplying arguments for parameters, very similar to what is shown in figure 15.1. Any program in any algorithmic language can be translated into a lambda calculus program. Now it seems that we have two different ultimate abstractions from computers: lambda calculus and the Turing machine. How can that be? It turns out that these two abstractions are equivalent, which means that any program for a Turing machine can be translated into an equivalent lambda calculus program, and vice versa. Moreover, every known formalism for expressing algorithms[6] has been shown to be no more expressive than Turing

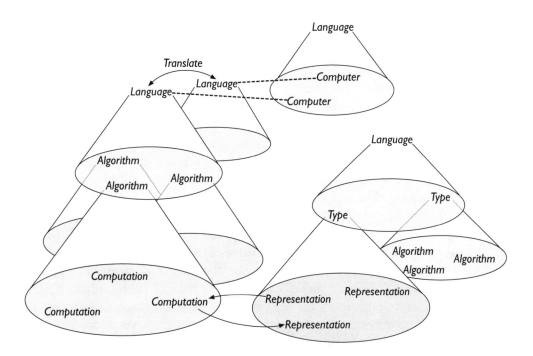

**Figure 15.5**   The tower of abstractions. An algorithm is a (functional) abstraction from computations. An algorithm transforms representations, whose (data) abstractions are types. The acceptable inputs and outputs for an algorithm are also expressed as types. Each algorithm is expressed in a language, which is an abstraction from algorithms. A translation algorithm can transform algorithms from one language into another and therefore makes algorithms independent from a particular computer or abstract machine that understands the language in which it is expressed. Language is also an abstraction of computers, since translation can effectively eliminate the differences between computers. Types are also expressed as part of a language. The abstraction hierarchy illustrates that all abstractions in computer science are expressed in some language.

machines or lambda calculus. Therefore, it seems that any algorithm can be expressed as a Turing machine or a lambda calculus program. This observation is known as the *Church-Turing thesis*, named after the two pioneers of computer science. The Church-Turing thesis is about the expressiveness and reach of algorithms. Since the definition of an algorithm is based on the idea of an effective instruction, which is an intuitive notion tied to human abilities, an algorithm cannot be formalized mathematically. The

Church-Turing thesis is not a theorem that could be proved but rather an observation about the intuitive concept of an algorithm. The Church-Turing thesis is so important because it implies that everything that can be known about algorithms can be found out by studying Turing machines and lambda calculus. The Church-Turing thesis is accepted by most computer scientists.

✳ ✳ ✳

Computation is used for the systematic solving of problems. Although electronic computers have facilitated the unprecedented growth and reach of computation, they are just one tool of computing. The concept of computing is more general and more widely applicable. As we have seen, Hansel and Gretel already knew how to execute an algorithm and how to successfully employ abstractions in representing paths through pebbles. Sherlock Holmes was a master of signs and representations, and he manipulated data structures to solve crimes. And Indiana Jones didn't employ an electronic computer for any of his exciting searches. The language of music might not have solved any problem directly, but it incorporates every bit of syntax and semantics you can imagine. Phil Connors may not have known any theoretical computer science, yet he faced the same problem that illustrates the fundamental limits of computation: the unsolvability of the halting problem. Marty McFly and Doc Brown lived recursion, and Harry Potter revealed to us the magic power of types and abstraction.

The heroes of these stories may not be heroes of computing, but their stories have told us a lot about what computation is. As this book ends, I want to leave you with one more story—*the story of computer science*. This is a story about abstractions for conquering the concept of computation. Its main protagonist is the *algorithm*, which can systematically solve *problems* through the transformation of *representations*. It does that by skillfully applying its basic tools, *control structures* and *recursion*. Although problems can be solved in different ways, the algorithm doesn't settle for any specific solution but aspires to be as general as possible by employing its secret weapon, the *parameter*. However, any of its concrete missions is a constant struggle, since the algorithm always faces serious opposition from its arch enemy *complexity*:

Computation = Story(algorithm, solving problems)

The story unfolds as new and larger problems push the algorithm to its limits. But in its struggle it enjoys the friendship and support of its relatives from the *abstraction* family: its sister *efficiency*, who counsels it about the prudent use of precious resources; its brother *type*, who shields it relentlessly from programming errors and incorrect inputs;

and its wise grandmother *language*, who bestows on it expressiveness and makes sure it is understood by its trusted companion the *computer*, on whom it relies for executing any of its plans:

Computer Science = Story(abstractions, capturing computation)

The algorithm is not all powerful and cannot solve all problems, and it is particularly vulnerable to inefficiency and errors. But it is well aware of this fact. And this knowledge about its own limitations makes it strong and confident about the adventures that lie ahead.

# Further Exploration

The magic in Harry Potter illustrates the concepts of types and typing rules and how they can help making predictions about the future. A rigorous system of magic can be found in L. E. Modesitt Jr.'s series of fantasy novels *The Saga of Recluce*, where magic is a person's ability to control the chaos and order that is inherent in all matter. The protagonist in Jim Butcher's book series *The Dresden Files* is a private detective and wizard who investigates cases involving supernatural phenomena. The stories contain different types of magic, laws of magic, and tools for magic.

Many examples of creatures with specific abilities, which can be described as types, can be found in the world created by J. R. R. Tolkien in his novels *The Lord of the Rings* and *The Hobbit*. The superheroes in the *X-Men* comic series and corresponding movies have special abilities that are well defined and interact in a precisely defined way with the natural world. Some of the superheroes define a type that has exactly one element, namely, themselves. Other types have multiple members.

Using a device incorrectly often amounts to a type error and can lead to malfunction. This is regularly exploited for dramatic effect, as in the movie *The Fly*, where the improper use of a teleportation device causes mixing of the DNA of a human and a fly. Type errors also occur when people change or switch roles, playing on stereotypes associated with the roles. For example, in the movie *Freaky Friday*, the minds of a teenager and her mother switch their bodies, which leads to behaviors that violate the expectations associated with the roles of teenager and adult. In Mark Twain's *The Prince and the Pauper*, a prince switches roles with a poor boy.

Abstractions come in many different forms. Dioramas are abstractions often used to represent important events in history. Some examples occur in the movie *Dinner for Schmucks*. A voodoo doll is an abstraction of a person and is used to inflict pain on the person over a distance. Examples occur in *Indiana Jones and the Temple of Doom* and in *Pirates of the Caribbean: On Stranger Tides*. In Jim Butcher's *The Dresden Files*, voodoo dolls are used several times. Similarly, an avatar is representations of oneself that can act in distant environments, which is a major theme of the movie *Avatar*. The movie

*Inside Out* represents the mind as a space inhabited by five people that personify basic emotions.

Money is an abstraction of value and is an essential tool for exchanging goods in economies. The fact that money is a socially constructed abstraction and works only when all participants agree on its value is nicely illustrated in stories that use non-traditional currencies, as in *Mad Max 2*, where gasoline is the major currency, or in the movie *In Time*, where one's own life span is used as a currency. In Frank Herbert's *Dune*, water and spice are currencies, and Douglas Adam's *The Hitchhiker's Guide to the Galaxy* contains a number of weird currency examples.

Abstractions of behavioral rules can be found in Isaac Asimov's *I, Robot* collection of short stories in the form of three laws of robotics that are intended to ensure that robots serve humans well without harming them. These laws represent an abstraction of morality. The stories illustrate the application of these laws and their limitations, which has led to modification and extensions of the laws. And in Max Barry's *Lexicon* a secret society has developed a novel language that is not a tool for communicating ideas but for controlling the actions of other people. While natural languages typically provide abstractions for describing the world, the special language in *Lexicon*, is based on abstractions for neurochemical reactions that steer human actions, similar to how some magic spells can directly affect behavior.

# Glossary

This glossary summarizes important terms in the book. The entries are grouped in sections by story and major concepts. Some entries appear in more than one section.

Important terms used in definitions are labeled with a section letter indicating the section where they themselves are defined. For instance, *algorithm*[A] indicates that the term *algorithm* is defined in section A.

## A. Computation and Algorithms

**algorithm.** A method for solving a problem[A]. An algorithm is applicable to different problem examples and must be given by a finite description in a language[D] that is understandable by a computer[A]. All steps of the method must be effective. Execution[A] of an algorithm on a particular problem example generates a computation[A]. An algorithm should terminate[E] and produce a correct[A] result for any problem it is executed on, but that is not always the case, and these properties are difficult to ensure. An algorithm that is understandable by a machine is called a program[A].

**computation.** A process that solves a problem[A] in a number of steps by systematically transforming a representation[A] of the problem. A computation is what happens during the execution[A] of an algorithm[A] by a computer[A].

**computer.** A person, machine, or other actor that can execute[A] an algorithm[A]. A computer must understand the language[D] in which the algorithm is given.

**correctness.** The property of an algorithm[A] to always produce the desired result for any given valid input[A]. If an algorithm gets stuck or doesn't terminate[E] for some input, it is not a correct solution to a problem[A].

**execution.** The process of following the steps in an algorithm[A] for a particular problem[A] example. Execution is performed by a computer[A] and generates a computation[A].

**input.** The variable part of a problem[A] that distinguishes different problem examples. The input is part of the problem representation[A] and can consist of several parts. An algorithm[A] applied to a specific input leads to a computation[A] for the problem instance for that input. In the algorithm, the input is represented by parameters[A].

**parameter.** A name used by an algorithm[A] to refer to its input[A].

**problem.** A representation[A] of a situation, deemed in need of a solution, that facilitates solutions through computation[A]. Refers to both individual problem examples that are subject to transformation by computation[A] and the class of all such problems that can be the input[A] for an algorithm[A].

**program.** An algorithm[A] that can be understood and executed[A] by a machine.

**representation.** An entity that stands for something in the real world. A representation must be modifiable by the steps of a computation[A]. See also **representation**[B].

**runtime.** A measure for the number of steps an execution[A] of an algorithm[A] is expected to take. Expressed as a rule that captures how the runtime is related to the size of the input[A]. Commonly occurring runtime measures are linear[C], quadratic[C], logarithmic[C], and exponential[C].

**worst case.** The longest possible runtime[A] of a computation[A] generated by an algorithm[A]. The worst case serves as an estimate to judge whether an algorithm[A] is efficient enough to produce a solution to a problem[A].

| Concept | How It Appears in *Hansel and Gretel* |
|---|---|
| Algorithm | Method to follow pebbles |
| Computation | Finding a way home |
| Computer | Hansel and Gretel |
| Correctness | Tracing pebbles leads home and doesn't get stuck or lead to a loop |
| Execution | When Hansel and Gretel perform the pebble-tracing algorithm |
| Input | Placement of all the pebbles |
| Parameter | The expression "shining pebble that was not visited before" |
| Problem | Survival; finding the way home |
| Program | A description of the pebble-tracing algorithm in machine-readable form |
| Representation | Locations and pebbles |
| Runtime | Steps needed to follow the pebbles home |
| Worst case | Hansel and Gretel have to visit each pebble at most once |

# B. Representation and Data Structures

**array.** A data structure[B] for representing a collection of items. Akin to a table with two rows, one row of which contains names or numbers (indices) for the items stored in the array. An index[B] is used to look up items in an array. An array is a good choice for implementing a set[B] because it facilitates constant-time lookup for items. But, since an array has to reserve space for all possible items, it can be used only if the number of possible items that might be stored in it is small. Is also used to represent the buckets in bucket sort[C].

**data structure.** A representation[B] used by an algorithm[A] that provides distinct access and manipulation. Frequently used data structures are arrays[B], lists[B], and trees[B].

**data type.** A description of a representation[B] whose behavior is given through a set of operations that can manipulate the representation[B]. Must be implemented by a data structure[B]. One data type can often be implemented by different data structures, which typically implement the operations with different runtimes[A]. Frequently used data types are sets[B], dictionaries[B], stacks[B], and queues[B].

**dictionary.** A data type[B] for associating information with keys[B]. Provides operations for inserting, removing, and updating the information for specific keys as well as an operation for looking up information given a key. A set[B] is a special form of dictionary in which the elements are the keys and which doesn't store any information with those keys.

**icon.** A sign[B] that represents based on similarity with the signified[B].

**index.** A sign[B] that represents based on a law-like relationship with the signified[B]. Also, a way to look up elements in an array[B].

**key.** A value used to find information in a dictionary[B]. See also **search key**[C].

**list.** A data structure[B] for representing a collection of elements in a specific order. The elements can be accessed one by one, starting with the element at the front of the list. Can also be viewed as a tree[B] in which each node[B] (except the last) has exactly one child. Can be used to implement data types[B] such as stacks[B], queues[B], or sets[B].

**node.** An element in a data structure[B] that is connected to other elements. Examples are the elements of trees[B] and lists[B]. In a tree[B] the elements that can be directly accessed from a node are called its children, and the node from which a node can be accessed is called its parent. Each node can have at most one parent, and the topmost node in a tree, the root, has no parent. Nodes with no children are called leaves.

**priority queue.** A data type[B] for a collection from which elements are removed in the order of a given priority. Realizes the HIFO (highest in, first out) principle for accessing elements in a collection.

**queue.** A data type[B] for a collection from which elements are removed in the same order in which they were inserted. Realizes the FIFO (first in, first out) principle for accessing elements in a collection.

**representation.** A sign[B] that stands for something in the real world. See also **representation**[A].

**set.** A data type[B] for representing a collection of elements that provides operations for insertion, removal, and finding of elements. Can be represented as a dictionary[B] in which the elements are the keys[B]. The set data type is important, since it facilitates the representation of properties.

**sign.** A specific form of representation[B] consisting of a signifier[B] (its visible part) and a signified[B] (what the signifier stands for).

**signified.** The part of a sign[B] represented by the signifier[B]. Not a concrete object in the world but a concept about objects that people have in their minds.

**signifier.** The part of a sign[B] that is perceived and that stands for the signified[B]. One signifier can represent different concepts.

**stack.** A data type[B] for a collection from which elements are removed in the opposite order in which they were inserted. Realizes the LIFO (last in, first out) principle for accessing elements in a collection.

**symbol.** A sign[B] that stands for the signified[B] based on an arbitrary convention.

**tree.** A data structure[B] for representing a collection of elements as a hierarchy. Its elements are called nodes[B]. Any node higher up in the hierarchy is connected to zero or more nodes lower in the hierarchy and to at most one node higher in the hierarchy.

| Concept | How It Appears in *The Hound of the Baskervilles* |
|---|---|
| Array | Representation of suspect set with check marks |
| Data structure | List of suspects, family tree |
| Data type | Set of suspects |
| Dictionary | Sherlock Holmes's notebook with entries about the suspects |
| Icon | Portrait of Sir Hugo Baskerville; map of the Devonshire moor |
| Index | The hound's footprints and the cigar ashes at the crime scene |
| Key | Names of suspects |
| List | The list of suspects Mortimer→Jack→Beryl→Selden→ . . . |
| Node | Name of family member in the family tree |
| Priority queue | Inheritance ordering for the heirs of Baskerville |
| Queue | Watson's list of things to do at Baskerville Hall |
| Representation | Suspect list or array; map of the Devonshire moor |
| Set | Set of suspects |
| Sign | Engraving on Dr. Mortimer's walking stick |
| Signified | Charing Cross Hospital (by signifier CCH) |
| Signifier | Acronym CCH (for Charing Cross Hospital) |
| Stack | Repeatedly computing descendants of children before siblings |
| Symbol | A number (2704) for a taxi cab |
| Tree | Family tree of the Baskervilles |

# C. Problem Solving and Its Limitations

**approximation algorithm.** An algorithm[A] for computing[A] solutions that might not be completely correct[A] but are good enough in most cases.

**balanced tree.** A tree[B] in which all leaves have about the same distance from the root (their distances differ by at most 1). A balanced tree has the smallest height among all trees with the same number of nodes[B]; it is as wide as possible. This shape guarantees that if a binary search tree[C] is balanced, finding elements has logarithmic runtime[C] in the worst case[A].

**binary search.** An algorithm[A] for finding an element in a collection. Compares the element to be found with one element in the collection, which partitions the collection into two regions. Depending on the outcome of the comparison, the search continues in only one of the two regions. When elements for splitting are chosen well so that they always partition the search space into two regions of approximately the same size, as in a balanced binary search tree[C], binary search takes logarithmic runtime[C] in the worst case[A].

**binary search tree.**  A binary tree[C] with the property that for each node[B] in the tree[B], all the nodes in its left subtree are smaller, and all the nodes in its right subtree are larger.

**binary tree.**  A tree[B] in which each node[B] has at most two children.

**bucket sort.**  A sorting algorithm[A] that scans the list[B] to be sorted and places each element into one of a number of specifically reserved and initially empty spaces (buckets). After all list elements have been placed into buckets, the buckets are inspected in order, and all the elements from nonempty buckets are put into the result list. Bucket sort typically uses an array[B] to represent the buckets. It requires that the set of elements that may possibly occur in the list be not too large, so that each potential bucket can be assigned only a few or even only one element. In that case bucket sort has linear runtime[C].

**divide-and-conquer.**  An algorithm[A] schema in which the solution is obtained by splitting the input into separate parts, solving the problems for the parts independently of one another, and then combining the solutions for the parts into a solution for the original problem[A]. Divide-and-conquer is not an algorithm itself, but an algorithm structure. Mergesort[C] and quicksort[C] are examples.

**exponential runtime.**  An algorithm[A] has exponential runtime when its execution time doubles (or increases by a factor greater than 1) whenever the size of the input[A] grows by 1. This means that if the size of the input increases by 10, the algorithm will take 1,000 times longer. Algorithms with exponential runtime are not practical solutions, since they work only for inputs of small size.

**generate-and-test.**  An algorithm[A] schema that consists of two major phases. In the first phase, it produces potential solutions, which are then systematically checked during the second phase. Generate-and-test is not an algorithm itself, but an algorithm structure. Trying out all combinations for a combination lock is an example, as is trying out all combinations for solving a knapsack problem[C].

**greedy algorithm.**  An algorithm[A] is called greedy if it always picks the currently best available option. Picking elements from a sorted list for solving a knapsack problem[C] is an example.

**insertion sort.**  A sorting algorithm[A] that repeatedly picks the next element from an unsorted list[B] and inserts it at the right place in the sorted list. Insertion sort has quadratic runtime[C] in the worst case[A].

**intractable problem.**  A problem[A] for which only algorithms[A] with exponential runtime[C] are known. Examples are the knapsack problem[C] and the traveling salesman problem.

**knapsack problem.**  An example of an intractable problem[C]. The task is to fill a knapsack of limited capacity with as many items as possible to maximize the total value of all items that fit in the knapsack.

**linear runtime.** An algorithm[A] has linear runtime[A] when its execution time grows proportionally to the size of the input[A]. Linear runtime is better than linearithmic runtime[C] but not as good as logarithmic runtime[C]. Finding the smallest element in a list has linear runtime in the worst case[A].

**linearithmic runtime.** An algorithm[A] has linearithmic runtime[A] when its execution time grows proportionally to the size of input[A] multiplied by the logarithm of the size. Linearithmic runtime is not quite as good as linear runtime[C] but much better than quadratic runtime[C]. Mergesort[C] has linearithmic runtime in the worst case[A].

**logarithmic runtime.** If an algorithm[A] has logarithmic runtime, its runtime[A] increases only by 1 for input[A] twice the size. Logarithmic runtime is much faster than linear runtime[C]. For example, binary search[C] in a balanced[C] binary search tree[C] has logarithmic runtime.

**lower bound.** The complexity of a problem[A]. Gives the growth rate of the minimum number of steps any algorithm[A] must take to solve a problem. Any algorithm whose worst-case[A] runtime[A] is the same as the lower bound is an optimal algorithm[C].

**mergesort.** A divide-and-conquer[C] sorting algorithm[A] that first splits the list[B] to be sorted into two sublists of equal length, then sorts these sublists, and finally merges the sorted sublists into the sorted result list. Mergesort has linearithmic runtime[C] in the worst case[A]. Since the lower bound[C] for sorting is also linearithmic, mergesort is an optimal algorithm[C] for sorting.

**optimal algorithm.** An algorithm[A] whose worst-case[A] runtime[A] is the same as the lower bound[C] of the problem[A] it is solving.

**quadratic runtime.** An algorithm[A] has quadratic runtime[A] when its execution time grows proportionally to the square of the size of input[A]. Quadratic runtime is worse than linearithmic runtime[C] but much better than exponential runtime[C]. Insertion sort[C] and selection sort[C] have quadratic runtime in the worst case[A].

**quicksort.** A divide-and-conquer[C] sorting algorithm[A] that first splits a list[B] to be sorted into two sublists that each contain all the elements that are, respectively, smaller and larger than a chosen pivot element. These two lists are then themselves sorted, and the results are concatenated, with the pivot element in the middle, into the sorted result list. Quicksort has a quadratic runtime[C] in the worst case[A], but performs very well in practice and has linearithmic runtime[C] in the average case.

**search key.** A piece of information that identifies something to be found. In some cases it is derived (then it is an index[B]); in other cases it is a separate, unrelated value (then it is a symbol[B]). Identifies the boundary that separates relevant from irrelevant elements with regard to the current search. See also **key**[B].

**selection sort.** A sorting algorithm[A] that repeatedly finds the minimum from an unsorted list[B] and puts it at the end of the sorted list. Selection sort has quadratic runtime[A] in the worst case[A].

**trie.** A tree[B] data structure[B] for implementing sets[B] or dictionaries[B] that represents each key[B] as a sequence of nodes[B]. A trie is particularly efficient when the stored keys share common parts.

| Concept | How It Appears in *Indiana Jones* |
|---|---|
| Approximation algorithm | Using an inflatable boat as a parachute |
| Balanced tree | Some of the search trees for letter frequencies |
| Binary search | Finding tiles on the tile floor |
| Binary (search) tree | Representing letter frequencies for the words Iehova, etc. |
| Bucket sort | Computing letter frequencies using an array |
| Divide-and-conquer | Reducing the search for Henry Jones, Sr., to Venice |
| Exponential runtime | Determining the exact weight of the idol |
| Generate-and-test | Systematically trying out all weight combinations |
| Greedy algorithm | Trying weights in descending order |
| Insertion sort | Sorting the tasks for finding the Well of Souls |
| Intractable problem | Finding the exact weight of the idol with a balance scale |
| Knapsack problem | Collecting treasure items in the temple of the crystal skull |
| Linear runtime | Executing the list of tasks |
| Linearithmic runtime | Finding the idol's weight by trying |
| Logarithmic runtime | Finding a letter frequency in a binary tree |
| Lower bound | Minimum time to sort list of tasks |
| Mergesort | Sorting the tasks for finding the Well of Souls |
| Optimal algorithm | Using mergesort for sorting |
| Quadratic runtime | Using selection sort for sorting |
| Quicksort | Sorting the tasks for finding the Well of Souls |
| Search key | Venice; Iehova |
| Selection sort | Sorting the tasks for finding the Well of Souls |
| Trie | Tile floor |

# D. Language and Meaning

**ambiguity.** A property of a grammar[D]. When a sentence[D] can have two or more syntax trees[D].

**abstract syntax.** The hierarchical structure of a sentence[D], represented as a syntax tree[D]. The abstract syntax of a language[D] as defined by a grammar[D] is the set of all syntax trees that can be built using the grammar.

**compositionality.** A property of the semantics definition$^D$ of a language$^D$. A semantics definition is compositional if the meaning of a sentence$^D$ is obtained from the meanings of its parts. Implies that the structure of a sentence determines how the meanings of its parts are combined in a systematic way.

**concrete syntax.** The appearance of a sentence$^D$ as a sequence of terminals$^D$ (or arrangements of visual symbols).

**derivation.** A sequence of sentential forms$^D$, each of which is obtained from the previous one by substituting a nonterminal$^D$ according to a grammar rule$^D$. The first element of a derivation must be a nonterminal, and its last element must be a sentence$^D$.

**grammar.** A set of grammar rules$^D$ that map nonterminals$^D$ to sentential forms$^D$. Defines a language$^D$. One language can be defined by different grammars. The language defined by a grammar consists of all sentences$^D$ for which a derivation$^D$ from the start symbol$^D$ exists.

**grammar rule.** A grammar rule has the form $nt \rightarrow$ RHS where $nt$ is a nonterminal$^D$ and RHS is a sentential form$^D$. Used to substitute nonterminals in sentential forms as part of a derivation$^D$.

**language.** A set of sentences$^D$, each of which has an appearance as a sequence of words or an arrangement of visual symbols (concrete syntax$^D$) and an internal structure (abstract syntax$^D$ or syntax tree$^D$). The definition of a language is given by a grammar$^D$. A language is the set of all sentences that can be derived$^D$ from the grammar's start symbol$^D$. Some, but not all, languages also have a semantics definition$^D$.

**nonterminal.** A symbol that occurs on the left-hand side of a grammar rule$^D$; a symbol that can be substituted by a sentential form$^D$. The start symbol$^D$ of a grammar$^D$ is a nonterminal.

**parsing.** The process of identifying the structure of a sentence$^D$ and representing it as a syntax tree$^D$.

**semantic domain.** A set of values that are relevant in a particular application area. Used in the semantics definition$^D$ of a language$^D$.

**semantics definition.** A mapping of the syntax trees$^D$ of a language$^D$ to elements of a semantic domain$^D$.

**sentence.** An element of a language$^D$ given by a sequence of terminals$^D$.

**sentential form.** A sequence of terminals$^D$ and nonterminals$^D$. Occurs on the right side of a grammar rule$^D$.

**start symbol.** A designated nonterminal$^D$ of a grammar$^D$. Any sentence$^D$ of a language$^D$ defined by a grammar must be obtainable through a derivation$^D$ from the start symbol.

**syntax.** The definition of which sentences$^D$ belong to a language$^D$. Typically defined by a grammar$^D$, which consists of rules for forming or recognizing a sentence$^D$. The rules define both the concrete syntax$^D$ and the abstract syntax$^D$ of a language.

**syntax tree.**  A hierarchical representation of the structure of a sentence[D] in the form of an upside-down tree[B] diagram. The leaves of the tree are terminals[D], while all the other nodes are nonterminals[D].

**terminal.**  A symbol that only occurs on the right-hand side of a grammar rule[D]; cannot be substituted. A sentence[D] of a language[D] consists of a sequence of only terminals.

| Concept | How It Appears in *Over the Rainbow* |
| --- | --- |
| Ambiguity | A verse without bar symbol |
| Abstract syntax | Tree of measures and notes |
| Algorithm[A] | The score in staff notation or tablature |
| Compositionality | Sound of the song is concatenation of the sounds of its measures |
| Computer[A] | Judy Garland as a singer or musician |
| Concrete syntax | Staff notation; tablature |
| Execution[A] | Singing or playing |
| Derivation | Expanding *melody* into the score using the grammar rules |
| Grammar | The grammar for melodies |
| Grammar rule | *note* → ♩ |
| Language | All valid staff notations |
| Nonterminal | *measure* |
| Parsing | Identifying the structure given through verses, chorus, measures, etc. |
| Semantic domain | Sounds |
| Semantics definition | Mapping of syntax tree to sounds |
| Sentence | The song given in staff notation |
| Sentential form | ♩ *note* ♩ *melody* |
| Start symbol | *melody* |
| Syntax | Rules for typesetting staff notation |
| Syntax tree | Tree of measures and notes |
| Terminal | ♩ |

# E. Control Structures and Loops

**body (of a loop).**  A group of operations to be repeated by a loop[E]. Must modify the program state to allow the termination[E] of the loop.

**conditional.**  A control structure[E] for deciding between the execution[A] of one of two groups of operations.

**control structure.** A part of an algorithm[A] for organizing the order, application, and repetition of operations. The three major control structures are loops[E], conditionals[E], and recursion[F].

**for loop.** A loop[E] whose body[E] is executed a fixed number of times.

**halting problem.** Will an algorithm[A] always terminate[E] for any given input[A]?

**loop.** A control structure[E] for repeating the body[E] of the loop. The number of repetitions is determined by the termination condition[E], which is checked after each execution[A] of the loop's body and which depends on the program state that can be changed by the operations of the loop's body. In general, it is not clear how many repetitions the loop generates and thus whether the loop terminates. Two major kinds of loops are the repeat loop[E] and the while loop[E]. For these loops the termination condition determines how often the body will be repeated, which is generally not known before executing the loop. In contrast, the number of repetitions of a for loop[E] is fixed at the beginning of the loop, which guarantees the termination[E] of for loops[E].

**repeat loop.** A loop[E] whose termination condition[E] is checked always after the operations of the loop's body[E] have been executed.

**termination.** A property of an algorithm[A] or computation[A] that holds when the computation ends. The termination of an algorithm[A] cannot be determined automatically by another algorithm; it is an undecidable[E] problem[A].

**termination condition.** A condition that determines whether a loop[E] ends or continues to run.

**undecidability.** A property of a problem[A]. A problem is undecidable if it cannot be solved by an algorithm[A]. A famous undecidable problem is the halting problem[E].

**while loop.** A loop[E] whose termination condition[E] is always checked before the operations of the loop's body[E] are executed.

| Concept | How It Appears in *Groundhog Day* |
|---|---|
| Body (of a loop) | Events that happen during Groundhog day |
| Conditional | Any decision taken by Phil Connors |
| Control structure | The Groundhog Day loop |
| For loop | The number of repetitions in the movie is fixed in the script |
| Halting problem | Will the Groundhog day loop ever come to an end? |
| Loop | The repeating Groundhog day |
| Repeat loop | The Groundhog Day loop |
| Termination | The happy ending |
| Termination condition | Is Phil Connors a good person? |
| Undecidability | Inability to judge a priori whether Groundhog Day will end |
| While loop | The Groundhog Day loop |

# F. Recursion

**base case.** The nonrecursive part of a recursive definition[F]. When a recursive algorithm[A] reaches a base case, the recursion[F] will stop at that point. A base case is required, but not sufficient, for a recursion to terminate[E].

**bounded recursion.** A recursion[F] that terminates[E].

**descriptive recursion.** When the definition of a concept contains a reference to itself, usually through the use of a name or symbol. Sometimes called self-reference.

**direct recursion.** When the definition of a name or object contains a reference to itself.

**fixed point.** A solution to a recursive equation.

**indirect recursion.** When the definition of a name or object does not contain a reference to itself but rather contains another name that contains the reference.

**interpreter.** A computer[A] that executes[A] an algorithm[A] using a stack[B] data type[B] to keep track of recursive[F] (and nonrecursive) calls and multiple copies of arguments that arise as a consequence of recursive calls[F].

**paradox.** A logical contradiction, which is caused by a descriptive recursion[F] that cannot be executed to yield a bounded[F] unfolded recursion[F]. A recursive equation describes a paradox if it doesn't have a fixed point[F].

**recursion.** Refers either to descriptive recursion[F], unfolded recursion[F], or the execution[A] of a recursive definition[F].

**recursive call.** A call to an algorithm[A] from within its own definition (direct recursion[F]) or from the definition of another algorithm that it calls (indirect recursion[F]).

**recursive definition.** When the definition of a name or object contains a reference to itself. In a recursive definition of an algorithm[A], the reference is also called a recursive call[F].

**substitution.** The process of replacing parameters[A] by concrete values. Replacing the call of an algorithm[A] by its definition while substituting the arguments for the parameters.

**trace.** A sequence that captures the different states a computation[A] went through. Helpful in illustrating the execution[A] of an algorithm[A] that is given by a recursive definition[F].

**unbounded recursion.** A recursion[F] that does not terminate[E]. This happens when the recursive definition[F] lacks a base case[F] or when the base case is not reached by the recursive calls[F]. Examples are never-ending songs, infinite lists[B] of numbers, or some nonterminating computations[A].

**unfolded recursion.** When an artifact, typically a picture or text, contains a (sometimes scaled) copy of itself. Sometimes called self-similarity. Fractals and geometric patterns, such as Sierpinski triangles, are examples of unfolded recursion in pictures, and a never-ending song or poem is an example of unfolded recursion in text. Matryoshka dolls are an example of a recursive physical object.

| Concept | How It Appears in *Back to the Future* |
|---------|----------------------------------------|
| Base case | Marty saves Doc Brown in 1885 |
| Bounded recursion | Time travel happens only a fixed number of times |
| Descriptive recursion | The description of time travel in *ToDo* or *Goal* |
| Direct recursion | Marty travels to 1885 after traveling to 1955 |
| Fixed point | The actions taken by Marty and others are consistent |
| Indirect recursion | If *Goal* were split into two functions, say, *Easy* and *Hard* |
| Interpreter | The universe executing the time travel actions |
| Paradox | Jennifer sees her older/younger self |
| Recursion | Marty traveling into the past |
| Recursive call | The call *ToDo*(1885) in the definition of *ToDo*(1955) |
| Recursive definition | The definition of *ToDo* or *Goal* |
| Substitution | The sequence of actions obtained for a call of *ToDo* or *Goal* |
| Trace | The linear sequence of actions from *Back to the Future* |
| Unbounded recursion | If Marty never stopped traveling back in time |
| Unfolded recursion | The sequence of actions resulting from time travel |

# G. Types and Abstraction

**abstract machine.** A high-level description of a machine, often given as a mathematical model, that ignores details of actual machines and thus provides a unifying view on a large number of different but similar machines. The Turing Machine[G] is an example.

**abstraction.** The process of ignoring the details in a description and summarizing it. Also the result of that process. To facilitate the use of an abstraction, it is given an interface[G].

**axiom.** A rule that is always true. A typing rule[G] is an axiom if it has no premises[G].

**Church-Turing thesis.** The claim that any algorithm[A] can be expressed as a program[A] for a Turing machine[G] or lambda calculus[G]. Is believed to be true by most computer scientists.

**conclusion.** A part of a typing rule[G]. The conclusion of a typing rule[G] is true only if all its premises[G] are true.

**data abstraction.** When abstraction[G] is applied to representation[A,B]. Provides a common view on a number of different data. Types[G] are a major form of data abstraction.

**dynamic type checking.** Checking types[G] during the execution[A] of an algorithm[A].

**functional abstraction.** When abstraction[G] is applied to computation[A]. Provides a common view on a number of different computations. Embodied in the concept of an algorithm[A], which describes a class of similar computations.

**instance.** An instance of an abstraction[G] is obtained by the substitution[F] of arguments for the parameters[A] in the definition of the abstraction.

**interface.** A name plus parameters[A] that is assigned to an abstraction[G] to facilitate its use.

**lambda calculus.** A language[D] abstraction[G] for algorithms[A]. If the Church-Turing thesis[G] is true, any algorithm can be expressed as a lambda calculus program[A]. In its expressiveness to describe algorithms and computation[A], lambda calculus is equivalent to a Turing machine[G].

**premise.** A part of a typing rule[G] that must be true for the conclusion[G] of the typing rule to hold.

**static type checking.** Checking types[G] before executing[A] an algorithm[A].

**Turing machine.** An abstract machine[G] for computers[A]. Serves as a mathematical model of computation[A]. In this regard it is equivalent to lambda calculus[G]. If the Church-Turing thesis[G] is true, any algorithm[A] can be translated into a program[A] for a Turing machine.

**type.** A data abstraction[G] that provides a unifying description for a group of representations[A].

**type checker.** An algorithm[A] that checks whether another algorithm violates any typing rules[G].

**typing rule.** A rule for constraining the admissible inputs[A] and outputs of algorithms[A] that can spot mistakes in algorithms. Can be checked automatically by a type checker[G].

| Concept | How It Appears in *Harry Potter* |
| --- | --- |
| Abstract machine | — |
| Abstraction | Potion, Marauder's map |
| Axiom | Muggles cannot perform magic |
| Church-Turing thesis | — |
| Conclusion | ..., he or she can cast spells |
| Data abstraction | The types of wizards and muggles |
| Dynamic type checking | Trying a spell without checking the requirements |
| Functional abstraction | Spells |
| Instance | Using Wingardium Leviosa spell on a feather |
| Interface | A spell has a name and needs a wand and an incantation |
| Lambda calculus | — |
| Premise | If somebody is a wizard, ... |
| Static type checking | Predicting that muggles can't do magic |
| Turing machine | — |
| Type | Spell, wizard, muggle |
| Type checker | The world of magic |
| Typing rule | If somebody is a wizard, he or she can cast spells |

# Notes

## Introduction

1. John Dewey, "The Pattern of Inquiry," in *Logic: Theory of Inquiry* (1938).

## Chapter 1    A Path to Understanding Computation

1. Quotations are taken from the free online version of *Grimms' Fairy Tales* by Jacob Grimm and Wilhelm Grimm that is available at www.gutenberg.org/ebooks/2591.

2. The terminology can get a bit confusing here, since the term *problem* is generally used for one particular problem instance as well as for a whole problem class. For example, we talk about the "problem of way-finding" in general as well as the concrete "problem of finding a way between two specific locations." In most cases, however, the ambiguity is resolved by the context.

3. This is true only under certain assumptions that are discussed later.

## Chapter 2    Walk the Walk: When Computation Really Happens

1. The amount of ground coffee follows the National Coffee Association's recommendation; see www.ncausa.org/i4a/pages/index.cfm?pageID=71.

2. The first recorded use of the word *computer* dates back to 1613. The first idea of a mechanical computer was the Difference Engine, designed by Charles Babbage in 1822. The first programmable computer, the electro-mechanical Z1, was built around 1938 by Konrad Zuse.

3. This assumes that Hansel and Gretel do not take any shortcuts and that they do not have to backtrack to resolve dead ends (see chapter 1).

## On Your Way

1. If you have never driven in the United States, Canada, or South Africa, you may not know this traffic rule. For somebody who first learned how to drive in Germany, four-way stop

streets are a truly amazing concept, in particular, the fact that they cause so few accidents and quarrels about who came first.

2. This follows, since signs are representations and since we have identified computation as the systematic transformation of representations.

## Chapter 3　The Mystery of Signs

1. A binary number is a sequence of 1s and 0s. The first few natural numbers are represented in binary as follows: $0 \mapsto 0, 1 \mapsto 1, 2 \mapsto 10, 3 \mapsto 11, 4 \mapsto 100, 5 \mapsto 101, 6 \mapsto 110, 7 \mapsto 111, 8 \mapsto 1000, 9 \mapsto 1001$, and so on.

2. If you think this is complicated, consider this. I am writing this chapter in early 2015, and we are close to Superbowl XLIX, which is the Roman way of saying 49. L means 50, placing an X before it means to subtract 10. Now we have to add 9 more, which can be achieved by appending IX, which itself means to subtract 1 from 10.

3. Doubling in the binary system is as easy as multiplying by 10 in the decimal system: simply add a 0 at the right end.

4. In general, the intersection operation can produce multiple points (or no point) in case the road crosses the river more than once (or not at all).

5. *The Hound of the Baskervilles* does not contain computations with individual symbols; however, it does contain computations with collections of symbols (see chapter 4).

## Chapter 4　Detective's Notebook: Accessory after the Fact

1. Quotes are taken from the free online version of *The Hound of the Baskervilles* by A. Conan Doyle that is available at www.gutenberg.org/files/2852/2852-h/2852-h.htm.

2. There are more sophisticated versions of lists, for example, lists whose elements are connected in both directions. However, this chapter discusses only the simple singly linked list.

3. In principle, the order of elements could be of importance, and the position in the list could be used, for example, to express the degree of suspiciousness of each member. But in the story there is no indication that Sherlock Holmes maintains such an order.

4. Note that this assumption is generally *not* justified; it is usually *not* possible to use names as identifiers for array cells and get efficient access to array cells. This limitation can be overcome, in part, by employing more advanced data structures such as hash tables or so-called tries, which are discussed in chapter 5. We can ignore this limitation in what follows because the comparison of lists and arrays is not affected by it.

5. See wikipedia.org.

6. A wiki is a program for collaboratively editing and sharing information over the internet.

7. Their ultimate goal is, of course, to trim the set down to contain exactly one element.

## Lost and Found

1. In case you forgot how to do it, there are numerous instructions to be found on the internet, although finding instructions that are just right for you might again be a difficult search in itself.

## Chapter 5    The Search for the Perfect Data Structure

1. See www.youtube.com/yt/press/statistics.html; web site checked on September 16, 2015, see web.archive.org/web/20150916171036/http://www.youtube.com/yt/press/statistics.html.

2. The inside is not guaranteed to contain the element, since the element we are looking for may not exist at all in the search space.

3. See en.wikipedia.org/wiki/Boggle.

4. This assumes that the tiles do not have to be stepped on in a particular order and that all safe tiles do not have to be visited.

5. Thus, to ensure that each letter of a word is only counted once, we have to maintain a set data type when processing the word. We check that the set does not contain the letter before updating its count, and we add the letter to the set afterwards to prevent further updates to the count from later occurrences in the same word.

6. In fact, it takes time proportional to the number of elements times the logarithm of this number. This time complexity is also called *linearithmic*.

7. The word was originally pronounced "tree" as in re*trie*val, from which it was derived, but today many people pronounce it "try" to emphasize the special features that distinguishes it from search trees in general.

8. Half of the nodes in a binary tree are contained in its leaves.

## Getting Your Ducks in a Row

1. An algorithm has linearithmic runtime if it requires time proportional to the size of the input (here the number of students or exams) times the logarithm of that number.

2. Even taking into account that the list of exams gets shorter in each step.

## Chapter 6    Sorting out Sorting

1. More precisely, $1 + 2 + 3 + \cdots + n = \frac{1}{2}n^2 + \frac{1}{2}n$.

2. Since we have removed the pivot.

3. Referring to logarithms to the base 2. Thus, $\log_2 100 < 7$, since $2^7 = 128$, and so on.

4. John von Neumann is probably best known in computer science for describing a computer architecture on which most of the computers existing today are based.

5. This is because between any two names that might be used as adjacent array indices, there exist infinitely many other names. Say you decide that index "aaa" should be followed by "aab"; then indices such as "aaaa," "aaab," "aaaaa," and infinitely many others would not occur as indeces in the array and could not be counted. For the same reason arrays cannot be indexed by real numbers, and therefore counting sort cannot be used for sorting lists of real numbers.

6. Or at least one of the Holy Grails, since there can be multiple optimal algorithms.

7. All possible lists of length $n$ (containing different elements) can be constructed as follows. Any of the $n$ elements can be in the first position. Then any of the remaining $n-1$ elements can be in the second position, and so on. Altogether this amounts to $n\times(n-1)\times\cdots\times2\times1 = n!$ possibilities, which means that there are $n!$ different lists of length $n$.

8. An algorithm that uses no more than $k$ comparison operations can distinguish between $2^k$ different cases. Thus to cope with all possibilities for a list of length $n$, it must be that $2^k \geq n!$, or $k \geq \log_2(n!)$. One can then show that $k \geq n \log_2 n$, which yields the linearithmic lower bound.

## Chapter 7    Mission Intractable

1. This includes the empty combination, which is the solution for the case when the weight should be zero. This case is not important in this example, but it is a possibility in general. Excluding the empty set does not change the fact that the number of possible combinations is exponential in the number of available objects.

2. In fact, Moore's law, which had its 50-year anniversary in 2015, is coming to an end, since the miniaturization of electronic circuits has reached fundamental limits imposed by physics.

3. A quadratic algorithm for input of size $n$ performs about $n^2$ steps. Doubling the computer's speed means that it can execute in the same time twice as many steps, that is, $2n^2$ steps. This is the number of steps that the algorithm takes for input of size $\sqrt{2}n$, since $(\sqrt{2}n)^2 = 2n^2$. In other words, since $\sqrt{2} \approx 1.4142$, the algorithm can process input that is approximately 1.4 times as large.

4. About 30 billion atoms would have to be split to produce the energy needed to light up a 1 watt lamp for 1 second.

5. The *P* stands for *polynomial* and refers to the class of problems for which a solution can be constructed by an algorithm whose runtime is proportional to a polynomial such as $n^2$ or $n^3$.

   The *N* stands for *nondeterministic*, and *NP* refers to the class of problems for which a solution can be constructed by an algorithm with polynomial runtime on a nondeterministic machine, which is a hypothetical machine that can always make a correct guess for each decision needed in the algorithm. For example, we can generate a solution for the weighing problem in linear time if we can correctly guess for each weight whether it is included in the solution. Equivalently, *NP* refers to the class of problems whose solutions can be verified by an algorithm with polynomial runtime. For example, a proposed solution to the weighing problem can be verified in linear time, since it requires only the summation of the weights and the comparison with the target weight.

6. However, if one has to repeatedly find and remove the smallest element from a list, the sorting-based method becomes more efficient at some point.

7. Consider the first object added. It either weighs more than half of the target weight (which proves the case) or it weighs less than half, which means that we can add the next object, since its added weight (which is less than the first and thus also less than half the target weight) does not exceed the target weight.

   Now we can again distinguish two cases. If the two objects together weigh more than half of the target, their weight is less than 50% off the target weight. Otherwise, if they weigh less than half, each object must weigh less than one-fourth of the target, and so does the next object, since it weighs even less and can thus be added. Following this line of reasoning shows that we can continue to add objects at least until we have reached half the target weight. This argument assumes there are enough objects available to reach the target weight, but this assumption is already contained in the assumption that we can find an optimal solution.

## Doctor's Orders

1. Ludwig Wittgenstein, *Tractatus Logico-Philosophicus* (1921), para 5.6, trans. K. C. Ogden. www.gutenberg.org/files/5740/5740-pdf.pdf

## Chapter 8   The Prism of Language

1. The Recording Industry Association of America and the National Endowment for the Arts have listed it as the number one entry on their "Songs of the Century" list.

2. Music by Harold Arlen; lyrics by E. Y. "Yip" Harburg.

3. The objective in the telephone game is to transmit a sentence or phrase from one person to the next through whispering. When played with a large group, after a number of transmissions, the phrase often gets distorted in funny ways.

4. Unfortunately, tablature is ambiguous with regard to the duration of notes and can therefore only effectively be used when the performer knows the piece already.

5. To clearly distinguish nonterminal from terminal symbols, the former are always given by a name with a dotted frame around it, similar to the dotted underlining used to represent parameters in chapter 2. This notation evokes the notion of a placeholder that is to be substituted.

6. To represent $n$ different pitches and $m$ different durations, we need $n \times m$ rules. This number can be drastically reduced to about $n + m$ rules by decomposing a note into two nonterminals for pitch and duration plus rules for producing these two aspects independently of one another.

7. Idiomatic expressions are an exception to this rule (see chapter 9).

8. Oops. I forgot the last two words "it doesn't," which prevented you from successfully parsing the sentence. In this case, you could probably fix the sentence by adding the missing part, but sentences for which that doesn't work will be left without meaning—a very frustrating experience for the reader or listener.

## Chapter 9    Finding the Right Tone: Sound Meaning

1. More precisely, I should say that each sentence has *at most* one meaning, since some syntactically correct sentences might lack a meaning, for example, what is the meaning of "The green thought ate"?

## Chapter 10    Weather, Rinse, Repeat

1. A town in India that holds records for the highest annual and monthly amounts of rainfall.

2. Recall that *step* and *condition* are nonterminal symbols that stand for actions and conditions. When these nonterminals are replaced by an action and a condition, respectively, this program schema becomes instantiated to a concrete program.

3. This is often attributed to Albert Einstein or Benjamin Franklin, but the authorship is not clear. Early written references can be found in Rita Mae Brown's 1983 novel *Sudden Death* and in a 1980 Alcoholics Anonymous pamphlet.

4. Alternatively, you can expand the first *step* to *get up* and the second one to *take a shower; have breakfast*, which leads to the same result.

5. There are some important exceptions. For example, most spreadsheet systems do *not* have a loop to apply, say, one formula, to a number of values or cells. This is typically accomplished by copying rows and columns in the spreadsheet and is much like the expansion of the loop **repeat** *fold three times* into the sequence *fold; fold; fold*.

6. The condition of a repeat loop is appropriately called a *termination condition*; the condition of the while loop is better called an *entry condition*.

7. The for loops that can be found in most programming languages actually have the following slightly more general form, which provides the body of the loop with information about the number of iterations that have passed:

for :*name*: :*= :*number*: to :*number*: do :*step*:

This form introduces a nonterminal :*name*: that acts as a counter bound to the current iteration number. It can be used in the body of the loop, as in **for** *n* := 1 **to** 10 **do** *compute the square of n*.

## Stop at Nothing

1. Recursion can also be a source of nontermination. However, since any recursive algorithm can be transformed into a nonrecursive one that uses loops, it is sufficient to consider only loops.

## Chapter 11  Happy Ending Not Guaranteed

1. Of course, the really important part of the algorithm has been left out. We only assume that the condition that tests termination can be defined in some way, which, as shown later, is actually impossible to do.

2. See en.wikipedia.org/wiki/Barber_paradox.

3. If a problem asks for a yes or no answer, as in the case of the halting problem, it is called a *decision problem*. A decision problem that has no algorithmic solution is called *undecidable*; otherwise it is called *decidable*.

   If a problem asks for a specific output value for any given input value, it is called a *function problem*. A function problem that has no algorithmic solution is called *uncomputable*; otherwise it is called *computable*.

4. If you know the difference between "countably many" and "uncountably many," the number of decidable problems is countable, whereas the number of undecidable problems is uncountable.

## Chapter 12  A Stitch in Time Computes Fine

1. Incidentally, Carl Sagan thought that *Back to the Future II* was the best movie ever made based on the science of time travel; in "Q&A Commentary with Robert Zemeckis and Bob Gale," *Back to the Future Part II*, Blu-Ray (2010).

2. Remember that the semicolon is the control structure that sequentially composes steps of an algorithm.

3. The situation is a bit more complicated than this, but the analogy is still valid.

4. The recursive description is longer because the name of the algorithm has to be mentioned explicitly.

5. One can also distinguish between *generative* and *structural* recursion, but that distinction is not so important for the fundamental understanding of the concept of recursion itself. Moreover, one can distinguish between *linear* and *nonlinear* recursion (see chapter 13).

6. See en.wikipedia.org/wiki/Drawing_Hands and en.wikipedia.org/wiki/Print_Gallery_(M. _C._Escher).

7. Only when the algorithms are applied to nonnegative numbers.

8. From David Hunter, *Essentials of Discrete Mathematics* (2011).

## State of the Art

1. Note that it is not simply the collection of results that define an algorithm, because different algorithms for solving the same problem are distinguished by how they solve the problem.

## Chapter 13   A Matter of Interpretation

1. This is way of passing arguments to parameters is called *call-by-value*.

2. In this example, the parameter values are actually not needed anymore, and the computation of *Isort* is also completed.

3. Maybe that's because young Biff is not aware that the old man who gives him the sports almanac is his older self.

4. In practice, one can stop the recursion with lists of length 1, which are sorted and can also be returned unchanged.

## Chapter 14   The Magical Type

1. If the alarm clock uses a 12-hour time format, it requires an additional a.m./p.m. indicator.

2. Types that can be described in this way are called *polymorphic*, since they can have many different forms. Since all the different forms can be described using one parameter, this kind of polymorphism is called *parametric polymorphism*.

3. However, the power of typing rules is limited. They cannot, for example, guarantee the termination of algorithms.

4. This all depends on the context. Usually, one would also say that it doesn't make sense to multiply the height of a person with itself, but the square of a person's height is actually used to divide the weight of a person to compute the so-called body-mass index.

5. Published in the United Kingdom as *Harry Potter and the Philosopher's Stone*.

## Chapter 15   A Bird's Eye View: Abstracting from Details

1. The word *abstraction* has its origin in Latin where the verb *abstrahere* means "to draw away."

2. This definition could be further extended to work with lists of arbitrarily many protagonists. However, such a definition would be a bit more complicated.

3. For brevity, rules for expanding the nonterminals *protagonist* and *challenge* have been omitted.

4. The conic visualization of an abstraction is itself an abstraction with the abstract concept at the top and the concepts abstracted from at the bottom.

5. Ignoring here the fact that a runner will eventually get tired, which places a natural limit on the length of runs.

6. In this context, the word *algorithm* refers more narrowly to methods for computing mathematical functions, which does not includes, for example, recipes.

# Index

*Page numbers in italics refer to figures and tables.*

abbreviation, 52, 53, 56
abstract machine, 278, *279*
abstract syntax, 142, 151
abstract syntax tree, 151
abstract syntax tree ↔ parse tree, 151, 153, *153*
abstraction, 10, 261, 264–265, *267*
    algorithm, 10, *272*, 271–273
    application of, 266
    computation, of, 271, *272*
    computers, of, *279*, *281*
    data, 273, *281*
    design of, 268–271
    examples of, 10, 264
    functional, 273, *281*
    hierarchy, *281*
    instance of, 265, *267*
    interface, 265, *267*
    machines, of, 278, *279*
    mechanisms, 270
    representation, of, *272*
    representations as, 273–275
    runtime, of, 275–276, *277*
    type, *272*
access pattern, *see* data access pattern
algorithm, 17, 25, 281, 311n6
    approximation, 120, 129, 257
    complexity, *see* runtime
    correctness, 27–29
    defining characteristics, 26–27
    desirable properties, 27–29
    divide-and-conquer, 103, 112, 236

effect of, 25
execution, 18, 19, 35, *36*, 166
    *see also* computation
generate-and-test, 123
greedy, 130
hard-wired, 36
input, *see* input
linear, *see* runtime, linear
optimal, 114
output, *see* output
quadratic, *see* runtime, quadratic
recursive, 8, 75, 113
resource requirements, 32, 38
runtime of, *see* runtime
step, 38
termination, *see* loop, termination, 29
*see also* algorithm examples;
        Church-Turing thesis; program;
        recursion examples
algorithm ↔ computation, 26, 35, 38, 177
algorithm examples
    binary search, *see* binary search
    data compression, 3
    *Halts*, 194, *196*
    *Loop*, 194, *195*
    making coffee, 34
    page rank, 3
    path finding, 25, 218
    *see also* problem examples, path finding
    recipe, 2
    *Selfie*, *196*

set intersection, 71
sorting, *see* sorting algorithms
square root, 1, *2*
tree traversal, 73, 76
*see also* algorithm
ambiguity, *see* language, ambiguity;
      representation, ambiguity
ambiguity ↔ nondeterminism, 162
ancestor (tree), 73
application typing rule, 251
approximation algorithm, 120, 129, 257
argument, *see* input
array, 62, 67, *69*, 86, 113
    index, 67, 86
    notebook analogy, 67
    *see also* data structure
array ↔ list, 67, *69*, 90
artificial intelligence, 141
axiom (typing rule), 251

Babbage, Charles, 303n6
barber paradox, 197
Bertillon, Alphonse, 57
binary numbers, 50, 53, 304n6
binary representation, *see* binary numbers
binary search, 82, 203
    property, *92*
    tree, *92*, 91–96
    tree, balanced, 95, 97
    *see also* tree
binding, 233
boundary (search), 85, 91, 111
bounded ↔ unbounded recursion, 219
bucket sort, 272

Church, Alonzo, 280
Church-Turing thesis, 281
collection, 61, 63
    ordering of elements, 72
complexity
    algorithmic, *see* runtime; space
        requirements
    problem, *see* lower bound
compositionality, 159, 165
computation, 18–20, *22*, 23, *144*
    description of, *see* algorithm

essence of, 23, 25
limits of, *see* computer science, principal
    limitations
resources, 1, 38
role in society, 1–10
step, 21, 38
stuck, *28*, 254
with signs, 57, 58
*see also* algorithm, execution;
    representation, transformation of
computation ↔ algorithm, 26, 35, 38, 177
computation ↔ problem solving, 23, *24*
computation examples, *see* algorithm examples
computation representation, *22*, 52
    *see also* representation
computer, 31, 36
    requirements, 37
    universal, 36
    *see also* computer examples
computer examples
    alarm clock, 36
    difference engine, 303n6
    human, 36, 139, *144*, 158
    laptop, 36
    pocket calculator, 36
    ribosome, 37
    smart phone, 36
    Z1, 303n6
    *see also* computer
computer science
    essence of, 262, 264, 282–283
    objectives, 18, 32, 122, 129, 140, 269
    principal limitations, 103, 198
    science of problem solving, 4, 18, 282
computing, *see* computation
conclusion (typing rule), 251
concrete syntax, 142, 151
condition, 178, 185
conditional, 179
control structure, 7, 173, 179
    conditional, 179
    loop, *see* loop
    sequential composition, 173, 179
    *see also* recursion
Cook, Stephen, 128
correctness, 27–29, 193, 246, 255

data abstraction, 273, *281*
data access pattern, 61, 63
data structure, 62, 64, *69*
    recursive, 91
data structure ↔ data type, 64, 66, 275
data type, 61, 63, 66, *69*, 275
data type ↔ data structure, 64, 66, 275
de Saussure, Ferdinand, 51
decidability, *see* problem, unsolvable
decimal numbers, 50, 53
decimal representation, *see* decimal numbers
decomposition, *see* problem decomposition
denotational semantics, *164*, 165–167
derivation (grammar), 150
descendant (recursion example), 205
descendant (tree), 73
descriptive ↔ unfolded recursion, 214
dictionary, 70, 90
    implementation, 68, 69, 90
    key, 70
    *see also* data type; set
direct ↔ indirect recursion, 220
distributed computing, 47, 182
divide-and-conquer, 103, 113, 236
    *see also* recursion
Droste effect, 9
dynamic ↔ static type checking, 256–258

efficiency, *see* space requirements; runtime
encryption, *see* public key encryption, 5, 131
enerate-and-test, 123
Escher, M. C., 162, 220
execution, *see* algorithm, execution
execution time, *see* runtime
exponential ↔ nonexponential runtime, *125*
exponential algorithm, *see* exponential runtime
exponential growth, *see* exponential runtime
exponential runtime, 5, 120, 122, 124–126

FIFO (first in, first out), 72, 247
first come, first serve, 61, 72
first in, first out, 72, 247
fixed point, 215–217
flowchart, 180, *181*, 183, *184*
for loop, 185
for loop ↔ repeat/while loop, 186

fractals, 9
Frege, Gottlob, 165
functional abstraction, 273, *281*

Gödel, Kurt, 128
Google, 3, 5, 81
grammar, 145
    derivation, 150
    nonterminal, 146, 147
    recursive rule, 148
    rule, 147
    sentential form, 147
    start symbol, 150
    terminal, 146, 147
    *see also* language; syntax
grandfather paradox, 214
greedy algorithm, 130

halting problem, 189, 194, 257
    unsolvability, 194–197, 278
HIFO (highest in, first out), 73
highest in, first out, 73
Hindu-Arabic numerals, 3, 50
histogram, 90, 102
Hoare, Tony, 108
homonym, 54
HTML (hypertext markup language), 6, 151
hypertext markup language, 6, 151

icon (sign), 56
index
    array, 67, 86
    sign, 56, 144
indirect ↔ direct recursion, 220
input, 34, 246, 247, 252
    *see also* parameter; substitution; type
insertion sort ↔ selection sort, 107
interface, 262
internet search, 5
interpreter, 166, 225, 231
    trace, *232*, *234*
intractable problem, 4, 120, 126–129
intrinsic problem complexity, *see* lower bound
iteration, *see* loop, iteration

JavaScript, 6, 151
jump instruction, 209

key
>    dictionary, 70
>    private, 131
>    public, 131
>    search, 84, 85

lambda calculus, 280, 281
language, 5, 139, 141
>    ambiguity, 5, 145, *161*, 159–163
>        *see also* ambiguity ↔ non-determinism
>    compositionality, 165
>    grammar, *see* grammar
>    meaning, *see* language, semantics
>    semantics, 157, *164*, 163–165
>    sentence, 142, 145
>    structure, 139
>    syntax, *see* syntax
>    translation, 167, 278, *281*
last in, first out, 73, 247
lazy evaluation, 117
>    *see also* precomputation
LIFO (last in, first out), 73, 247
linear ↔ linearithmic ↔ quadratic runtime, *110*
linear recursion, 236
linear runtime, 40, *110*
linear storage space, 42
linearithmic runtime, 110, *110*, 305n6
list, 62, 64, *69*
>    finding element in, 66
>    infinite, 220
>    notation, 65
>    ring-binder analogy, 66
>    *see also* data structure
list ↔ array, 67, *69*, 90
logical paradox, 197, 214
loop, 7, 173, 176
>    body, 176, 179
>    condition, 178, 185
>    iteration, 176, 183, 185, 190
>    termination, 178–179, 185, 187
>    unfolding, 192, *192*
>    *see also* control structure
loop ↔ recursion, 185, 218–219
lower bound, 103, 115, 128

machine abstraction, 278, *279*

Mars Climate Orbiter, 10, 55
meaning (language), *see* language, semantics
meaning (sign), 47
mergesort, 272
method (for solving problems), *see* algorithm
music notation, 143–145
mutual recursion, *see* recursion, indirect

NASA, 10, 55
Necker cube, 162
nondeterminism, 161, 307n6
>    *see also* ambiguity ↔ non-determinism
nondeterminism ↔ ambiguity, 162
nonlinear recursion, 236
nonterminal, 146, 147
nontermination, 204
>    *see also* loop, termination
NP-complete problem, 126–129
number representation, *see* representation,
>        number

order, *see* collection, ordering of elements
output, 26, 247, 252
>    *see also* type

P = NP problem, 122, 128, 307n6
paradox
>    barber, 197
>    grandfather, 214
parallel computing, 182, 236
parallelism, 182
parameter, 31, 34–35, 261, 265
>    *see also* input; substitution
parameter binding, 233
parse tree, 151
parse tree ↔ abstract syntax tree, 151, 153, *153*
parsing, 153, *154*
partition (of search space), 81, 85
pattern matching, 211, 270
Peirce, Charles Sanders, 56
Penrose triangle, 162
pivot element, 108, 111
pointer
>    between list elements, 65
>    to input, 35
policy, *see* data access pattern

precomputation, 102, 116
    *see also* lazy evaluation
predicate, 71
prefix tree, 99
    *see also* trie
premise (typing rule), 251
preorder traversal, 76
    *see also* algorithm examples, tree traversal
pretty printing, 154, *154*
priority queue, 61, 72
    *see also* data type; highest in, first out
problem, 17
    class, 26, 303n6
    intractable, 4, 120, 126–129
    intrinsic complexity, *see* lower bound
    NP-complete, 126–129
    P = NP, 122, 128, 307n6
    uncomputable, 198
    undecidable, 198, 257
        *see also* halting problem
    *see also* problem examples
problem complexity, *see* lower bound
problem decomposition, 17, 21, 103, 108, 111
    *see also* divide-and-conquer
problem examples
    finding home, 20, *22*
    getting up, 17
    halting problem, *see* halting problem
    knapsack, 127
    path finding, 20, 88
    searching, 5, 82, 83, 87
        *see also* binary search
    sorting, *see* sorting
    traveling salesman, 5, 127
    weighing, 123
    *see also* algorithm examples; problem
problem reduction, 128
problem representation, *22*, 52
    *see also* representation
problem simplification, *see* problem
        decomposition
problem solving, 4, 19, 103
problem solving ↔ computation, 23, *24*
program, 37
    *see also* algorithm
programming language, 37, 279

public key encryption, 5, 131

quadratic runtime, 41, *110*
queue, 4, 61, 72, 247
    implementation by list, 73
    *see also* data type; first in, first out

recursion, 8, 184, 203
    base case, 220
    bounded, 219
    descriptive, 203, 213, 228
    direct, 206, 220
    indirect, 220, 224
    linear, 236
    nonlinear, 236
    unbounded, 206, 219
    unfolded, 214
    *see also* bounded ↔ unbounded recursion;
        descriptive ↔ unfolded recursion;
        direct ↔ indirect recursion;
        divide-and-conquer; recursion ↔
        loop; recursion examples
recursion ↔ loop, 185, 218–219
recursion examples
    99 bottles, 204
    *Count*, 211, *213*, 215, 249
    descendant, 205
    drawing hands, 220
    *Even*, 221
    *FindHomeFrom*, 218
    *Goal*, 210
    *GroundhogDay*, 185, 218
    *Isort*, 229, 233, *234*
    Matryoshka dolls, 204
    *Odd*, 221
    *Ones*, 220
    print gallery, 220
    *Qsort*, 236, 249
    room with TV, 205, 228
    Sierpinski triangles, 224
    *ToDo*, 208, 231
    *see also* algorithm, binary search;
        divide-and-conquer; recursion
recursive equation, 211, 221
recursive picture, *228*
    *see also* recursion examples, room with TV

recursive rule (grammar), 148
reduction, *see* problem reduction
repeat loop ↔ while loop, 183, *184*
repeat/while loop ↔ for loop, 186
representation, 21, *22*, *55*
    ambiguity, 54
    layers of, 22, 53
    music, 167
    number, 3, 10, 50, 52, 53
    transformation of, 33, 58
    *see also* computation representation;
        problem representation; sign
representation level, *see* representation, layers of
resource requirements, *see* algorithm, resource
        requirements
result, *see* output
reuse, 107
rewriting, 229
RHS (right-hand side), 147
right-hand side, 147
Roman numerals, 50
rule (grammar), 147
rule (typing), 9, 245, 251
runtime, 31, 38, 276
    constant, 67
    exponential, 5, 120, 122, 124–126
    linear, 40, *110*
    linearithmic, 110, *110*, 305n6
    logarithmic, 95
    of loops, 185
    quadratic, 41, *110*
    worst case, 39, 40
    *see also* exponential ↔ non-exponential
        runtime; linear ↔ linearithmic ↔
        quadratic runtime
runtime abstraction, 275–276
runtime complexity, *see* runtime

search
    in a list, 84
        *see also* dictionary, implementation
    in a tree, *see* binary search; trie
    key, 84, 85
search problem, *see* problem examples,
        searching
search space, 81, 84, 88

selection sort ↔ insertion sort, 107
self-application, 195
self-reference, 203, 205, 228, *228*
self-replicating machines, 9
semantic domain, 164
semantics, *see* language; semantics
semiotics, 51
sentence, 142, 145
sentence structure, 142
sentential form, 147
    *see also* sentence; grammar
sequential composition, 173, 179
set, 66, 67
    difference, 71
    intersection, 71
    *see also* data type; dictionary
sign, 51–53, *55*, 141
    icon, 56
    index, 56, 144
    interpretation, 47, 56
    meaning, 47
    signified, 51, *55*
    signifier, 51, *55*, 70, 89
    symbol, 56
    transitivity, 53
    *see also* representation
signified (sign), 51, *55*
signifier (sign), 51, *55*, 70, 89
solution, *see* problem solving
sorting, 101
    *see also* sorting algorithms
sorting algorithms
    bucket sort, 111
    counting sort, 113
    insertion sort, 106, *106*, 229, *230*
    mergesort, 111, *112*
    quicksort, 108, *109*, 236
    selection sort, 105, *105*, 185
    type of, 249
space complexity, *see* space requirements
space requirements, 38, 65
spaghetti code, 182, 209
spreadsheet, 6
stack, 62, 63, 72, 247
    implementation by list, 73
    used by interpreter, 231–235

*see also* data type; last in, first out
start symbol (grammar), 150
state, 191, 223
static ↔ dynamic type checking, 256–258
storage space, 32
    linear, 42
substitution, 34, 147, 226–229, *230*, 266
    *see also* parameter
symbol (sign), 56
synonym, 54
syntax, 6, 145
    abstract, 142, 151
    concrete, 142, 151
    *see also* grammar; parse tree
syntax tree, *see* abstract syntax tree; parse tree

terminal, 146, 147
termination, 178–179, 185, 187
termination condition, 178, 179, 183, 191–195,
    309n6
    *see also* loop, condition
textual language ↔ visual language, 181
time abstraction, *see* runtime abstraction
trace, 223, *230*, 231
tree, 73
    ancestor, 73
    child, 74
    descendant, 73
    height, 95
    internal node, 91
    leaf, 74
    node, 74
    parent, 74
    path, 92
    root, 74
    subtree, 91

*see also* data structure
trie, 97–99, *100*
    *see also* data structure
Turing machine, 278, 281
Turing test, 141
Turing, Alan, 194, 278
type, 9, 142, 243, 247, 274
    algorithms, for, 247, 248, 253
    *see also* data type
type checker, 246, 256
    *see also* dynamic ↔ static type checking
type correctness, 246, 255
type error, 10, 244, 246, 255
type parameter, 249
type-directed programming, 254
typing rule, 9, 246, 251

unbounded ↔ bounded recursion, 219
uncomputable problem, *see* problem,
    undecidable
undecidable problem, *see* problem, undecidable
unfolded ↔ descriptive recursion, 214
unsolvable problem, *see* problem, undecidable
use-mention distinction, 51

variable, 146, 177, 191
    *see also* parameter
visual language ↔ textual language, 181
von Neumann, John, 111, 115, 306n6

way finding, *see* problem examples, path
    finding; algorithm examples, path
    finding
while loop ↔ repeat loop, 183, *184*
worst-case complexity, *see* runtime, worst case

Zuse, Konrad, 303n6